An Illustrated History of

LMS

LOCOMOTIVES

Top: Former Midland Railway 4—4—0s, No. 1011 (Class 4P 'Compound') and No. 525 (Class 2P) flanking Stanier 'Jubilee' 4—6—0 No. 5633 *Trans-Jordan* at Derby on June 11 1937, nicely symbolise two of the major locomotive design trends during LMS days. The MR influences form the theme of this Volume whilst *Volume 5* will cover the LMS Standard designs, as represented here by No. 5633. *L. Hanson.*

Above: Smartly turned-out ex-MR Class 3P Belpaire 4—4—0 No. 748, pictured at Chinley in the early 1930s, represents one of the best express passenger classes built at Derby in pre-Grouping days — see *Chapter 1. Authors' Collection.*

An Illustrated History of
LMS
LOCOMOTIVES

Volume Four:
Absorbed Pre-Group Classes,
Midland Division.

by Bob Essery & David Jenkinson

Silver Link Publishing

Below: The LMS standard Class 4 0—6—0 formed perhaps the strongest single statement of the Midland dominance of early LMS locomotive affairs. This example, No. 4252 at Derby in 1926, was given a very elaborate works grey paint treatment suggestive of the red livery. It did not, of course, get one, modellers, take note! *Authors' Collection.*

Lower: Stratford-upon-Avon & Midland Junction Railway 0—6—0 No. 3 in the condition in which it was withdrawn by the LMS in 1924. See also page 200. *Authors' Collection.*

© Bob Essery and David Jenkinson, and Silver Link Publishing Ltd, 1987
Reprinted September 1992

Printed in Great Britain by Woolnough Bookbinding Ltd, Irthlingborough, Northants.

Designed by Nigel Harris

Previous page, upper: A head-on view of former 'Somerset & Dorset' 2—8—0 No. 13806 taken in 1949 — see *Chapter 9. Ivo Peters.*

Previous page, lower: No. 7100, the first of the Midland-inspired LMS standard Class 3 0—6—0Ts, pictured ex-works when new in 1924 — see *Chapter 5. BR (LMR).*

Essery, R.J.
   An illustrated history of LMS locomotives.
   Vol. 4: Absorbed pre-group classes, the
   Midland division.
   1. London, Midland and Scottish Railway —
   History   2. Locomotives — Great Britain —
   History.
   I. Title.   II. Jenkinson, David
   625.2'61'0941   TJ603.4.G72L6695

ISBN 0-947971-16-5

CONTENTS

Footnote: Readers wishing to have a full stock list and other associated data for the pre-group engines covered in this volume are recommended to consult *British Locomotive Catalogue, 1825-1923, Vol 3A,* published by Moorland Publishing Co.

This page: The 'Tilbury Tanks' were a distinctive element of the LMS scene in their home area, in spite of much standardisation elsewhere. These views show (top) LTSR '51 Class' 4—4—2T No. 2163 (later No. 2097) shortly after the Grouping and (above) sister engine No. 2098 (formerly No. 2164) some ten years later at Plaistow in 1934, by this stage with extended smokebox and other 'Derby' modifications — see *Chapter 8. Authors' Collection.*

TO OUR READERS — AN EXPLANATION

BEFORE we continue with our survey of LMS locomotives we feel we should explain why this series is continuing under a new publishing imprint. Many readers will know that during 1986-7 our former publishers, OPC, were twice taken over by other companies. Our original agreement was for a three-volume series, later expanded to five. However, it proved impossible to reach a satisfactory arrangement with OPC's former owners regarding publication of the final two books in the series. Fortunately, Silver Link Publishing Ltd heard of our difficulty and offered to produce the final two parts of the series on mutually acceptable terms, so we would like to start this volume by offering our very sincere thanks to Jayne and Nigel Harris for their considerable gesture of confidence.

This volume has been prepared to match, as nearly as possible, the style and format of the first three books, save for any inevitable differences caused by the change of publisher. Our endeavour has always been to try and provide as definitive work of reference as we could, and we hope that it may continue to be regarded as such for many years to come.

AUTHORS INTRODUCTION TO VOLUME FOUR

THIS part of our survey of LMS motive power concludes the pre-Grouping coverage of the LMS locomotive fleet by considering the engines of the Midland Division. At the same time, having positioned it at the end of the pre-1923 surveys, we are also using it to introduce the LMS standard types (most of which will appear in *Volume Five*), by way of including in this book the four Midland designs which were perpetuated by the LMS, the 'Compound' 4—4—0, the '2P' 4—4—0, the '3F' 0—6—0T and the Class 4 0—6—0. We explain this further on page 9.

We realise that some readers, knowing of our Midland susceptibilities, might feel that we would favour the Midland product above others inherited by the LMS. We are well aware of this possibility and have striven even harder to be as objective as possible. Admirable though the Midland Railway was in many ways and much though we like its products, its influence on the LMS locomotive department was not wholly beneficial and we have tried our best not to 'over gild' the lily. We hope we have succeeded.

We are also conscious that in parallel with this series of LMS books, we are preparing a second series of volumes, for Wild Swan Publications, devoted to the pre-1923 history of Midland Railway locomotives. This is largely because, uniquely among the larger constituents of the LMS, there is no single work on Midland locomotives in the pre-group period to which we can refer our readers. We had no such problems with *Volumes Two* and *Three* of the LMS account. There is some degree of factual overlap but we have done our best to ensure, as far as possible, that a strict dividing line is observed. We have, therefore, only transgressed 'across the great divide' where we feel some repetition to be essential to better understanding. Furthermore, the two series are structured quite differently. Nevertheless, we express our sincere thanks to both publishers for trusting us in this matter!

Finally, we must again thank our many friends for checking, advising and helping search for pictures. As always however, any factual mistakes and/or incorrect pictorial attributions should be laid at our door. Some errors already spotted in previous volumes are included in Appendix 1; we are glad there are so few. They are mostly trivial, but nevertheless irritating. We must also apologise for the fact that because of the problems already mentioned, *Volume Five* could not be started in any serious way until we had settled the issue. Consequently there will be a somewhat longer interval between the current volume and the final part, compared with those between *Volumes Two* to *Four*. This should, however, enable us to incorporate a more comprehensive correction list in the final part. We therefore hope that readers will continue to send us comments and observations via our new publisher.

DJ
Knaresborough
1987.

RJE
Solihull
1987.

LOCOMOTIVE LIVERY KEY LIST

WE repeat, below, *Table 10* from page 204 of *Volume One* in order to help the reader. The list should adequately define the vast majority of liveries carried by LMS locomotives from 1923 to 1947 and is, in essence, a tabulated summary of the livery section of *Volume One*. In virtually all the photographs in this volume, liveries are described by reference to the code letters and numbers in the left hand column of this list, augmented by such other detail as seems relevant in context. The main variable (apart from totally non-standard paint schemes) was in the centre-to-centre spacing of the letters 'LMS' during the 1928-47 period. Where a particular class of engine displayed some consistency in this respect, we shall say so in the narrative, but where much variety was evident, we shall either try to provide some sort of valid generalisations where we can or simply draw attention to the problem.

LIVERY CODE

CRIMSON LAKE LIVERY VARIATIONS

Code	Description	Detail
A1	Pre-1928 standard, 18in figures	LMS Coat-of-Arms
A2	Pre-1928 standard, 18in figures	Individual Letters 'LMS'
A3	Pre-1928 standard, 14in figures	LMS Coat-of-Arms
A4	Pre-1928 standard, 14in figures	Individual Letters 'LMS'
A5	Post-1927 standard, Gold/Black insignia	10in numerals
A6	Post-1927 standard, Gold/Black insignia	12in numerals
A7	Post-1927 standard, Gold/Black insignia	14in numerals (Midland pattern)
A8	Post-1927 standard, Straw/Black insignia	10in numerals (Midland pattern)
A9	Post-1927 standard, Straw/Black insignia	12in numerals
A10	Post-1927 standard, Straw/Black insignia	14in numerals (Standard pattern)
A11	Post-1927 standard, Gold/Red insignia	12in numerals
A12	Post-1927 standard, Gold/Red insignia	1936 pattern
A13	Post-1927 standard, Yellow/Red insignia	10in numerals
A14	Post-1927 standard, Yellow/Red insignia	12in numerals
A15	Post-1927 standard, Yellow/Red insignia	12in numerals (Midland pattern)

LINED BLACK LIVERY VARIATIONS

Code	Description	Detail
B1	Lined Black livery, Horwich/St. Rollox style	18in Midland figures
B2	Post-1927 standard, Gold/Red insignia	10in numerals
B3	Post-1927 standard, Gold/Red insignia	12in numerals
B4	Post-1927 standard, Gold/Red insignia	14in numerals (Midland pattern)
B5	Post-1927 standard, Gold/Black insignia	10in numerals
B6	Post-1927 standard, Gold/Black insignia	12in numerals
B7	Post-1927 standard, Gold/Black insignia	14in numerals (Midland pattern)
B8	Post-1927 standard, Yellow/Red insignia	10in numerals
B9	Post-1927 standard, Yellow/Red insignia	12in numerals
B10	Post-1927 standard, Yellow/Red insignia	14in numerals (Midland pattern)
B11	Post-1927 standard, Gold/Red insignia	1936 pattern
B12	1946 standard livery — full lining style	
B13	1946 standard livery — simpler original lining style	

PLAIN BLACK LIVERY VARIATIONS

Code	Description	Detail
C1	Pre-1928 standard, 18in figures	Standard cab/bunker panel
C2	Pre-1928 standard, 18in figures	Round cornered cab/bunker panel
C3	Pre-1928 standard, 18in figures	Individual Letters 'LMS'
C4	Pre-1928 standard, 14in figures	Standard cab/bunker panel
C5	Pre-1928 standard, 14in figures	Round cornered cab/bunker panel
C6	Pre-1928 standard, 14in figures	Individual Letters 'LMS'
C7	Crewe 'hybrid' style, 18in figures	LMS Coat-of-Arms
C8	Crewe 'hybrid' style, 14in figures	(Midland pattern), LMS Coat-of-Arms
C9	Crewe 'hybrid' style, 14in figures	(Standard pattern — straw), LMS Coat-of-Arms
C10	Crewe 'hybrid' style 18in figures	Individual Letters 'LMS'
C11	Crewe 'hybrid' style 14in figures	(Midland pattern), Individual Letters 'LMS'
C12	Crewe 'hybrid' style 14in figures	(Standard pattern), Individual Letters 'LMS'
C13	Post-1927 standard, Gold/Black insignia	10in numerals
C14	Post-1927 standard, Gold/Black insignia	12in numerals
C15	Post-1927 standard, Gold/Black insignia	14in numerals (Midland pattern)
C16	Post-1927 standard, Plain Straw insignia	10in numerals
C17	Post-1927 standard, Plain Straw insignia	12in numerals
C18	Post-1927 standard, Plain Straw insignia	14in numerals (Standard pattern)
C19	Post-1927 standard, Gold/Red insignia	1936 pattern
C20	Post-1927 standard, Gold/Black insignia	1936 pattern
C21	Post-1927 standard, Yellow/Red insignia	10in numerals
C22	Post-1927 standard, Yellow/Red insignia	12in numerals
C23	Post-1927 standard, Yellow/Red insignia	14in numerals (Midland pattern)
C24	Post-1927 standard, Plain Yellow insignia	10in numerals
C25	Post-1927 standard, Plain Yellow insignia	12in numerals
C26	Post-1927 standard, Plain Yellow insignia	14in numerals (Midland pattern)
C27	1946 standard insignia — smaller size	
C28	1946 standard insignia — larger size	

INTRODUCTION TO THE MIDLAND DIVISION

THE Midland Division locomotives of the LMS consisted mainly of those formerly belonging to the Midland Railway. At the Grouping, these also included engines of the former London Tilbury & Southend Railway, absorbed by the MR in 1912. To these, the LMS added in 1923 a handful of engines from the Stratford-upon-Avon & Midland Junction Railway and, in 1930, the locomotives of the former Somerset & Dorset Joint Railway, when this system was divided between the Southern and LMS Railways, the LMS taking the locomotive fleet, the Southern obtaining the rolling stock. These three smaller concerns are considered separately in this survey. The ex-North Staffordshire Railway engines were also, initially, numbered in the Midland Division series but have already been dealt with in *Volume 2,* being operationally more associated with the Western Division.

The former Midland locomotives mostly retained their number identity in 1923, since they were already bearing numbers allocated in 1907 along similar principles also adopted by the LMS for the whole system after the Grouping. This avoided a considerable amount of renumbering and, in the event, also avoided a fair amount of repainting as well, as a result of the Midland livery being continued by the LMS. For many

ex-MR engines, all that really changed during the 1923-7 period was indication of ownership, rather than basic livery.

An important factor relevant to this part of our survey was the perpetuation by the LMS of four basic MR designs as new post-Grouping 'standard' types. These were the Class 4 'Compound' 4—4—0, the Class 4 0—6—0 (both little changed) together with the '483 Class' superheated Class 2 4—4—0 and the Class 3 0—6—0T, only slightly modified. We have elected to put these four classes into this volume along with the Midland engines in order both to keep them in a broadly homogeneous group and so that they appear in the same book wherein we also deal with the evolution *towards* their LMS standardised form. These four classes are given separate chapters and are dealt with in slightly more detail than the pre-group classes, in order to establish a pattern we shall adopt for the remainder of the LMS standard types and classes in *Volume 5.* However, their ancestry is covered in this volume in the appropriate chapters of the Midland coverage and in the 'Somerset & Dorset' chapter.

At the Grouping, the Midland Division number series ran from 1-4026 and the LMS eventually filled up most of the gap from 4027-999 with hundreds more Class 4 0—6—0s and, later, with the Beyer Garratts and Stanier Class 5 4—6—0s.

Above: The 'Crimson Ramblers', to use a popular if not always flattering pseudonym for the famous Class 4 'Compound' 4—4—0s, represented a strong statement of Derby influence in early LMS days. This fine study at Crewe South on June 16 1929 shows an LMS standard example, No. 1131, shortly after the change to the 1928 style of company markings — see also *Chapter 2. H.C. Casserley.*

CHAPTER 1:

MIDLAND RAILWAY

INTRODUCTION
&
PASSENGER TENDER CLASSES

THE Midland Railway originated in 1844 when three separate concerns, all with Derby as a common factor, amalgamated. These were the Midland Counties, the Birmingham & Derby and the North Midland Railways. The three systems formed a rough inverted 'Y' shape with Derby at the junction of the three arms. Thereafter, this tight nucleus effectively formed the centre of the spider's web by which the Midland gradually extended its system.

The reasons for the Midland's expansion are not difficult to understand. Its central position in England meant that it was continually fighting for outlets for traffic as railway business increased. At first, the MR tended to hand over traffic at strategic points to other systems for onward movement; for example, traffic for London was handed over at Rugby to the London & Birmingham Railway (later the LNWR). However, as time went by, the competitor companies gave less and less priority to the Midland traffic and the Company was thereby forced to seek alternatives. Sometimes it did so by alliance with another competitor, rather than its original partner, such as the GNR rather than the LNWR for the London traffic, but increasingly, the Derby-based system found itself forced to build its own independent routes to gain truly independent freedom of action. Thus, it reached Manchester via the Peak Forest in 1867, London (St. Pancras) on its own lines in 1868, and after the most epic battle of all, Carlisle, via the Settle - Carlisle line, in 1876.

Prior to these aggressive and expansive thrusts, the MR had already reached Bristol, Lincoln and the West Riding of Yorkshire, so all told, one must concede that well before the Grouping, the Midland had proved itself to be a persistent 'thorn in the flesh' of its competitors — and thus far there has been no mention of its activities in Wales and Northern Ireland!

The extraordinary thing about the Midland Railway was that for all that it became one of England's three or four major systems, it never forsook its provincial base. In this it may be compared with the North Eastern Railway, the principal difference being that unlike the Midland, the North Eastern never aspired to or built a London main line. By 1923, the MR ranked third in terms of size after the LNWR and the GWR and, sadly for the LMS, both Midland and LNWR were incorporated in the 'grouped' railway. One says 'sadly' largely because in its infancy the LMS suffered grievously from the LNWR/MR rivalry — yet independently both had much to contribute and, had the LMS been better managed in the 1920s, the LNWR and MR working in harmony could have produced a formidable system. That for ten years or so they did not can only be a source of regret, regardless of one's sentimental affinity to either Company.

In the event, Midland locomotive policy became dominant for reasons already outlined in *Volume 1*. This was not too surprising in management terms, but it was somewhat extraordinary if viewed objectively from purely locomotive criteria. We have a strong and well-known personal affinity for the Midland — it was in many ways the most magnificent of railways, as others have averred — but we must admit that in purely locomotive matters it was not the best in the business by 1923. This in itself was also surprising, for in the late 19th century it had been second-to-none in motive power matters. Even in the early 20th century it continued to progress under R.M. Deeley but when he retired things tended to degenerate into rather self-satisfied complacency as 'management' began to rule the roost. It need not have been so and it is interesting to note that even the famous Great Western Railway fell into much the same trap during the 1930s and 1940s. Funnily enough, it was a GWR man, William Stanier, somewhat frustrated by his own complacent Railway, who came to the LMS as Chief Mechanical Engineer in 1932 and began to remove some of the more obvious manifestations of the 'dead hand of Derby'. Even so, by this time the LMS was well embarked on a 'first generation' standardisation based on MR methods and many of the visibly 'Midland' features were never totally removed from LMS locomotives. Therefore, it is essential in understanding the LMS standard engines to first comprehend those of the Midland itself. Since we have given a comprehensive 1883-1922 summary in our companion work *Midland Locomotives (Vols. 1-3)* — Wild Swan Publications we will confine ourselves here to what might be called the 'inherited' situation.

By 1923, Midland engines, always long-lived, bore visible signs of the three 'generations' of designers which had created them. First, chronologically, were those survivors of the Kirtley era (1844-1873) which still displayed recognisable marks of their ancient origin — double frames particularly. These were mostly 2—4—0s, 0—6—0s and a handful of 0—4—4Ts. They had all been rebuilt by Johnson (and later engineers) but most never totally lost their original character — see *Plate 1*. The second group comprised those engines built during Johnson's Superintendency (1873-1903). Like the Kirtley classes, these too had been mostly rebuilt (many extensively) but a great number of them still carried the unmistakeable and graceful hallmarks of the 'Johnson era', such as attractively curved splashers and cab side sheets. This group comprised mostly 0—6—0s, 2—4—0s, 4—2—2s and 0—4—4Ts, but there were also included a few 4—4—0s. A typical, fairly original Johnson product is depicted in *Plate 2*. Finally, and most significantly from the LMS standpoint, were the products of the Deeley-Fowler era (1903-1909 and 1909-1923). The basic visual lines of these locomotives were quite different from those of Kirtley and Johnson and by 1923 they had been particularly applied also to 0—6—0s and 4—4—0s — the main stalwart types of the Midland fleet by the Grouping years. Moreover, the

(Plate 1): **The Kirtley 'look' as inherited by the LMS — 6ft 8in Class 1 2—4—0 (believed to be No. 42) in red livery (Code A1) at about the time of the Grouping. Note the lack of any company markings.** *Authors' Collection.*

characteristic Deeley-Fowler front-end treatment (chimney/smokebox) had been grafted on to just about everything else by 1923! *Plate 3* is fairly typical of an undiluted Deeley-Fowler design and *Plate 4* shows a good example of a modified earlier engine.

To be truthful, most of the latter day changes in appearance must properly be attributed to R.M. Deeley. Henry Fowler, never an innovator, generally went along with management views and tended to produce the mixture as before. The 'as before' was usually Deeley-inspired by late Midland days — and this extended to livery as well. However, apart from superheating, this lack of progressive development during the Fowler years did not augur well, either for the Midland or the LMS and it was most unfortunate. In his time, Matthew Kirtley had been one of the true 'greats' of British locomotive engineering. He did, after all, introduce the brick arch into the firebox, allowing steam locomotives to successfully burn coal rather than coke (without a brick arch, coal burns with excessive smoke and minimal efficiency) and his engines were most certainly 'built to last'. Samuel Johnson moreover (1873-1903) was really a 'big engine' man. At a time when the LNWR was still churning out small 2—4—0s and the GWR was trying to decide whether or not to keep the broad gauge, Johnson was building at Derby a superb series of 4—4—0s and 4—2—2s which gave the 19th century Midland Railway a real 'edge' over its competitors. He also initiated the 20th century with his 'Belpaire' 4—4—0 and the first of the celebrated 'Compound' 4—4—0s — both types were very much abreast of the times and 'big' engines by most contemporary standards.

From 1903, Deeley carried on the good work with bigger 0—6—0s, more 'Compounds' and better 4—4—0s, but when he left in 1909, motive power matters began to slide — with the noteworthy exception of steam superheating. The MR continued sending heavy coal trains to London behind two small 0—6—0s (one could almost say *too* small 0—6—0s!) and piloting was required for any reasonable load on express passenger duties which outfaced a modest 4—4—0 or 4—2—2.

Yet Derby had designed (and built) a very good 2—8—0 for the Somerset & Dorset Joint Railway, and there were several unfulfilled 4—6—0 proposals which might have eliminated the double-heading of many expresses — but management decreed otherwise. It is tempting to blame Fowler for the lost opportunities, but even the early LMS showed no signs of repentance, so perhaps he was just unlucky. In all events, this manifestly inappropriate mix of too many, too small engines became the dominant traction factor in 1923 and, in consequence, the ex-Midland types, even if not standardised by the LMS for new construction, were assured of 'most favoured nation' treatment. Because of the powerful Midland element in the infant LMS hierarchy, Derby's locomotives survived much longer than they ought to have done — and they certainly outlived other non Midland designs of probably greater practical use, which were scrapped simply because they were 'non-standard'. Only the ex-Caledonian engines fared as well and this was probably based on rather *better* reasons in thermodynamic and traffic terms!

Perhaps this is all a little unfair to the Midland. After all, it was a very profitable railway, it was held in high esteem by the public, it had a fabulous public 'presence', not the least of which was its inspired (and unique) colour scheme — 'any colour you like provided it is crimson lake', to paraphrase Henry Ford — and it was better managed than most of its contemporaries — except in the one crucial area of motive power. To this 'Achilles heel', the LMS motive power department fell heir. It was all the more ironic that in almost every significant aspect of locomotive affairs, save for the design of the engines themselves, the Midland could more than 'hold its own' and it is worth recording that its basic train reporting and control system stood the test of time through LMS days to the end of steam traction on BR itself in 1968. Even the GWR, LNER and SR engines had to 'suffer' Midland-inspired front number plates to the very end!

The Midland engines might have been less than perfect, but less than influential they certainly were not!

Above *(Plate 2):* Virtually undiluted Johnson — Class 1 4—2—2 No. 641 (Livery Code A1) rostered as pilot to a down express at St. Pancras in early LMS days. The train engine is an unidentified Class 3 Belpaire 4—4—0. *Authors' Collection.*

Right *(Plate 3):* Class 3 Belpaire 4—4—0 No. 733 dated back to the Johnson era but when the LMS inherited it, the visual lines were pure Deeley-Fowler. The picture was taken at Kentish Town in the early 1930s — Livery Code B4. *Authors' Collection.*

Above *(Plate 4)*: The tender, cab and graceful splashers of 2—4—0 No. 177 reveal its Johnson origins but the Belpaire boiler and front-end treatment are much later modifications carried out circa 1924/5. This picture was taken at Kings Norton on March 7 1925. *Authors' Collection.*

MIDLAND TENDERS

Midland tenders, especially in the Johnson/Deeley period, were characterised by considerable variety. Essentially however, as far as passenger engines were concerned in LMS days, one of two fundamental types of tender were utilised, either the familiar 'flared coping' Johnson variety (see *Plate 4*) or the Deeley 'flat sided' variety (see *Plate 3*). Within each of these two basic styles, several variations could be seen. The Deeley designs are dealt with in the Class sections to which they apply (Class 3 and Class 4 4—4—0s), but the Johnson tenders merit a preliminary note. A more comprehensive analysis is given in *Chapter 6* for the goods engines, because it was in this area that the whole panoply of designs could be seen. For the passenger section, it is probably sufficient at this point to state that by far the most common Johnson tenders used in LMS days were those of 2,950, 3,250 and 3,500-gallon capacity. These vehicles were often difficult to tell apart visually in many photographs, being dimensionally similar.

In general, the 2—4—0s were most commonly paired with 2,950-gallon tenders, whilst the 4—4—0s/4—2—2s had the larger variety, generally the 3,250-gallon variant. The largest 3,500-gallon type was confined to the fourth series of 4—2—2s and the last 40 or so of the Class 2 4—4—0s. In each section of the following analysis we state the type of tender which should officially have been used by the class concerned. Inevitably, there were exceptions, but perhaps not quite as many variants as might have been the case, for example, on the ex-LNWR lines. More often than not, Midland engines were generally returned to traffic after repair with the correct type of tender, as per the official diagram book.

PASSENGER TENDER CLASSES

By 1923, the Midland placed its faith in the 4—4—0 type for most of its important trains, but secondary services were frequently the preserve of a considerable number of 2—4—0s, some of them dating back well into the Kirtley era, together with a modest number of 4—2—2s, which had originated in the graceful Johnson times. The evolution of the 2—4—0 and 4—2—2 had long-since finished, but the MR 4—4—0 carried on its development into LMS days. All told, the Midland bequeathed 673 passenger tender engines to the LMS, of which more than half were 4—4—0s, the bulk of the remainder being 2—4—0s.

The analysis which follows will deal with the Midland engines according to wheel arrangement, rather than in strict numerical order. This is because the Deeley rebuilding of many early Johnson 4—4—0s, originally all Class 1 and numbered ahead of the 4—2—2s in 1907, tended to 'mix up' the 'power class by wheel arrangement' principles of the 1907 Midland re-numbering. By LMS days, many of the erstwhile Class 1 4—4—0s had long since become Class 2, even though they retained their original numbers. In consequence, the 4—2—2s will be considered before the 4—4—0s.

KIRTLEY DOUBLE-FRAMED 2-4-0 (LMS Nos. between 1-67; Power Class 1 later 1P)

This group of engines, which even by 1923 standards was looking more than a little archaic, consisted of two separate series of locomotives:

LMS Nos. 1-22: 6ft 3in driving wheel type, original '156 Class' engines, built 1866-74.

LMS Nos. 23-67: 6ft 8in driving wheel type, '800 Class', built 1870-1.

These running numbers were allocated in 1907 and by 1923 there were gaps (as a result of withdrawals), namely: 20/3/6-7/ 30/4/42-5/8/51-2/5-9/61/3/5-6. Essentially, these engines retained their original double-framed Kirtley characteristics, but their cabs were basically of Johnson origin, and the front-end configuration was Deeley-Fowler — *Plate 5*. By LMS times, all examples had lost their original tenders in favour of the flared coping plus coal rail Johnson type, generally of 2,950 — gallon capacity, although some of the 6ft 3in engines had 2,750-gallon tenders — see *Plate 6*. All examples were passed to the LMS in crimson livery but by no means all lasted long enough to receive LMS ownership markings in lieu of their previous MR insignia. It is not possible to state how many were properly repainted in LMS days, but the following are known to have received LMS markings in the 1923-8 period with the full red livery and circular emblem:

6ft 3in series: 1/3/4/5/8/13/5-7/22 (plus No. 7 Code A2 — *Plate 7*).
6ft 8in series: 24/49/62

Visually they did not change during the post-1922 period and by the 1928 livery change, the majority had been withdrawn,

Above: *(Plate 5)*: **Large-wheeled Kirtley 2—4—0 No. 53 at Bedford on August 4 1923. These engines defied all attempts to place either a Midland or an LMS badge on the cabside with the standard Code A1 livery.** *A.G. Ellis.*

especially from the larger-wheeled series, but a few survivors did achieve the post-1927 black style of painting. They are all believed to have carried red lining and the following have all been confirmed in the style represented by *Plates 8 & 9*, with letter spacing at consistently 40 in between centres, with the 'M' always just to the rear of the central vertical tender beading:

6ft 3in series: 2/12/9/21-2, all Code B3, Nos. 2, 12 with 2,750 gallon tenders.
6ft 8in series: 60, Code B2.

Interestingly, No. 60 was the only large-wheeled example to receive the later LMS style, all the others having been scrapped

Right: *(Plate 6)*: **The Johnson pattern 2750-gallon tender is clearly shown in this rear view of 6ft 3in 2—4—0 No. 2 in LMS livery (Code A1) at Derby in 1926. This engine is now preserved in the National Collection as pre-1907 No. 158A, but paired with the wrong tender for its current physical configuration.** *H.C. Casserley.*

by early 1929, and it survived until 1936, by which time it had been renumbered as 20060 on the LMS duplicate list (*Plate 10*).

Five of the smaller-wheeled engines also received 2XXXX series numbers: 20002/8/12/8/22. Of these, three examples at least (Nos. 20002/8/12 ran for some time with rather small cabside numbers some 6in high, no doubt hand-painted — *Plate 11*. There may have been others, but the last survivor (No. 20002) served out its time with standard 10in figures somewhat uncomfortably squeezed on to the cabside — *Plate 12*. A contemporary (circa 1938) colour slide suggests that red lining continued to be carried, but No. 20002 might have been plain black at withdrawal in 1947.

This engine is preserved in the National Collection as MR 158A, with a Kirtley-pattern tender. Since the locomotive is basically in its final condition, it would have been better to leave it as shown in *Plate 12*, with Johnson tender and carrying one of the later MR/LMS styles of painting, but it seems unlikely that this option is now available, owing to the lack of a suitable tender. Nevertheless, it is one of the most significant engines in the National Collection and is likely to be displayed at York from 1987/8 onwards in chronological sequence with the few other mid-Victorian survivors of the British scene.

Above (*Plate 7*): **A few ex-MR engines received the 1923-style of LMS ownership markings (Code A2), but No. 7 was probably the only ex-Kirtley 2—4—0 to be repainted in this fashion. This picture was taken at Derby on August 11 1923.** *Authors' Collection.*

Above & Left (*Plates 8 & 9*): **Post-1927 lined black liveries, Codes B3 and B2 respectively, on 2—4—0s Nos. 12 (above) and 60 (left) circa 1930. The red lining and insignia counter-shading barely register, but they are both there. The figure '6' on No. 60 is almost of Midland rather than LMS standard shape.** *A.G. Ellis/Authors' Collection.*

Right *(Plate 10):* Hand-painted unshaded cabside numerals were applied to No. 20060 in 1934 when the engine reached the LMS duplicate list. The engine was still lined-out when this picture was taken on June 2 1934. *L. Hanson.*

Left *(Plate 11):* 6ft 3in Kirtley 2—4—0 No. 20008, still probably in lined black livery but with small hand painted numerals, circa 1934. *Authors' Collection.*

Right *(Plate 12):* The standard 10in numerals (Code B8) were carried by No. 20002 towards the end of its life and probably originated circa 1938. Note too the 1936-pattern front numberplate. The Johnson tender is not the same as shown in *Plate 6* — note the lack of horizontal bottom-edge beading, adjacent to the running plate top, which identifies the vehicle as the 2950-gallon capacity type. *BR (LMR).*

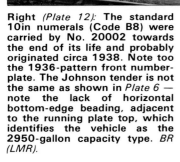

16

The expression 'Kirtley-Johnson' seems apt for this group, if technically less than precise, because although the engines were designed at the end of the Kirtley era, by the time the survivors reached the LMS, they were all but indistinguishable from the genuine Johnson product. Moreover, many of them appeared, even when new, after Kirtley had died and they embodied Johnson

modifications from the outset. Again, two separate series were involved, neither of which changed appreciably in appearance during the LMS period:

LMS Nos. 68-126: 6ft 8in driving wheels, survivors of Kirtley '890 Class' (*Plate 13*) built 1871-5.
LMS Nos. 127-146: 6ft 3in driving wheels, survivors of the '1070 Class', essentially a posthumous Kirtley design and sometimes attributed to Johnson (*Plate 14*); built 1874-5.

As with all the earlier ex-MR engines, there had been some withdrawals between 1907 and 1923, so the number series was not continuous. The gaps were: 73/9/86/8/91/106/11/4/25/41, of which only one was from the 6ft 3in series. The engines all carried Johnson cabs and tenders with the Deeley/Fowler front-end. By LMS days, their Johnson tenders were dominantly of the 3,250-gallon variety — the officially 'correct' type for the class.

They were all painted red (Code A1) when the LMS was formed but, as usual with ex-MR engines, it is not possible to state how many received LMS ownership markings. Scrapping naturally continued through the 1920s and 1930s and it is obvious that some of them must have retained MR markings to the end. The confirmed list of LMS insignia with full red livery is quite comprehensive but includes only a few of the smaller-wheeled type (such as No. 127 — *Plate 15*):

Code A1 - 69/70/2/6-7/81-2/5/7/92/7-8/100-2/5/7/9-10/2/5/7/20/2-4/6-7/9/32/6-7.
Code A2 - 82 (*Plate 16*)

After the livery change, several examples were given the new type insignia, retaining red livery. It seems possible that this may, in some cases, have been coincidental with removing the earlier insignia and that their limited life expectancy would not justify a full repaint. The engines concerned were Nos. 84/102/8, all Code A5 with 40in letter spacing. We believe No. 84 kept this style until withdrawn in 1932 — *Plate 17*. Only three reached the duplicate list (Nos. 20087/92/115) and No. 20092 was the

Top *(Plate 13)*: Kirtley-Johnson '890 Class' 2—4—0 No. 100, pictured in almost ex-works condition in early LMS livery, Code A1. *Authors' Collection.*

Above *(Plate 14)*: Small-wheeled Kirtley-Johnson 2—4—0 No. 138 was photographed on November 2 1923 bearing Livery Code A1 without ownership markings of any kind. Several examples ran like this in early LMS days. *W.L. Good.*

last withdrawal in 1938. Some of them, but not very many, did receive the post-1927 black livery, usually lined out; and there was enough room to permit the 10in figures to be employed in most cases — *Plates 18 & 19*. The list of known examples is as follows (all lined black), Code B2: Nos. 70/1/7/100/15/23/17/32/7/42, also No. 20115.

Above *(Plate 15):* **6ft 3in 2—4—0 No. 127 (livery Code A1) is the only example of this particular series we can confirm to have received an LMS emblem. It was photographed at St. Albans, circa 1925.** *A.G. Ellis.*

Above *(Plate 16):* **A rare livery for the type, Code A2, applied to 6ft 9in 2—4—0 No. 82 at Derby circa 1923/4.** *Authors' Collection.*

Left, top *(Plate 17)*: Post-1927 red livery (Code A5), was carried by quite a few non-entitled ex-Midland engines, probably because they did not justify a full repaint. 6ft 9in 2—4—0 No. 84, seen at Derby in 1928, was one such example. Note the 'bulkhead' pattern of Johnson 3250 — gallon tender. *Authors' Collection.*

Left & below *(Plates 18 & 19)*: Conventional post-1927 livery (Code B2) is seen here applied to 2—4—0s Nos. 127 (left) and 20115 (below) of the 6ft 3in series. The figure shapes have a distinct 'Midland' shape, compared with the somewhat coarser pattern of the LMS standard type. *L. Hanson/Authors' Collection.*

JOHNSON 2-4-0 (LMS Nos. between 147-282; Power Class 1, later 1P)

What might be termed the 'proper' Johnson 2—4—0s came to the LMS in four varieties, differentiated principally by small changes in wheel diameter. In 1907, they had been renumbered in order of building which meant that, apart from the 6ft 3in engines (the first type to be built in 1876), the next three versions tended to be intermixed, since the MR never quite decided which of the three larger-wheeled types to build in quantity. In consequence, batches of all three varieties emerged between 1876 and 1881. They are considered here in ascending order of driving wheel diameter and, as usual, there were a few 1907-22 withdrawals before the LMS was formed. The types can be summarised as follows:

6ft 3in driving wheels: LMS Nos. 147-156: built 1876 (Nos. 148/51 withdrawn pre-1923)
6ft 6in driving wheels: LMS Nos. 157-191/217-21: built 1876-80 (No. 160 withdrawn pre-1923)
6ft 9in driving wheels: LMS Nos. 192-6/207-16/222-71: built 1876-81 (all to the LMS)

7ft 0in driving wheels: LMS Nos. 197-206/272-81: built 1877-81 (No. 199 withdrawn pre-1923)

All examples were painted red (Code A1), on receipt by the LMS and all had Deeley/Fowler front ends. Otherwise, they were little changed from their original Johnson condition. All carried round-top boilers and were paired either with 2,950-gallon or 3,250-gallon tenders, roughly according to the following breakdown, based on accurate contemporary observation:

6ft 3in series: Generally 2,950-gallon.
6ft 6in series: Approximately equal proportions 2,950/3,250-gallon.
6ft 9in series: 2,950-gallon.
7ft 0in series: 2,950-gallon, but also a few 3,250-gallon.

Plates 20-23 illustrate examples of each of the four types in round-top boiler condition.

Above & opposite page *(Plates 20 - 23):* **The four varieties of Johnson 2—4—0 in round-top boiler configuration as received by the LMS: No. 155 (above) Code A2; No. 170 (opposite page, top) Code A1; No. 254 (opposite page, centre) Code B3; No. 201 (opposite page, lower) Code A2. The engines are illustrated in ascending order of driving wheel diameter.** *A.C. Roberts Collection/A.G. Ellis/Photomatic/Authors' Collection.*

This page: Johnson 2—4—0s Nos. 170, 254 and 201 — further details on opposite page.

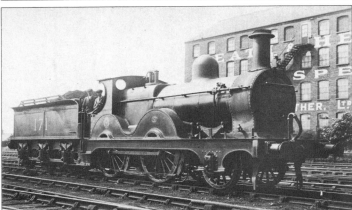

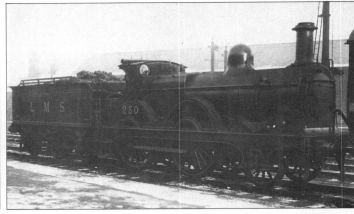

This page: *(Plates 24 – 27):* Illustrated here are Belpaire-boilered rebuilds of the four Johnson 2—4—0 types, again presented in ascending wheel diameter: No. 150 (top) Code A1; No. 171 (above, left) Code A1; No. 250 (above, right) Code A5; No. 20204 (right) Code B2. Perhaps the most interesting single feature is the post-1927 lined red livery on No. 250. *Authors' Collection (3)/ L. Hanson.*

In 1926, the LMS began to fit Belpaire boilers to many of these Johnson 2—4—0s, including examples from all four series. Not only was the boiler shape altered (from round-top to Belpaire) so too were the dome and safety valves — 'pop' valves replacing the original Salter fittings. Although their operating life was extended by this rebuilding, the changes did nothing for their appearance, even though something of the original Johnson elegance still managed to 'fight through' *(Plates 24-27)*. The bulk of the Belpaire rebuilding was applied to the 6ft 9in engines (the old Johnson '1400 Class') probably because these were more numerous anyway and newer than all the 6ft 3in engines and most of the 6ft 6in types. Virtually all the long-term survivors to the 2XXXX duplicate series were of the rebuilt Belpaire type. The 2XXXX survivors were:

6ft 3in series: Nos. 20153/5
6ft 6in series: Nos. 20157*/79*/83/5/8/219/21
6ft 9in series: Nos. 20194/207/11*/3-6/25/8/38/42/5*/6*/51/3/4*/61/6-7/9
7ft 0in series: No. 20204
*Still round top, remainder Belpaire

Three of these engines (Nos. 20155/85/216) lasted until BR days and were allocated BR Nos. 58020-2, although these were never carried. No. 20155 was the last survivor (1950). During their lifetime, most engines continued to be paired with the original tenders but there were a few changes as illustrated in *Plate 28*.

Above *(Plate 28)*: The 'bulkhead' Johnson 3250-gallon tender is clearly featured in this picture of Belpaire-boilered 6ft 9in 2—4—0 No. 268, still carrying livery Code A1 at Grimesthorpe Motive Power Depot in the winter of 1932. *Gordon Coltas.*

Left *(Plate 29)*: Red lining and countershaded 12in figures (Code B3) are clearly visible on 6ft 6in 2—4—0 No. 219 at Northampton, December 8 1934. Note the Midland-style '9'. *L. Hanson.*

Above *(Plate 30):* 2—4—0 No. 162 also carried countershaded insignia and lining, (Code B3) when pictured in June 1931 at Nottingham — but it hardly registered on the photograph. *Authors' Collection.*

Right, upper *(Plate 31):* 6ft 9in 2—4—0 No. 260 was given lined black livery with 10in figures in April 1928 — at which time they would, undoubtedly, have been either black-shaded or unshaded — Code B5. *W.L. Good.*

Right, lower *(Plate 32):* No. 20155, with hand-painted smokebox number. The livery is likely to have been Code C21 by this time. *Authors' Collection.*

Turning now to LMS livery, there is the usual problem of confirming those locomotives which received proper LMS markings during the 'all-red' 1923-8 period, but a reasonable cross-section is given in the summary. After the livery change, at least two examples received the post-1927 red livery, but most became lined black. Although the lining frequently failed to register on contemporary pictures, it is felt likely that it was always there, usually with countershaded insignia. The engines were always 'shopped' at Derby and it is very improbable that at this place they would not receive the officially correct style! The summary is based on this presumption and it is not thought that very many received plain black, save for any post-1939 repaints. Post-1927 liveries tended to favour 12in numerals with letter spacing consistently at 40in centres, but there were exceptions as shown in *Plates 29-31*.

An interesting small detail which was quite often seen on these engines when placed on the 2XXXX lists, was the somewhat crude rendering of the new smokebox number in paint rather than on a cast plate. This practice (see *Plate 32*) was common to many ex-MR types but was by no means universally followed, as shown in *Plate 33*. Likewise, while it was quite common for duplicated ex-MR engines not to receive new five-figure number plates, some of them did. As usual in these matters, a dated photograph is the only sure confirmation.

In *Plates 34-38*, we offer further examples of interesting LMS period variations in the Johnson 2—4—0s and the following summary attempts to cover most of the significant livery differences, especially the Belpaire rebuilds.

Below *(Plate 33)*: **No. 20216, renumbered in 1937, carried no smokebox number-plate when photographed at Bedford (Livery Code B2) on April 25 1937.** *A.G. Ellis.*

Left *(Plate 34)*: **No. 245 (Livery Code B3) was one of the longer-lasting Johnson 2—4—0s to retain a round-top boiler in 1935, and is pictured here on May 25 that year.** *Vic Forster Collection.*

Above *(Plate 35):* **The majority of Belpaire-boilered 2—4—0s quickly received 'pop'-type safety valves, but No. 185 (Livery Code B3) was still carrying Ramsbottom-type valves when photographed at Carlisle Upperby on June 10 1936.** *A.G. Ellis.*

Left *(Plate 36):* 6ft 9in 2—4—0 No. 213 (Livery Code B3) has both lining and countershading — although this is not very clear to see in this view. Note the added 'P' painted next to the metal power class figure on the cabside, and the rolled-up stormsheet at the back of the cab roof. *Authors' Collection.*

Right *(Plates 37 & 38):* 2—4—0 No. 155 was quite a celebrated engine. Not only was it the last ex-MR 2—4—0 to survive (until 1950) but it also ran as 'Engineer South Wales' between 1933 and 1936. Right upper: No. 155 at Bath, where the leading right-hand spring is apparently the subject of the shed fitters attentions. Note also the tablet-catcher fitted to the tender, for use on single line sections. Right, lower: No. 155 as 'Engineer South Wales' inside the shed at Abergavenny. Both pictures feature Livery Code B3. *Photomatic/Authors' Collection.*

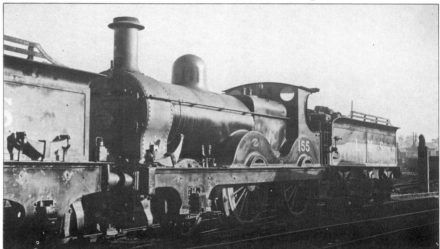

Above *(Plate 39):* **MR No. 614 was one of only two of the first series of Johnson 'Bogie Singles' to reach the LMS, and the only one with original Johnson cab. It is seen here at Chinley before the cabside MR emblem was replaced by that of the LMS**. *Authors' Collection.*

The Johnson 'Bogie Singles' dated from 1887, when the single driving wheel type made a surprising comeback, largely because of the invention of steam standing equipment by Works Manager Holt at Derby. Single driving wheel types were especially prone to slipping — particularly in view of increasing train weights — but the introduction of steam sanding gear assisted adhesion considerably and gave the type a new lease of life. They were built until the end of the 19th century but, by LMS days, heavy inroads had been made into their numbers and the fifth and final series — the so-called 'Princess of Wales' type — had all been scrapped. In consequence, the LMS received examples of only the four earlier types — but only 43 of the 85 examples which had been built.

Their relatively short life might suggest that they were less than effective — but this was not so. Essentially they did not (by virtue of their 4—2—2 configuration), lend themselves to the larger boilers which Deeley and Fowler so successfully fitted to the bulk of the contemporary 4—4—0s. Quite a number of the 'singles' were reboilered in the Edwardian period but the new boilers were limited in size because of the requirement to fit 'between' the driving wheels. In consequence, and apart from the inevitable Deeley style front-end, the survivors came to the LMS still bearing most of their original Johnson elegance — and it was a very high standard of elegance, much commented on throughout their lifetime.

The four series of 'singles' received by the LMS were in two principal groups, slide and piston valve respectively; but to some extent, each of the three later types represented a progressive improvement on the earliest series. Before scrapping commenced, they were divided as follows, using the 1907 Midland numbers and listing the more obvious differences:

MR Nos. 600-24: Slide valves, 7ft 4½in wheels (Nos. 608-9/20-4 had 7ft 6in wheels), leaf springs to the driving wheels; built 1887-90.

MR Nos. 625-59: Slide valves, 7ft 6in wheels, coil springs to driving wheels, modified (deepened) frame top between smokebox and driving wheel; built 1891-3.

MR. Nos. 660-69: Piston valves, 7ft 6in wheels, coil springs and much deeper frames below smokebox; built 1893 and 1896.

MR Nos. 670-84: Piston valves, 7ft 9in wheels, coil springs and further front frame shape modifications. (Nos. 675-84 had a further variation of the front frame modification). Built 1896-7 and 1899.

By LMS times, the survivors were:

1st series: Nos. 600/14 only
2nd series: Nos. 627-8/32-3/5/8-41/3-5/9/51-2/4-5/7/9
3rd series: all to LMS
4th series: all to LMS except Nos. 675/81/4

All examples had 3,250 gallon tenders except the last series which had the 3,500-gallon type. The four varieties are shown in *Plates 39-42* and the variant of the fourth type (with the slightly changed front frames) in shown in *Plate 43*. Connoisseurs of these matters generally rated this fourth series (the old MR '115 Class') as the 'flower of the flock' visually, and we are inclined to agree. It is, of course, one of these, No. 673, which is preserved at the National Railway Museum in its post-Deeley configuration. This locomotive was kept for nearly half a century as MR No. 118 in a quite extraordinary version of the old MR pre-1905 livery, until one of the authors managed to get most of the mistakes corrected in 1976, when it was repainted at Derby. Along with No. 679 *(Plate 43)*, it was one of the last two examples to survive, until 1928, but as preserved, its tender is not of the correct pattern for the class, being of only 2,950-gallon capacity.

The engines were never painted any colour but red (essentially Code A1) and most of them probably went for scrap during 1925/6, with their MR markings on the cabsides. However, a few did receive the LMS emblem, including the one and only rebuild, No. 600 (the pioneer engine), which also lasted until 1928 and was mainly used for inspection train duties in its final years — *Plate 44.*

Known examples of engines which carried LMS markings are Nos. 600/14/38/41/4/9/65/79 (all Code A1) of which No. 665 also ran as Code A2 for a short time *(Plate 45)*. It is likely that there were a few more, possibly No.s 633/40/5/69/73, none of which were withdrawn before 1927.

Above *(Plate 40)*: No. **638** represents the second series of 4—2—2s, fitted with coil springs and slightly deepened frames, Livery Code **A1**. *National Railway Museum.*

Left *(Plate 41)*: Much deeper upper frames distinguished the third series of 4—2—2s of which the first example, No. **660**, in MR markings is pictured, exactly as it came to the LMS in **1923**. *Authors' Collection.*

Right *(Plate 42):* **No. 672 of the old '115 Class' was one of five engines of the fourth series of 4—4—2s to display the 'convex plus concave' frame shape ahead of the smokebox. The preserved No. 673 is virtually identical.** *Authors' Collection.*

Left *(Plate 43):* **No. 679, resplendent in newly applied LMS livery (Code A1) represents the alternative front frame arrangement of the fourth series of 4—2—2s. Note also the double curve of the 'lifters' to the Salter safety valves on the dome casing.** *Authors' Collection.*

Below *(Plate 44):* **The 'odd man out' from the first series of 4—2—2s was No. 600 with Deeley cab, seen here at Derby in July 1926 coupled to an officers' saloon, itself a rebuild from a former steam railmotor.** *W.L. Good.*

JOHNSON CLASS 1 4-4-0 (LMS Nos. between 300-327; Power Class 1, later 1P)

With the exception of the Class 3 'Belpaires' and Class 4 'Compounds' (below), all Midland 4—4—0s from the Johnson period were originally of the slim-boiler kind. By LMS days, most of them had been rebuilt to one of several 'Class 2' configurations, but there were still some left more or less in original state, these being the 16 surviving examples of the first 30 built (in 1876/7), twenty eight examples were given new numbers (300-27) in 1907 and, by LMS days, the following were still in existence:

6ft 6in driving wheel series: Nos. 300/3-6/8 (six of the original ten); built 1876/7, generally 2,950-gallon tenders.
7ft 0in driving wheel series: Nos. 310-1/4/7/9-20/3/5-7 (ten of the original 20) built 1877, generally 3250-gallon tenders.

Smokeboxes and chimneys excepted, these engines were still unmistakeably Johnson in appearance, as shown in *Plates 46 & 47*. They all passed into LMS ownership in red livery. All but

Above (Plate 46): **Unrebuilt 6ft 6in Johnson 4—4—0 No. 306, Livery Code A1**, with circular LMS emblem on the rear driving wheel splasher. *Authors' Collection.*

one stayed that way since most were withdrawn in the mid-1920s, many without even receiving LMS emblems. Those known to have had the cabside LMS device were Nos. 305-6/8/11/20/3/5-6 but again, it is believed that there were a few more. One example, No. 323 (*Plate 48*) was fitted with an extended smokebox which did nothing for its appearance. It was withdrawn in 1929, still paired with a 3,250-gallon tender.

The last survivor was No. 311, outliving the rest by some four years and particularly associated in some of its later years with the M & GN services. It was the only example to receive post-1927 lined black livery (*Plate 49*) and was withdrawn late in 1934.

Above: *(Plate 47):* Unrebuilt 7ft 0in Johnson 4—4—0 No. 320, Livery Code A1. *BR (LMR).*

Right: *(Plate 48):* No. 323, (Livery Code A1) was an unrebuilt 7ft 0in 4—4—0 with an extended smokebox which is just discernible at the left-hand side of this picture, taken circa 1926. *Authors' Collection.*

Below: *(Plate 49):* No. 311, the only unrebuilt Johnson 4—4—0 to receive the post-1927 lined black livery, was painted thus before the red counter-shaded insignia were introduced in 1929. The locomotive is seen here in the condition in which it ran from 1928 to 1934, Livery Code B6. *Authors' Collection.*

JOHNSON (REBUILT BY DEELEY) SATURATED STEAM CLASS 2 4-4-0
(LMS Nos. between 328-481; Power Class 2, later 2P)

These were unquestionably the most confusing 4—4—0 engines, in terms of visual style and appearance, which the Midland bequeathed to the LMS, having all undergone at least one rebuilding (often more) after they took to the rails in slim-boilered form during the Johnson period. In fact, 'renewal using the old number' would be a better description than 'rebuild'. Quite a number of different 'slim boiler' classes were involved, but all had been modified well before the LMS period.

Essentially, the renewal of the Johnson 4—4—0s from Deeley's time onwards had taken three basic forms. The first chronologically was the fitting of new and larger round-top boilers with new cabs but retaining original frames. These were known as 'H' boiler rebuilds and representatives of three wheel diameters came through to the LMS with few further modifications (Plates 50-52). The next Deeley phase was to fit a standard Belpaire boiler, again usually with original frames and

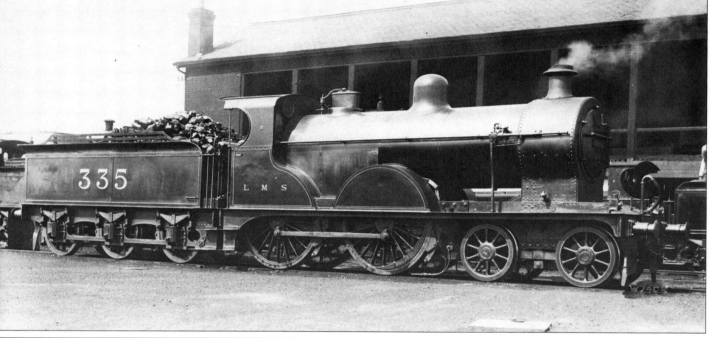

This Page: (Plates 50 - 52): Three 'H' boilered 4—4—0s, illustrated in order of ascending driving wheel dimension from 6ft 6in to 7ft 0in are pictured in LMS colours: No. 475 (top) Livery Code A1; No. 335 (centre) Livery Code A2 and No. 373 (left) with MR markings, as received by the LMS. Note particularly the continuous splasher style of the 6ft 6in engine (No. 475) compared with the separate leading splasher (plus coupling rod box) of the larger-wheeled series.
Bernard Matthews (2)/Authors' Collection.

This Page: (Plates 53 – 55): Saturated Belpaire-boilered Class 2 4—4—0s, in ascending wheel sizes: No. 381 (top) Livery Code A1; No. 338 (above) Livery Code A1 and No. 374 (right) Livery Code A1. Note the separate leading splasher in all three wheel sizes. Interestingly, No. 338 was photographed as late as 1934, still in red livery. *All: Authors' Collection.*

the engines so fitted also varied considerably in appearance, depending on wheel diameter *(Plates 53-55)*.

This phase more or less concludes the Deeley part of the story, save to remark that some engines received both 'H' boilers and saturated Belpaire boilers in their time; and it is with engines in one of these various saturated configurations that this section is mainly concerned. However, and to maintain an adequate link to the LMS standard part of the story, it should also be mentioned that many of this 328-481 series were further rebuilt (this time with new frames) to form the superheated '483 Class' type (below) during the Fowler regime, and this rebuilding went on into the LMS period in and after 1923. Including the LMS examples, those engines which were further rebuilt as the '483 Class' were as follows, this effectively being the third basic form, following the two saturated variations. The process was complete early in 1924: Nos. 332/7/51/3/6/9/62/4/70/7/ 94-7/400-27/30/2-4/6-9/43-4/6-8/50/2-6/8-9/61-4/6/8/ 70-2/7-80.

These superheated rebuilds will not be considered further in this chapter, since none of them received LMS markings except in '483 Class' configuration — see *Chapter 2*.

Turning now to the remaining saturated engines, the breakdown of types within the residual 328-481 series was as follows:

Between 328 and 357: 6ft 9in engines (both 'H' boiler and Belpaire); original frames
Between 358 and 377: 7ft 0in engines (both 'H' boiler and Belpaire); original frames
From 378 to 392: 6ft 6in engines, all Belpaire and new frames
Between 393 and 481: 6ft 6in engines, all 'H' boiler except 460/5 (Belpaire as 378-92, but retaining original frames)

In the 328-77 series, the 'H' boiler and Belpaire breakdown was:

6ft 9in 'H' boiler: Nos. 331/3/5/41/3-5/8/52/4-5/7
6ft 9in Belpaire: Nos. 328-30/4/6/8-40/2/6/9-50
7ft 0in 'H' boiler: Nos. 360/7/71/3/5
7ft 0in Belpaire: Nos. 358/61/3/5-6/8-9/72/4/6

All examples served out their days without significant further change, although there was one known maverick (*Plates 56 & 57*). The 'H' boiler survivors were quite speedily scrapped, but the Belpaire-fitted examples lasted a few years longer, three of the 6ft 6in series actually lasting to reach BR ownership. These were Nos. 383/5/91 (*Plate 58*).

Below (*Plate 58*): **No. 40383 was one of only three saturated ex-MR Class 2 4—4—0s to reach BR and the only example to receive the fully lined BR livery. Note the LMS (Stanier) pattern chimney and 'pop' safety valves. This picture was taken at Derby on June 12 1949.** *Authors' Collection.*

Having hopefully resolved the visual identification problems of the engines themselves, attention can now be focussed on the somewhat simpler matter of tenders and livery. By the time the LMS received these engines, all were running with the Johnson 3,250-gallon tender and this pattern never changed, regardless of the variable locomotive anatomy. Livery too, was straightforward. All came to the LMS in crimson lake and quite a number received correct new company markings without any other change. The last of the H-boilered engines had gone before 1928 was over and none received 1928-style painting. Many were undoubtedly scrapped with MR insignia in place.

Scrapping of the Belpaire-boilered examples began just before the elimination of the H boiler series and it is likely, but not confirmed, that most of them received LMS identification during the red period. At the livery change, one or two examples (see *Plate 59*) received 10in figures, in some cases retaining red livery, but the consistent style was lined black livery with 14in gold-coloured Midland numerals in the red countershaded form. Many were doubtless scrapped in red livery, circa 1928-30, but a fair number have been confirmed in the correct post-1927 intermediate livery as shown in *Plates 60 & 61*.

Virtually all examples had gone before the war and the only candidates for wartime black livery were the three 6ft 6in engines which survived to BR ownership (Nos. 383/5/91) plus No. 378, withdrawn in 1947. These lasted longer, probably by virtue of the new frames fitted when first rebuilt with saturated Belpaire boilers.

LIVERY SAMPLES – *for precise wheel diameter and boiler type, see breakdown of number list above.*	
CODE A1:	328/30-1/4/6/8-42/6/8/50/5/8/61/6/72-5/9-82/5-8/91-2/8/429/31/5/42/60/73/5-6
CODE A2:	335/67/476
CODE A5:	369
CODE A7:	380
CODE B4:	329/36/8/65-6/8-9/72/4/6/8/80-3/5-7/9-92
CODE B5:	350
CODE C22:	391
CODE C23:	378

Letter spacing: 40in centres for all post-1927 styles

Above *(Plate 59)*: **6ft 9in saturated Belpaire 4—4—0 No. 350 was an early post-1927 repaint to lined black with 10in numerals and unshaded insignia (Livery Code B5). The picture was taken at Derby in June 1928.** *Authors' Collection.*

Left (upper & lower) *(Plates 60 & 61)*: **7ft 0in and 6ft 6in saturated Belpaire 4—4—0s Nos. 369 and 387 in the normal post-1927 style, Code B4.** *Authors' Collection / Bernard Matthews Collection.*

FOWLER '483 CLASS' 4-4-0
(LMS Nos. between 332-480, plus 482-562; Power Class 2, later 2P)

This design was a superheated renewal rebuild of many older 4—4—0s and dated from 1912. The process continued into the LMS period and was completed by 1924, all remaining unrebuilt 4—4—0s being scrapped in an earlier configuration (see previous sections). The '483 Class' rebuilds all had 7ft diameter driving wheels and a 9ft 6in wheelbase regardless of their previous dimensions, and all had piston valves.

This type was adopted in 1928 as an LMS standard design for new construction with but few changes — mainly a slight reduction in wheel diameter — and is analysed in detail in *Chapter 2*. However, in *Plates 62 & 63*, two views are offered of

Above & below: (Plates 62 & 63): **Superheated '483 Class' rebuilt 4—4—0s Nos. 425 (above) Livery Code A1 and 409 (below) Livery Code B4, represent possibly the most common versions of this familiar type during the LMS period. Both had been rebuilt in MR days from earlier types. Their Johnson tenders made them look rather more different from the LMS standard version than was really the case. Johnson 4—2—2 No. 641 is also featured in the upper picture.** *National Railway Museum.*

these eventually very familiar engines, one each in the two main LMS liveries.

JOHNSON/DEELEY CLASS 3 'BELPAIRE' 4-4-0
(LMS Nos. 700-779; Power Class 3, later 3P)

Above *(Plate 64):* **Saturated Class 3 Belpaire No. 751 (Livery Code A1) leaving Kings Norton on June 30 1926. Note the different front footplate and cab roof profile, compared with the superheated series. It is also worth drawing attention to the mixed train formation.** *W.L. Good.*

This series of 4—4—0s was second only to the Class 2 engines in terms of visual variation, especially in Midland days. Even by the LMS period there were four or five quite noticeably different engine configurations, and a great deal of tender variety was also to be observed. Although a detailed examination of Midland locomotive evolution is not appropriate here, it is still necessary to summarise the basic situation in 1923, to aid understanding of the LMS continuation.

The 80 engines of this class originated in 1900 with the building by Johnson of a new large Belpaire-boilered 4—4—0 type. Subsequently, all succeeding engines were often referred to as 'Johnson Belpaires', even though the last 20 examples (Nos. 760-79) were actually built by Deeley and all the earlier ones had eventually been rebuilt to his 'visual' style. The MR actually identified several different classes in this series but in LMS days they came to be regarded as one class.

Fowler began to fit these 4—4—0s with superheaters in 1913 but this process was not complete by 1923. During 1923-5 most of the residual saturated engines were superheated by the LMS but a few were scrapped in saturated form. In summary, this was carried out as follows:

a) Withdrawn (saturated) by LMS: Nos. 737/42/9/72/8/9
b) Superheated by LMS: Nos. 707/12/6/20/34/47/50-1/1/3/ 5/8-9/62-4/71/4-5/7
c) Superheated pre-1923: all others.
NB: *No. 751 may have been withdrawn in saturated form – confirmation is lacking.*

It is not thought that any of those examples superheated by the LMS were given new company liveries until after rebuilding, but at least three of those which were never superheated did receive LMS markings — *Plate 64.*

Turning now to visual variations, the saturated engines represented by *Plate 64* could always be identified by their considerably shorter smokeboxes and their retention of earlier pattern front frames and cab roof. However, additional to this differentiation was a basic four-fold division of the whole class as follows:

Nos. 700-9 'Shallow depth' cabside panel, 'straight' (vertical) front footstep plate fixed behind the running plate (footplate) angle *(Plate 65).*
Nos. 710-29. 'Normal' cab panel, very deep footplate angle with 'cranked' front footsteps rivetted to the front of the footplate angle *(Plate 66).*
Nos. 730-59. As Nos. 710-29 but with (for the type) 'normal depth' footplate angle *(Plate 67).*
Nos. 760-79. Generally as Nos. 700-9 (vertical front footstep plates behind the valance) but with normal-sized cabside panel and displaying the same 'downcurve' of the footplate angle behind the front buffer plank as the 710-59 series *(Plate 68).*

These differences generally applied to the superheated engines but the cabside and footstep variations were also displayed on the few residual saturated examples.

There were also several types of tender paired with these engines. In theory these were supposed to stay behind distinct locomotive batches, but in practice it did not turn out this way, tender-changing adding further to the confusion. The basic types of tender were:

Deeley flat-side Type 1: Rebuilt from old bogie tenders and having a distinct rounded 'turn under' above the side frames *(Plate 69).*
Deeley flat-side Type 2: As Type 1, but with no 'turn under'

This page: *(Plates 65-68):* **The four basic types of superheated Class 3 Belpaire 4—4—0s (as defined in the main text and all bearing early LMS livery, Code A1) are represented, in order, by Nos. 701 (top left), 718 (top right), 753 (above) and 767 (right). Three tender variations are also shown — and are covered in more detail in the next group of four views.** *W.L. Good/Authors' Collection (2)/Bernard Matthews Collection.*

This page (Plates 69-72): The four common tender variations associated with the Class 3 'Belpaire' 4—4—0s (as defined in the main text) are represented, in order, coupled to superheated locomotives Nos. 748 (top), 708 (above left), 759 (above right) and 774 (left). The Livery Code is B4 in the first three cases, and B10 for No. 774. Three of the four basic locomotive variants are represented. *Photomatic/Bernard Matthews Collection/Authors' Collection (2).*

and displaying the edge of the footplate between front and rear steps (*Plate 70*).

Johnson 'Belpaire' Type 1: Johnson 3,500 gallon tender of normal type but with deep footplate angle (or valance), thus allowing the running plate to line up with that of the engine (*Plate 71*).

Johnson 'Belpaire' Type 2: As Johnson Type 1 but devoid of the vertical beading strip halfway along the tender side panel

(*Plate 72*).

The two Johnson tender types were designed for the Class 3 4—4—0s, having a higher than normal running plate, and were rarely seen attached to any other engine type. The Deeley version, however, could also be seen operating with some of the 'Compound' 4—4—0s since a few of these and many of the 'Belpaires' had originally carried large bogie tenders. In point of fact, some of these flat-sided tenders had come from the former

Left (Plate 73): Class 3P 4—4—0 No. 762, at Wellingborough on March 25 1932, was coupled to a '990 Class' tender, presumably supplied a few years earlier. The Livery Code is B4 and the tender livery is similar to the slightly higher-sided version shown in Plate 70. L. Hanson.

Below (Plate 74): Class 3P 4—4—0 No. 707 was photographed at Leicester on July 20 1935, (Livery Code B4) coupled to a hybrid tender comprising an LMS tank on Deeley frames. Note that the tank is shorter than the chassis frames at the rear. Authors' Collection.

'Princess of Wales' type 4—2—2s (whose bogie tenders had also been rebuilt) when the engines themselves were scrapped before 1923.

Additionally, in later days a few residual 'Belpaires' were seen trailing replacement tenders of the Deeley 990 type (Plate 73) or LMS rebuilds of earlier tenders (Plate 74). What seems to have happened is that the 'Belpaires' became a sort of 'dustbin' class for tenders (from withdrawn engines) which were in better condition than those originally provided.

Fortunately, the engines themselves did not undergo too many significant further changes in LMS days. Bogie brakes were gradually removed (Plates 75 & 76) and there was an equally gradual change to 'pop' safety-valves among the later survivors, along with a few replacement Stanier-type chimneys (Plate 77). One or two examples continued to carry bogie 'splash' plates during early LMS days — occasionally with experimental modifications as well (Plate 78). Generally however, the LMS tended to regard the Class 3 4—4—0s as non-standard and withdrew them slowly but steadily, without making too many changes of a basic anatomical nature.

LMS liveries for the class were consistent — either red pre-1928 or lined black thereafter. Most red examples probably received new company markings before the change in style and 14in Midland figures with red countershading were the norm during the lined black period (Plate 79). Quite a few received the 1936-style markings (Plate 80) while odd ones were fitted with new block-style numberplates retaining scroll/serif insignia (Plate 81). There were a few plain black wartime repaints and a few temporary styles in early BR days (Plate 78), before the

residual engines received the BR lined black style. A total of 23 examples reached BR: Nos. 711/5/20/6-9/31/4-6/9-41/3/5/7-8/56-8/62-3. The last survivor (No. 40726) was withdrawn in 1952.

Given that scrapping commenced in the 1920s, the engines really lasted rather well. Many would reckon them to have been a better basis for an LMS standard type than the Class 2 engines, and even though their days as the 'mainstay' of the Midland may have begun to decline during the building up of the 'Compound' fleet, they were always a popular type, if not the easiest group about which to generalise. The tabulated summary accompany-

LIVERY SAMPLES - (FOR LOCOMOTIVE CONFIGURATION, SEE PRECEEDING TEXT)

PRINCIPAL TENDER VARIATIONS

	TENDERS (SEE PAGES 39 & 41)			
LIVERY	DEELEY TYPE 1	DEELEY TYPE 2	JOHNSON TYPE 1*	JOHNSON TYPE 2*
CODE A1	706/11/2/8/25-7/9/37‡/41/4/6/8	700-2/8-9/45	751‡/3/5-9/61-3/5/7	770/4-7/9‡
CODE B4	706/12-3/8/21/3/6/8-9/30/2/4-6/41/8	708/45	724-5/43/50/6-60/3/5/7-8	726/47/73-7
CODE B11	—	—	725/57/9	743
CODE C21	731	—	—	—
CODE C22	—	—	—	775
CODE C23	735	—	—	739

*Letter spacing 40in centres on Johnson tenders, post-1927; remainder 53in centres.
‡Saturated locomotives.

Left & Below *(Plates 75 & 76)*: **Bogie brakes were removed from the Belpaire 4—4—0s in the early 1930s and the 'before and after' appearance is represented by Nos. 743 (left) and 721 (below), both painted in lined black livery, Code B4. Further engine/tender combinations are represented, also the change to 'pop' safety valves. The pictures were taken in 1931 and post-1935 respectively.** *G. Coltas. Authors' Collection.*

Above *(Plate 77)*: **A Stanier chimney and non-standard livery displayed on BR No. 40726 at Derby on September 25 1948. The livery is, effectively, Code C24.** *W.L. Good.*

ing this section attempts to cover as many of the points as can reasonably be mentioned, with apologies for its degree of complexity.

TENDER VARIATIONS (See also opposite page)		
LIVERY	DEELEY '990' TYPE	LMS 'HYBRID' TYPE
CODE A1	720	—
CODE B4	720/33/56/62/71	707/15-6/9/27/38/47/55/62
CODE B10	—	715
CODE B11	—	707/40
CODE C23	—	711/38

Right *(Plate 78):* Pioneer Belpaire 4—4—0 No. 700 with feedwater heater (on the running plate, adjacent to the smokebox) and bogie 'splash' plates (beneath the buffers) in early LMS days, Livery Code A1. Note also the bogie brakes. *Bernard Matthews Collection.*

Below *(Plate 79):* Perhaps the most visually harmonious combination of features on the Class 3 4—4—0s was the final engine series coupled to the purpose-built Johnson-style tenders — represented here by No. 776, painted in the typical post-1927 livery (Code B4). This engine was also interesting in that it was fitted with a Kylala blast pipe and slightly 'fatter' chimney. *Authors' Collection.*

Above *(Plate 80):* 1936-style insignia (Code B11) were carried by a few 'Belpaires', including No. 743. Note the detail changes compared with the same engine a few years earlier shown in *Plate 75. W.T. Stubbs Collection.*

Left *(Plate 81):* The application of a 1936-style front numberplate did not necessarily also mean that the engine in question had carried the proper 1936 livery. In many cases the numberplates were simply a replacement and this is believed to be the case here, with No. 723, still bearing countershaded 14in Midland figures (Code B4) when photographed at Derby on July 11 1937. *L. Hanson.*

DEELEY '990 CLASS' 4-4-0 (LMS Nos. 990-999, later between 800-809; Power Class 4)

In 1907, Deeley introduced a robust two-cylinder simple expansion 4—4—0 of comparable power to the three-cylinder 'Compounds', it being generally reckoned that the engines were built for comparative purposes. Ten examples only were built (all but the first in 1909) and apart from regular trips to workshops for attention and the odd venture further afield, they were perhaps most celebrated for having spent virtually their whole working lives on the Leeds—Carlisle main line. Originally saturated, all came to the LMS with superheaters fitted during the Fowler regime they were often referred to as '999s', after the first example built, but it is understood that the correct designation is '990 Class'.

They demonstrated no real advantage over the more numerous 'Compounds' and were somewhat less economical, even though their 6ft 6in diameter driving wheels may have shown some adhesive benefit over the 7ft 'Compounds' on the steeper grades. In consequence, the design was not developed and they were withdrawn in the late 1920s, little changed. They

Above & Below *(Plates 82 & 83):* **The clean and neat lines of the Class 4 '990' 4—4—0s are clearly shown in these views of (above) No. 999 (the pioneer engine) and (below) No. 992, both Livery Code A1. Note the prominent steam brake cylinders between the driving wheels.** *National Railway Museum/Authors' Collection.*

were always painted red *(Plates 82 & 83)* and ran with purpose-built Deeley flat-sided tenders.

In 1927, ostensibly to make room for more new 'Compounds' (to be numbered in the 9XX series), the engines were renumbered 800-9 in order, but Nos. 800/2/4 failed to be carried before scrapping commenced. The last withdrawal was No. 809 (the pioneer engine) in 1929.

Confirmed examples with LMS markings from the 9XX series are Nos. 991/2/9. There may have been others but all the renumbered 8XX examples did carry LMS emblems *(Plate 84)*.

Right *(Plate 84):* **Renumbered '990 Class' 4—4—0 running as LMS No. 808 during 1928, and with the circular LMS emblem on the cabsides.** *Authors' Collection.*

JOHNSON/DEELEY 'COMPOUND' 4-4-0 (LMS 1000-1044; Power Class 4)

The celebrated three-cylinder Midland 'Compound' loco-motives were developed by Johnson and Deeley in the 1901-9 period but, by LMS days, just over half of them had been further modified by Fowler to the superheated form. In this superheated configuration the type was adopted almost unchanged by the LMS as a standard design for new construction and, as such, the whole superheated class (MR and LMS) is considered together in *Chapter 2*. However, in *Plates 85 & 86* we offer views of two examples which were still in saturated state when the LMS took over. The full list of 'Compounds' received in saturated condition is: 1005/10/3/7-9/21-2/5-30/2-4/6/41/3-4.

The ex-MR 'Compounds', saturated or superheated, always ran during LMS days with flat-sided Deeley tenders. A few of these tenders were rebuilt from old bogie examples as was the case with the Class 3 4—4—0s (already described) but most tenders were newly built to a very similar design (also used on the '990 Class') and visually distinguishable mainly by the slightly shallower upper panelling above the top horizontal beading. After the LMS was formed, tender exchanging began to be widespread and added to the three or four Deeley varieties were several variations on the 'LMS standard' theme. This matter will be discussed in *Chapter 2*, along with all the other ramifications of the superheated series.

The conversion to superheating was completed in January 1928 and the two pictures appended are the only ones we have managed to locate showing saturated 'Compounds' in LMS livery.

Opposite page, lower and above *(Plates 85 & 86):* Unlike many classes, most of the original ex-Midland 'Compounds' changed very little in appearance when superheated — mainly only by the slight lengthening of the smokebox. These two views of No. 1010 (opposite page) and 1043 (above) both in livery Code A1, show the shorter smokeboxes of the original saturated version. Note that No. 1010 (an earlier built engine) has a different front frame and smokebox support than No. 1043 — see also *Chapter 2*. Note also the two different styles of Deeley tender — one with continuous running plate and the other with the more typically Deeley 'interrupted' running plate — again see *Chapter 2*. The pictures were taken, almost symbolically, at opposite ends of the Midland division — Carlisle and Kentish Town. *Authors' Collection.*

CHAPTER 2:

THE MIDLAND/LMS STANDARD 4-4-0 CLASSES

S UCH was the dominance of former Midland Railway officers in the earlier locomotive story of the LMS, that for the first few years after the Grouping, affairs at Derby continued almost as though nothing at all of significance had happened. This led directly to the virtually unchanged continuance by the LMS of several Midland designs. At the same time however, the new engines were not precisely identical, either visually or mechanically and this can cause a little confusion. Nevertheless, as far as the LMS was concerned, those MR designs which were 'adopted' by the new company were regarded as 'standard' types and indeed, the LMS-built engines were rarely differentiated in

popular nomenclature from their Midland predecessors, even if they differed slightly in outward styling. It therefore seems more logical to try and give the outline story as one continuous line of evolution.

Of the four types concerned, two were 4—4—0s and these probably showed rather more differences between the MR and LMS types than did the 0—6—0Ts (Chapter 5) and particularly the 0—6—0 tender engines (Chapter 7). The four-coupled designs were, of course, the Class 2 inside-cylinder type and the Class 4 three-cylinder Compound. We deal with them separately.

THE CLASS 2 (LATER 2P) 4-4-0 (See text for number lists)

The inside cylinder 4—4—0 had a long history in Midland days and in the previous chapter we have taken the story of the non-superheated examples down to the point where Fowler introduced a superheated development in 1912 — the so-called '483 Class'. It was this design which formed the basis of the LMS standard version introduced in 1928, the main difference being that whereas all the Midland examples were, at least officially, rebuilds the LMS series were all new engines.

Starting first with the Midland examples, the '483 Class' took its name from the first running number of the first series of non-superheated engines to be rebuilt, although No. 483 itself was not the first example to appear in superheated form. The engines were, for all practical purposes new machines, although they retained their original Johnson tenders for the most part. Rebuilt from locomotives with varying driving wheel diameters

Caption: See Opposite Page.

(6ft 6in to 7ft 0in) and variable coupled wheelbases (8ft 6in to 9ft 6in) all the '483 Class' 'renewals' (to use a more accurate description) came out with 7ft wheels at 9ft 6in wheelbase and a very consistent-looking series of engines resulted *(Plate 87)*. They were typically Midland — or, to be more accurate, particularly characteristic of the Deeley/Fowler school of styling — and their appearance hardly changed throughout their often lengthy lives.

By the time of the Grouping, the renewal programme had not embraced all the former saturated 4—4—0s and the process was never fully completed, as we have seen. However, by LMS days, the whole series of engines from Nos. 482-562 were in the '483'

Opposite page & Above *(Plates 87 & 88):* **These two views compare and contrast the basic configuration of the ex-MR '483 Class' 4—4—0 (No. 463) and the first member of the LMS derivative design (No. 563). The most apparent differences are the tender styles, the size of the boiler mountings, the type of safety valves and the left hand drive position for the LMS design. The liveries are (opposite page) Code A1 and a works grey version of Code B6 (above) — see also** *Plate 103. National Railway Museum/BR (LMR).*

L. M. S. R.

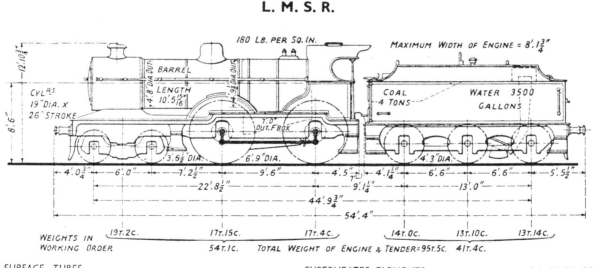

HEATING SURFACE, TUBES—							
LARGE AND SMALL	...	...	...	...	1,033·7 SQ. FT.
FIREBOX	...	...	...	...	123·8 ,,
TOTAL (EVAPORATIVE)	...	...	...	1,157·5 ,,
SUPERHEATER	...	...	...	...	252·7 ,,
COMBINED HEATING SURFACES	...	...	1,410·2 ,,

SUPERHEATER ELEMENTS ... ... 21—1½ IN. DIA. OUTS.

LARGE TUBES ... 21—5¼ IN. DIA. OUTS. { 10 FT. 10½ IN.

SMALL TUBES ... 146—1¾ IN. DIA. OUTS. { BET. TUBEPLATES

GRATE AREA ... ... 21·1 SQ. FT.

TRACTIVE EFFORT (AT 85 PER CENT. B.P.) ... ... 17,729 LB.

Recent changes not shown on drawing : length of boiler barrel decreased to 10 ft. 4 7/16 in. ; coal rails added to tender ; new shape chimney

" 2P " Class

configuration along with a fair number of earlier examples — for a full list of the latter, see page 36. To these machines were added, in 1930, five further examples of the '483' type which had, hitherto been in the stock of the Somerset & Dorset Joint Railway — see *Chapter 9.*

The LMS standard version of the '483 Class' appeared in 1928, the main differences mechanically being the reduction of driving wheel size to 6ft 9in, an increase of boiler pressure from 160psi to 180psi and a reduction in cylinder diameter from 20½in to 19in. This hardly affected the overall external appearance of the engines, but there were a few subtle differences, including left-hand drive, reduced-height chimney and dome fittings (mainly in order to clear the more restricted Scottish area loading gauge) and 'pop' safety-valves rather than

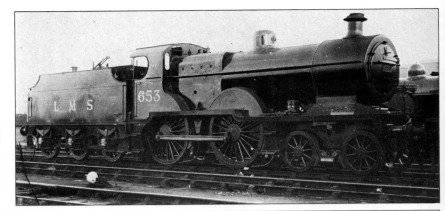

Right: *(Plate 89):* **LMS standard Class 2P No. 653, newly outshopped from Crewe in 1931 (Livery Code B4)** displays the taller chimney style fitted to this series of engines which were at the time, presumably, not expected to be working into Scotland. Note also the use of 40in letter spacing, somewhat unusual for most LMS-built Class 2Ps before No. 686 *(Plate 90)*. The fact that it was a Crewe-shopped engine may provide the explanation. *Authors' Collection.*

Above *(Plate 90):* **The first example of the final 15 LMS-built Class 2Ps was No. 686,** again pictured newly outshopped in 1932. The heavily rivetted nature of both engine and tender is readily apparent, as also is the different numeral size and 40in letter spacing adopted for this batch (Code B3). The GWR-style driving wheel balance weights should also be noted, along with the auxiliary coal rails on the tender. *Authors' Collection.*

the Ramsbottom type. In fact, by the time of their appearance, 'pop' safety valves were already beginning to replace the older type on the Midland series as well. However, the most obvious visual difference between the MR and LMS series was the fitting of Fowler LMS standard high-sided 3,500-gallon tenders to the post-Grouping engines. This created a far greater difference than any of the other detail changes and imparted a conceivably more 'modern-looking' appearance to the LMS-built series. These characteristics are well brought out in *Plate 88.*

Towards the end of the building of the LMS series, a few further detail changes took place. Nos. 628-660 were put into service with the taller MR type chimney *(Plate 89)* and the final 15 examples (Nos. 686-700) were given the visibly rivetted pattern of 3,500-gallon tender, fitted also with coal rails *(Plate 90).* These latter 15 engines, some also having taller chimneys

(Plate 91), carried GWR-style balance weights in the driving wheels and since visible rivetting was also a GWR characteristic, one can perhaps see something of the hand of Stanier in this final 1932 build. The full build of the LMS standard Class 2P 4—4—0 was:

ENGINE NOS.	BUILDER	DATE
536-612	Derby	1928
572§	Derby	1928
575-6†	Derby	1929
580†	Derby	1929
613-28	Derby	1929
629-32	Derby	1930
633-5*	Derby	1928
636-60	Crewe	1931
661-5	Derby	1931
666-85	Derby	1932
686-700+	Crewe	1932

§ - *Second No. 572, replacing original No. 572 which was renumbered 601 after entering service, having been fitted with experimental valves.*
† - *Second engines to carry these numbers, originals having been sold to SDJR in 1928.*
* - *Original 575-6/580, absorbed from SDJR in 1930.*
+ - *Modified batch (see text) built with Stanier modifications.*

The LMS standard engines, which like the 483 Class proper, also included some former SDJR examples, (see also Chapter 9) were numbered immediately in sequence after the ex-MR

50

examples, the 6XX series taking the full allocation of numbers vacated by withdrawn 4—2—2s. The last example built (No. 700) took the number of the pioneer (now withdrawn) Class 3 'Belpaire'. It came out in 1932, two years after the absorption of the SDJR stock and at that point, the full series of engines was:

332—6: ex-MR 483 Class, absorbed from SDJR.
Between 332-480: ex-MR 483 Class (a discontinuous series of numbers).
482-562: ex-MR 483 Class.
563-700: LMS standard series (Nos. 633-5 ex-SDJR, originally built as LMS Nos. 575/6/80).

Turning now to some of the more characteristic changes which affected these engines during LMS days it can be said that, for Midland-styled engines, this class exhibited less variation than most. Not surprisingly, it was the ex-MR series which, marginally, showed most variation. The '483' type came to the LMS with tall chimneys and Ramsbottom safety valves (*Plate 92*) but fairly soon, the safety valves began to be replaced by the 'pop' type (*Plates 93 & 94*). In later days, extending into the BR period, some examples began to receive reduced-height boiler mountings of the same size given to the

Above *(Plate 91):* **A superb shed yard scene at Saltley, showing penultimate Class 2P No. 699, which was one of several members of the final 15 examples to carry a taller chimney, but the engine is otherwise similar to No. 686 —** *Plate 90.* **The picture is dated 1935, but the original Code B3 livery is still carried and is in good condition. The bogie brakes have been removed.** *H.C. Casserley.*

majority of the LMS-built engines (*Plate 95*). The style of replacement chimney, on both ex-MR and LMS-built examples, generally changed from the Fowler type with wind-guard (capuchon) on the upper front rim, to the plainer Stanier pattern. By no means all members received Stanier-type chimneys, but proportionally more of the ex-MR locomotives were so treated. However, even with this chimney style, both heights could be seen (*Plates 96 & 97*).

Below *(Plate 92):* **This posed, official view of ex-MR 483 Class No. 423 clearly shows the Midland-pattern boiler fittings and Ramsbottom safety valves. It is also an excellent reference view for the pre-1928 red livery, (Code A1). Note particularly the lined-out sideframes above the bogie and the black-painted coupling rod 'flutes'. These were characteristic MR Livery features perpetuated by the LMS until at least 1928 on many ex-MR 4—4—0s.** *BR (LMR).*

Right, upper & lower *(Plates 93 & 94):* **This interesting pair of pictures shows a couple of ex-MR Class 2s, Nos. 489 and 396, displaying (upper) an early change to 'pop' safety valves and (lower) a late retention of the Ramsbottom type. The pictures were taken in 1924 and 1931 respectively at Pear Tree (Normanton) and at Birmingham New Street. No. 489 carries the very early (1923 only) red livery (Code A2) and still retains its bogie 'splash' plates in front of the guard irons, while No. 396 is in the customary early 1930s configuration, wearing Livery Code B4.** *Bernard Matthews Collection/ Photomatic.*

Left *(Plate 95):* **Reduced-height boiler mountings were, by 1946, fitted to ex-MR No. 561 when photographed by Patricroft in wartime livery (Code C23). Somehow, the fundamentally shapely 'shorter' Stanier pattern chimney did not quite seem to suit most of the ex-MR engines to which it was fitted.** *W. Stubbs Collection.*

A considerable number of '2P' 4—4—0s, all from the ex-MR series, received exhaust steam injectors, revealed by a prominent steam pipe on the left-hand side below the smokebox wrapper *(Plate 98)*, but we are unable to give a full list of such examples. One or two of the MR series were paired, for a time, with Class 3 'Belpaire'-type tenders *(Plate 99)* and for a short period in the 1920s, a handful were converted for oil burning *(Plate 100)*. Again we are unable to give full lists and, not for the first time, we would again advise modellers in particular to make full use of pictorial sources to establish all details.

Both series of engines had bogie brakes and cylinder by-pass valves during the earlier days, the LMS examples having them fitted from new; but as with all other LMS engines so equipped, removal of these items took place from the mid-1930s. This apart, as far as the LMS-built series was concerned, variations were very few indeed and perhaps the most striking was the fitting of Dabeg feed water-heating apparatus to Nos. 633/53 in 1933. This was retained for a few years, *(Plate 101)* but we have been unable to ascertain the precise date of renewal — if any readers can assist we would be pleased to hear.

The livery treatment of the Class 2 4—4—0s was, as befits a standard type, very consistent indeed and as with most of the LMS standard classes both in this book and in *Volume 5*, we do not feel it necessary to tabulate every single style carried, since

Above (Plate 99): This view, taken in the Aire Valley, of a Leeds-Morecambe express in the early 1930s, shows ex-MR No. 455 (Livery Code B4) coupled to a Type 1 Johnson-pattern Belpaire tender. This was an unusual, but not unique situation and, as with the 'Belpaires' the tender valance and higher running plate gave a more harmonious visual balance. Note also the late retention of Ramsbottom safety valves. *Authors' Collection.*

valid generalisations are readily possible. The MR series all came to the LMS in standard red livery and an amazingly large number of them received LMS ownership markings, all with 18in figures, to Code A1 (*Plate 100*). A fair number also received the earlier version with individual 'LMS' (*Plate 102*), but since we cannot be certain that every single member received LMS markings, we have listed only the positively confirmed examples below. There may, of course, have been others.

Following the 1927/8 livery change, lined black was the universal treatment and LMS-built examples emerged in this style from new. Indeed, it was the first of this series, No. 563 (*Plate 88*), which was used as a 'model' for the new lined black livery, albeit initially with hand-painted insignia with 12in numerals. These new engines were introduced in March 1928, precisely at the time of decision-making as to insignia size (see *Volume 1, page 188*) and at least the first two examples carried these 12in figures (*Plate 103*).

Only a month later, in April 1928, the 14in Midland pattern numeral in gold transfer form became standardised and this style became universal. However, until the introduction of red countershaded insignia in 1929, plain gold figures were in use on both the LMS and ex-MR engines. As far as we can deduce, all LMS-built engines up to at least No. 623 (and probably a few beyond) were outshopped with plain gold insignia (Code B7) when new (*Plate 104*). By the time No. 635 had emerged, the gold transfer insignia with red countershading (Code B4) had been adopted (see *Volume 1, page 191*) and thereafter this became the 'norm' — (*Plate 101*). Except for one small group, Nos. 686-700 (below), we have every reason to believe that all members of both the ex-MR *and* the LMS series carried this style for most of the 1930s. Consequently, we have not listed this version in the summaries.

The exception alluded to above was the case of the LMS-built engines with rivetted tenders, all built at Crewe. These all seem to have entered service with 12in red-shaded figures, to Code B3

(*Plate 90*). Moreover, letter spacing with this variant was usually at 40in centres, rather than the 53in value for most of the LMS-built batches. We reckon that most of the 686-700 series probably received the standard Code B4 style at first repainting but we cannot be certain.

Since the decision to change insignia position dated from 1927, the adoption of lined black was in early 1928, standardisation of numeral size came later in 1928 and the red countershaded style of insignia did not, of course, appear for the first time until 1929, there was, naturally, a short period of hiatus as far as the ex-MR examples were concerned (*Plates 105 & 106*). One or two examples retained red livery for a year or two (with new type insignia) while a few more were repainted black with plain gold insignia in at least two sizes of numeral. Such examples as we have confirmed are listed below. Thereafter, the above-mentioned highly consistent pattern described for the LMS examples duly emerged on the MR series too.

Even after the livery experiments of 1936-7 (see *Volume 1*) the Class 2Ps did not seem to change very much, but there was a general reduction in overall consistency of appearance after this time, both in livery and visible detail — sometimes producing the odd, unique 'one-off', as illustrated in *Plate 107*.

Continued on page 58 . . .

Left (Plate 100): No. 487, in pre-1928 LMS red livery (Code A1) was one of several ex-MR Class 2 4—4—0s to be converted to oil burning for a period in 1926. The conversion was short-lived. *Authors' Collection.*

Right (Plate 101): LMS-built Class 2P No. 633 was one of three such engines absorbed from the SDJR fleet in 1930. Along with No. 653, it was also fitted, experimentally in 1933, with Dabeg feed water heating apparatus, clearly shown here in this circa 1936-vintage picture taken at Bath — Livery Code B4. *Bernard Matthews Collection.*

Left (Plate 102): Early LMS red livery with cabside lettering was given to No. 551, photographed at Derby in September 1923 — Code A2. Note that the engine has not yet acquired its replacement LMS worksplate on the leading splasher side. *A.C. Roberts Collection.*

Right *(Plate 103):* This view of No. 563 (see also *Plate 88*) confirms that the first of the LMS-built engines went into service with the non-standard insignia (Code B6). We have confirmed No. 564 as having been similar and there may have been one or two more, possibly Nos. 565-6. *W.T. Stubbs Collection.*

Above: *(Plate 104):* This well-known official ex-works view of No. 579 shows the classic layout of the Class 2P livery of the 1930s, embodying 14in Midland-style numerals. This was one of many engines manufactured before the introduction of the countershaded insignia, and the black shading to the transfer characters is clearly discernible on the original print. We have confirmed up to, at least, No. 623 of the LMS-built series as having emerged in this livery style (Code B7). *BR (LMR).*

Right - Caption details on opposite page

Left & opposite page, lower *(Plates 105 & 106)*: Several ex-MR Class 2Ps received 1928-pattern insignia before the full standardisation of the new livery. In these views, No. 545 (opposite page, lower) is seen still carrying red livery, but now Code A5; whereas No. 546 (left) has been repainted in black, but with the same small size numerals Code B5. *Authors' Collection/W.T. Stubbs Collection.*

Above, left *(Plate 107)*: This very unusual combination was photographed at Preston in 1949 and shows LMS-built No. 681, with replacement Stanier chimney, coupled to a Deeley high-sided tender of the 'Compound' '990' type — see *Chapter 1*. We know of no other like example. The LMS livery, as far as can be determined under all the grime, is Code C23. *H.C. Casserley.*

Above, right *(Plate 108)*: This splendid rear view of No. 535, taken at Cricklewood on July 7 1937, not only gives useful detail of the engine itself, but also offers a very clear impression of the 1936-pattern livery and insignia given to quite a number of the ex-MR series — Code B11. We have discovered no examples of the LMS standard series so finished. *H.C. Casserley.*

Above *(Plate 109)*: This interesting picture, taken early in 1948, shows one of the final batch of LMS-built Class 2Ps (note the rivetted and coal-railed tender) in a very short-lived BR style of plain black painting as No. M690. The engine has a new Stanier chimney and is also one of those to have received a replacement 1936-pattern LMS front numberplate. *Authors' Collection.*

A few members of the class (all ex-MR) received the 1936 style of letters and numbers *(Plate 108)* and a few of the engines received replacement block style front numberplates but to no apparent pattern *(Plate 109)*. Locomotives repainted after 1937 with scroll and serif insignia generally received the red-shaded yellow symbols, but this is not always possible to deduce from pictorial evidence. As with the 'Compounds', some members of the class received the Northern Division blue prohibition disc in 1939/40 *(Plates 110 & 111)*. These included 403/50/91/500/18/24/6/646. Repainted engines became plain black during the war, an early repaint being No. 656. When repainted in this style a considerable number received 10in numbers, being located in Scotland at the time *(Plate 113)*. As far as known, none received the 1946 insignia and with all liveries, Power Class markings were placed on the upper cabside panel between cabside cutaway and cab front. The Class changed from 2 to 2P in 1928.

The ex-SDJR 4—4—0s, assimilated into LMS stock in 1930, were an interesting group of engines. Many of them (probably all) when first given LMS numbers had the insignia applied by hand over the old S&D markings, which were simply erased.

This had the effect of giving the LMS some lined out *blue* engines for a short time — but for how long they lasted like this is not known. Those reported to have been blue with LMS markings are Nos. 323-6/634-5 of which accurately confirmed examples are listed in the summary. The five 7ft engines, Nos. 322-6, being of the MR Fowler 483 Class and which all lasted until after Nationalisation, were given numbers on the ex-MR sequence left blank by the scrapping of the original Johnson 4—4—0s (see *Chapter 1*) but there were three more ex S&D Class 2P 4—4—0s. These engines were built in 1928 to the LMS standard design, and then became S&D Nos. 44-6. In 1930 they came back to the LMS and were numbered with the Standard 2Ps. Initially Nos. 575/6/80 (before being sold to the SDJR) they came back as Nos. 633-5. This trio were probably all blue in 1930 and later on, one of them became a much photographed engine when fitted with Dabeg feed water heating apparatus, *(Plate 101)*.

The original hand-painted insignia given to these ex-SDJR engines had numerals of around 14in height, but they followed more closely the 1928 pattern than the Midland style of figure. They were applied in yellow paint along with very neatly hand-

painted smokebox and tender back numbers, pending the fitting of the cast smokebox and tender plates. They are illustrated in *Chapter 9, Plates 423 and 424.*

Wartime witnessed the adoption of plain black livery, accompanied by a gradual deterioration in appearance. It is quite likely that a number of examples survived the war with their lining intact, but it was rarely possible to distinguish such detail beneath the grime during the early 1940s. After Nationalisation, plain black livery was retained for a while with a variety of experimental numbering styles *(Plates 109, 111 & 114)* but very soon the class settled down in BR lined black livery with

Above & Below *(Plates 112 & 113):* These two views, both taken in 1948 at Rowsley (September 19) and Stranraer (April 23) respectively, show possibly the most characteristic final LMS liveries of the Class 2Ps, together with some very typical external changes as far as the Midland series was concerned. No. 520 (above) fitted with exhaust steam injector, together with replacement chimney and dome, displays the more common Code C23, livery, while LMS-built No. 600 (below), still with its original boiler fittings is carrying the characteristic Scottish variant with 10in figures, (Code C21). In both cases, the red shading to the yellow characters is still quite clear. *Both: H.C. Casserley.*

its LNWR-inspired lining and, dare we say it(?!) the engines looked rather good in this form — see *Plate 115*. 'British Railways' in full soon gave way to the familiar BR emblem on the tender — *Plate 116*. The smaller version was the common choice but there were exceptions *(Plate 117)*. Quite a few late survivors also achieved the later (1956 onwards) revised emblem. The whole class reached BR ownership, save for two premature accident withdrawals from the LMS series in 1934 (Nos. 591/639) and the last withdrawals were in 1962; MR series No. 40453 (in October) LMS series No. 40670 (in December). None were preserved.

The '2Ps' were never the most outstanding of British locomotives, but they ran millions of miles of useful service on lighter passenger workings, not to mention the occasional goods train, and at one time it rather seemed that every LMS shed had to have a mandatory allocation of at least one of these engines! As has been recorded elsewhere by E.S. Cox and others, they were the cheapest of all the LMS standard types in terms of repair cost (per mile run) and this figure gave a 'base' value by which all other classes could be compared, when the LMS introduced its meticulous engine costing system. We doubt, however, if they would have emerged quite so well from the calculations had repair costs been related to ton-mileage hauled.

We conclude this survey, as usual, with a tabulated summary of liveries (on page 61) — save for the standard Code B4 style carried by all (above) — along with a few more pictures which embrace further livery and detail variations *(Plates 118-122)*.

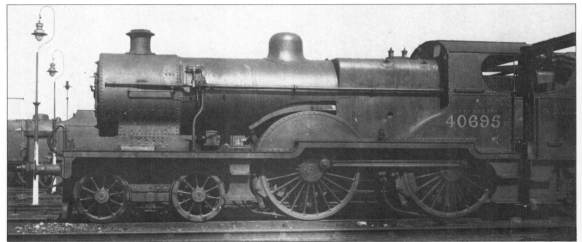

Right *(Plate 114)*: **One of the first BR styles of numeral painting in the 4XXXX series (see also** *Plate 111)* **was to utilise LMS-style characters, as shown here on No. 40695. This method was preceded by the short-lived 'M' prefix style** *(Plate 109)* **and soon gave way to the standard treatments** *(Plates 115 & 116)*. A.G. Ellis.

Above *(Plate 115)*: Ex-MR No. 40351, immaculate in the new LNWR-style lining with 'BRITISH RAILWAYS' in full on the tender, outside Derby works on September 25 1948. By this stage, replacement chimneys and domes were commonplace on the former Midland engines. *Vic Forster Collection.*

LIVERY SAMPLES

CODE A1:	332/53/395-7/400-1/4/6/9/12/5/9/23/30/6-8/ 44/8/50/61-3/70/83-8/92-3/5/7-9/500/5/7/ 10-1/3-8/20-1/5-7/30-1/3/43-5/5/8/52-5/7/9/ 60
CODE A2:	332/439/82/7/9/90/507/20/30/51
CODE A5:	407/503/45
CODE A10*:	323-4/6/634-5
CODE B3:	686-700 (when new - see text)
CODE B5:	546
CODE B6:	563-4 (when new - see text)
CODE B7+:	541/50/67-623
CODE B10:	492/500/13/36/45/60/653/5/96
CODE B11:	370/404/24/54-5/68/71/525/35/49/602
CODE C21:	576/600/4/7/10/6/22/6/44/687
CODE C22:	409/13-4/37/529
CODE C23:	337/407/15/27/34/44/54-5/68/79/84/90/9/ 520/5/34/7/44-5/54/7/9/61-2/81/3/93/659
CODE C26:	493

Notes:
1. All engines believed to have carried livery Code B4 at some time during the 1930s.
2. Letter spacing at 40in centres (MR tenders) and 53in centres (LMS tenders) save, at first for Nos. 686-700 (40in centres - see text).
* These were Ex-S&DJR locomotives in lined blue to the style indicated. Non confirmed ex-S&DJR examples are thought to have been similar when first absorbed by LMS.
+ This livery is difficult to identify from Code B4 and there were probably more ex-MR examples than the two confirmed – see text for amplifying details of LMS standard series when new.

Below *(Plate 116):* **LMS-built No. 40694 displays the most common BR livery for the Class 2Ps (with the smaller 'lion & wheel' emblem). By later BR days, many of the LMS series had also received new chimneys, as is clearly seen here.** *Photomatic.*

Left *(Plate 117):* **Class 2P No. 40592 was given somewhat unorthodox — and arguably unfortunate — tender lining, along with the larger tender emblem and the less common BR 10in cab side figures, when repainted in Scotland. As in LMS days, so too in the BR period, there were often quite distinct differences in the Scottish interpretation of standard liveries and No. 40592 was not unique. The picture was taken at Hurlford on March 13 1961, some five years after the abandonment of the original emblem and it seems likely that the engine was scrapped in this form.** *Authors' Collection.*

Top & Above: *(Plates 118 & 119):* These pictures of LMS-built 4—4—0s Nos. 619 (top) and 596 (above) reinforce some of the livery comments made in the main text. No. 619, pictured undoubtedly as built, has black-shaded insignia and 53in tender letter spacing (Code B7). No. 596 also appears to have unshaded characters but exhibits 40in letter spacing — most unusual for this class with the Fowler tender, especially since it was Derby-built. It is therefore likely to be a repaint, possibly at Crewe, which much favoured 40in spacing. The picture is undated but is probably circa 1930, therefore the insignia could possibly be countershaded (Code B4). We cannot be certain. Both engines must have been lined but there is no real visible sign of this either. *Authors' Collection.*

Left, upper *(Plate 120):* **We have included this rather poor picture since we can offer no explanation as to why No. 697 was wearing a sort of 'flower-pot' chimney. This was undoubtedly early in its life since the livery is that which was originally applied to the last 1 LMS built engines in 1932 — see main text. Perhaps a reader can help?** *Authors' Collection.*

Left & below *(Plates 121 & 122):* **Although tender changing was not particularly common amongst the Class 2P engines, these final pictures show interesting tender changes within the ex-MR series during early BR days — both in plain black livery. No. 40429 (left) has acquired a Fowler tender while No. 40413 (below) is paired with one of the rivetted Johnson-pattern flared-coping tenders, normally associated with ex-MR goods engines. Note that the raised brass MR power class figure '2' is still prominent on the cabside of No. 40413, but also that it has acquired much visible cabside rivetting as well — somewhat in the manner of Nos. 686-700 — see page 50.** *D.F. Tee Collection/Authors' Collection.*

THE CLASS 4 (LATER 4P) COMPOUND 4-4-0 (See text for number lists)

Right *(Plate 123):* **This view at Kings Norton, on July 22 1931, shows superheated, former Johnson 'Compound' No. 1002. Other than displaying the post-1927 livery (Code A6) it is otherwise little changed from its final Midland form. It has, however, exchanged its original Type D1 tender for the D2 version — see text.**
Authors' Collection.

We now turn attention to what must surely be the most famous of all Midland Railway designs, the three-cylinder, compound expansion 4—4—0. By the time the LMS was formed in 1923, the Midland 'Compound' had been in existence in one form or another for more than 20 years, and had undergone quite a number of changes. Yet, in spite of not being quite the latest thing in locomotive design, the 'Compound' was to become the first generation LMS standard express passenger type, the 45 Midland built examples being supplemented by no fewer than 195 further engines built under LMS auspices during the 1924-32 period, the last five examples actually appearing at the start of the Stanier period.

The version chosen by the LMS for standardisation was the superheated development, the prototype example of which, No. 1040, had appeared in 1913 as the first superheated rebuild of the original saturated series. A brief resume of the Midland part of the story has been given in *Chapter 1* and a much more comprehensive account of the Midland period of development will be found in our companion series, published by Wild Swan Publications. Our concern here is solely with the LMS story of the superheated engines, but before embarking on a more detailed analysis of what was an undoubtedly confusing series of engines, a few more background comments will hopefully be of help — particularly to those readers who are fairly new to the subject.

Firstly, we would draw attention (as we did with the LNWR

Right *(Plate 124):* **'Compound' No. 1005 was the first Deeley example built (originally as No. 1000 before 1907). It is seen here in superheated form at Derby in 1926, hardly different in any significant external form from the superheated rebuilds of the Johnson series. It has already lost its bogie 'splash' plates and is carrying livery Code A1. The tender is the correct pattern for this series as built, namely Type D3.**
W.T. Good.

—8—0s in *Volume 2*) to another highly-detailed and definitive RCTS monograph on the more technical aspects of the subject, this time entitled *The Midland Compounds,* written by David Tee and published in 1962. We have drawn heavily on the data provided by this source and must gratefully acknowledge David's further assistance in our own compilation. Secondly, we shall leave consideration of the equally confusing story of the tenders attached to the 'Compounds' until after the analysis of the engines themselves. Also, and in spite of slightly overlapping our other work, it will be necessary first to analyse the immediate pre-Grouping story.

Just as in the case of the superheated 'Belpaires' *(Chapter 1)* so too in the case of the 'Compounds', the physical characteristics of the superheated engines inherited by the LMS reflected their earlier history. There were three varieties:

1) **The original Johnson engines: LMS Nos. 1000—4:** These engines, already rebuilt and superheated when received by the LMS, were in the physical configuration represented by *Plate 123,* an appearance first manifested by the first ten non-superheated Deeley engines — (2) below — but with an extended smokebox, consequent upon superheating.

2) **The original Deeley engines: LMS Nos. 1005—14:** These engines were the first Deeley version of the 'Compound' type and set the eventual visual style for the whole class. Seven examples had been superheated by LMS days, the remainder being modified similarly soon afterwards. Whether saturated or superheated, their deep frames below the smokebox set them apart from the second series of Deeley engines — (3), below. As can be seen from *Plate 124,* the superheated version differed little from that displayed by the rebuilt Johnson engines.

3) **The final Deeley engines: LMS Nos. 1015—44:** This modified version of the Deeley type showed a slight modification in that the frames were much shallower below the smokebox which, in consequence, gave quite a different 'front-end' appearance, whether saturated or superheated, as *Plate 125* reveals. These engines were built in two batches, Nos. 1015—34 and Nos. 1035—44, separated by the 1907 MR renumbering — see *Numbering Note.* Although No. 1040 of this series was the first superheated 'Compound', less than half of them had been superheated when the LMS was formed — for a full list of surviving saturated engines see page 47.

Numbering Note: Although not strictly relevant to the LMS story, it is probably helpful to record that the original Midland 'Compounds' were built between 1902 and 1909 and that the first 30 Deeley engines (Nos. 1005-34) were, prior to 1907, numbered 1000-29. In 1907, the original Johnson engines took Nos. 1000-4 and the Deeleys had '5' added to their numbers. The final ten (Nos. 1035-45) did not suffer in this confusing way, not appearing until 1908-9!

This was the situation which the LMS inherited in 1923, and the superheating of the remaining saturated Deeley engines was completed by January 1928, No. 1017 being the last. At first, the shallow front frames were retained for those engines which had them, but eventually, the LMS began to fit deepened and stronger front frames to the 1015-44 series to match those of the 1000-14 batches *(Plate 126).* The change-over seems to have been in 1926, by which time only Nos. 1018/21-2/6-7/44 of the shallow frame series remained to be superheated. It is not known how many of these engines went directly from shallow frame saturated condition to deep frame superheated configuration but all the remaining engines in the No. 1015-44 series undoubtedly went through an intermediate shallow frame superheated phase during late Midland and early LMS days.

So much for the basic engine configuration of the Midland series in early LMS days, but before dealing with the LMS standard continuation of the class, it will be helpful to complete the Midland story with a note on tenders. As with the engines, there were three distinct series of tenders, each of which

Plate 125): No. 1039 was one of the final ten Deeley 'Compounds' which received their numbers after the MR 1907 confusion — see text. This magnificent study, taken in 1924, shows clearly the shallow-depth front frames of the final Deeley engines as built and as first superheated. The livery is Code A1 and the tender Type D4 is of the series fitted to the final 30 Deeley engines when built. *Authors' Collection.*

Above *(Plate 126):* **By the time this picture was taken, in the early 1930s, former 'shallow frame' compound No. 1033 had received the deeper, strengthened front frames. The livery code is A6 and the original pattern of tender for this series is still in evidence. Note the change to 'pop' safety valves.** *A.G. Ellis.*

Right *(Plate 127):* **The pioneer 'Compound' No. 1000, pictured at Derby in the mid-1930s carrying a very scruffy version of Livery Code A5. It is paired with a rebuilt ex-bogie tender, Type D1. Strictly speaking, as preserved, this engine should have this type of tender, but such a vehicle was not available at the time of preservation. Note the exhaust steam injector, added by the LMS.** *W. Stubbs Collection.*

coincided with the above-defined breakdown of the locomotive series. There were:

Nos. 1000-4: Fitted with Deeley rebuilds of former Johnson bogie tenders, having a distinct 'turn-under' at the side between the bottom of the side panelling and the top of the sideframes. These were identical to the Deeley Type 1 tenders defined in relation to the 'Belpaires' on page 39 and for convenience will henceforth be referred to as Type D1 tenders *(Plate 127).*

Nos. 1005-14: Fitted with a new Deeley design of flat-sided tender, somewhat similar to Type D1, but with a shallower depth upper side panel, no 'turn-under' and a continuous

running plate along the side — see *Plate 128.* For reference these will be called Type D3 (for Type D2, see *Tender Note* below).

Nos. 1015-44: Fitted with a second new Deeley design of tender generally similar to Type D3 but with a discontinuous running plate. This style of tender *(Plate 129)* was also associated with the '990' Class (Chapter 1) and will be referred to as Type D4.

Tender Note: There was a fourth variant of the Deeley flat-sided tender, also rebuilt from former bogie examples and described in relation to the 'Belpaires' as Deeley Type 2 on page 39. These were, more or less, a higher-sided version of Type D3 and although not specifically associated with the ex-Midland

Above (Plate 128): Possibly the rarest kind of Deeley pattern tender was the type of which only ten were ever built and were paired with his first series of 'Compounds'. They were probably the neatest in appearance too. We have codified them Type D3 and their nature is shown well here in this view of engine No. 1009, at Derby on July 22 1928. (Livery Code A1). *Authors' Collection.*

Left (Plate 129): The Type D4 tender was a numerous type of which 40 were built for Deeley's final 'Compounds' and '990s'. A good broadside impression is given here, the picture having been taken at Kentish Town during 1926 when several 'Compounds' were converted for oil burning for a short period, including No. 1041, shown here. Note again, (see also *Plate 125*) the shallow front frames of the engine (Livery Code A1). *Authors' Collection.*

Above (Plate 130): Several of the first series of LMS 'Compounds' emerged attached to ex-bogie tenders. No. 1051 (Livery Code A1) was one such and the tender is the version we have codified Type D2. Other than the reduction in driving wheel diameter by 3in, there was no major visual difference between this batch and the preceding Midland-built series. *Authors' Collection.*

'Compounds' in terms of 'official' pairings, were fairly speedily brought into the picture. One of them is seen in *Plate 130* and for reference purposes will be called Type D2. In point of fact, the two styles of rebuilt ex-bogie tenders drew their inspiration from the new Deeley design Type D4, but we have codified them to reflect the order in which they have appeared in this narrative. Our 'shorthand' has no official status — or counterpart, as far as we are aware!

It seems abundantly clear that Derby was well-satisfied with the superheated 'Compound' at the time of the Grouping, in spite of the apparent slowness with which the superheating programme had been undertaken after 1913, and had decided to build more of the type, superheated from new. These duly emerged in 1924 as Nos. 1045-64, following the customary MR numbering procedure, now also part of official LMS philosophy. Apart from a slight reduction from 7ft to 6ft 9in diameter in driving wheel size and slightly larger cylinders, these new engines (*Plate 130*) were almost identical to the 'deep frame' superheated Midland rebuilds previously described.

They were swiftly followed in the same year by yet another 20 examples, Nos. 1065-84. Thus, in no more than 12 months, the 'Compound' total had virtually been doubled — and more than doubled if one only counts superheated engines!

This second 1924 batch was given reduced height boiler mountings and 'pop' type safety valves from the outset, these features thereafter becoming standard (*Plate 131*). All the earlier engines were eventually given 'pop' safety valves, while reduced height boiler fittings were also fitted to many of the 1000-64 series at a later date (*Plate 132*). The final change, from No. 1085 onwards, was to move the driving position to the left-hand side of the cab and in this matter of left versus right-hand drive, Derby had to yield to the majority view on other parts of the LMS. The LNWR, LYR, Caledonian and Highland areas were all left-hand drive systems and collectively well outnumbered the right-hand drive school. Thus, the LMS became a left-hand drive railway (*Plate 133*). However, there was never any attempt made to convert erstwhile right-hand drive members of the adopted Midland 'standard' types to left-hand drive, unlike, for

Above *(Plate 131)*: Reduced height boiler mountings and 'pop' safety valves distinguished the second LMS batch of 1924 and, as with the first LMS series, many came into service paired with ex-MR tenders, rebuilt some years earlier from former bogie types. No. 1070, (Livery Code A1) was an example but compared with *Plate 130*, received the 'turn under' variety, Type D1. *Authors' Collection.*

Right *(Plate 132)*: This view of No. 1001, in very scruffy condition, probably in wartime black livery (Code C22) does, none the less, give a clear impression of the visual differences wrought to the ex-MR engines when given reduced height LMS standard boiler fittings. The tender is still Type D1, first fitted to this batch well before the Grouping. *Authors' Collection.*

example, on the LNER, where many right-hand drive Gresley 'Pacifics' were later converted to the left-hand option — including the famous *Flying Scotsman*.

Having established the 'standard' form for the 'Compound', the engines thereafter came out 'thick and fast' and by the end of 1927 some 190 new example had been added to the Midland total. This virtually coincided with the superheating of the final ex-MR example, so within just four years, the LMS had acquired a great number of superheated 'Compounds' — an extraordinary state of affairs. The number series up to No. 1199 had been totally filled and in 1927 a start was made on the 900 and upwards series. There must even have been some thought of continuing to No. 999, for the 990 Class engines (Chapter 1) were renumbered into the 8XX series, but in the event the story seemed to come to an end with No. 934 *(Plate 134)*. As it was, the

LMS and Midland 'Compounds' between them had already established quite a few statistical records which were never overtaken:

a) Britain's only really successful compound type built in quantity.
b) Britain's largest class of new 4—4—0s — of *any* type.
c) The largest single class of any express passenger type built by the LMS Railway, save, marginally, by adding together the Class 5XP 'Patriot' and 'Jubilee' 4—6—0s.
d) The largest single class of three-cylinder compound engines built *anywhere in the world!*

Whatever one's views of these often misunderstood engines, there can be no denying the fact that no railway, however

Top *(Plate 133)*: **An immaculate LMS standard left-hand drive 'Compound', No. 1152, (Livery Code A1) virtually brand new, as delivered by the North British Locomotive Company Ltd, in 1925. Note the all-red front buffer plank** — see also *Plate 149* and **page 77.** *Authors' Collection.*

Left *(Plate 134)*: **For a long time, No. 934 was the 'last of the line'** — and certainly it was the **final example built before the final Stanier modifications. It is seen here in the early 1930s, after being fitted with an exhaust steam injector, in the common post-1927 livery for this series, Code A7.** *Authors' Collection.*

blinkered in its approach to locomotive matters, could possibly have countenanced the building of such a quantity of machines had there not been some real merit in the design. That the 'Compounds' proved, in the fullness of time, to be a bit too small (in terms of absolute power output related to LMS requirements) is no fault of the engines themselves, nor is the fact that some enginemen never learned to drive them properly. What is certain is that some five years after the main build of 'Compounds', no less a person than William Stanier saw fit to authorise the building of a final five examples in 1932 (Nos. 935-9, see *Plate 135*) — and this does merit some additional comment.

The building of the last five 'Compounds' shows some close parallels with the construction of the last 15 Class 2P 4—4—0s,

which we have already considered and which also emerged in the same year as Stanier's appointment as Chief Mechanical Engineer to the LMS. The quite radically different constructional nature of the last few Class 2s has already been remarked upon and the last five 'Compounds' were not dissimilar. The difference was that there was scarcely any time interval between the last of the 'pre-Stanier' 2Ps and the final batch, whereas in the case of the 'Compounds', the gap was some five years. In consequence, whilst the Class 2s seemed to slip by, almost un-noticed, the different nature of the final 'Compounds' did *not* pass unremarked. They too displayed heavily rivetted-construction, including their tenders, not to mention the same adjustable driving wheel balance weights

L. M. S. R.

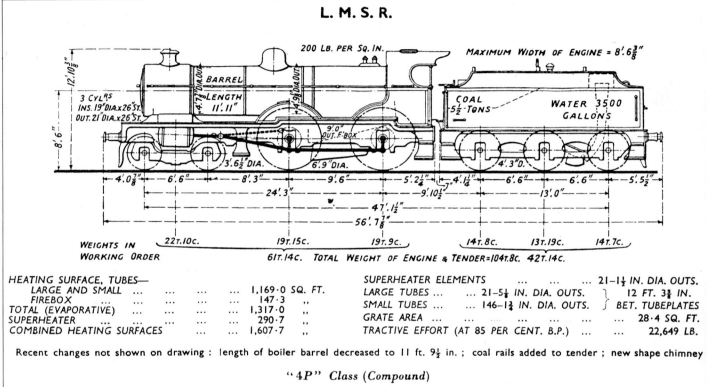

HEATING SURFACE, TUBES—						
LARGE AND SMALL	...	...	...	...	1,169·0 SQ. FT.
FIREBOX	...	...	...	...	147·3 ,,
TOTAL (EVAPORATIVE)	...	...	...	...	1,317·0 ,,
SUPERHEATER	...	...	...	...	290·7 ,,
COMBINED HEATING SURFACES	...	...	1,607·7 ,,

SUPERHEATER ELEMENTS	...	...	...	21—1½ IN. DIA. OUTS.
LARGE TUBES	...	21—5¼ IN. DIA. OUTS. ⎱ 12 FT. 3¾ IN.
SMALL TUBES	...	146—1¾ IN. DIA. OUTS. ⎰ BET. TUBEPLATES
GRATE AREA	...	...	...	28·4 SQ. FT.
TRACTIVE EFFORT (AT 85 PER CENT. B.P.)	...	...	22,649 LB.

Recent changes not shown on drawing : length of boiler barrel decreased to 11 ft. 9½ in. ; coal rails added to tender ; new shape chimney

"4P" Class (Compound)

Right *(Plate 135)*: No. 935, the first of the last five 'Compounds', appeared in 1932 and this view clearly shows the extended front frames, GWR-type balance weights to the wheels, coal rails on the tender and, perhaps less obviously, the much greater array of visible rivets. The reversion to a taller chimney is also obvious (compare with *Plate 134*). This picture was taken at Millers Dale in 1936, the engine being in Livery Code A7. *Vic Forster Collection.*

Above & left *(Plates 136 & 137)*: These two views show replacement shorter boiler fittings on a former 'tall' engine, No. 1048 (above) and replacement tall fittings on an erstwhile 'short' engine, No. 41074 (left), pictured in 1944 and 1950 respectively. Both are right-hand drive examples from the LMS-built series. The livery of No. 1048 cannot be determined — it could be grimy red — but No. 41074 is in early BR plain black. Note the Type D2 tender still carried by No. 1048 and the coal rails added to No. 41074's standard Fowler tender.
E. Blakey/Authors' Collection.

which were so characteristic of GWR practice. They also had extended front frames and reverted to taller chimneys. We are therefore inclined to think that, along with the 2—6—0s and, possibly, the 0—4—4Ts (as covered in *Volume 5*), the construction of the final series of Midland-inspired 4—4—0s, both simple and compound, was all part and parcel of a deliberate attempt by Stanier to 'play his team in' to the new ideas which he proposed to incorporate henceforth.

Thus it was that the 'Compounds' eventually totalled 240 examples and, as will be our normal practice in this and the next volume with all the new locomotives built to LMS standard design, we give in the table (right) a summary of the LMS build by works and year.

ENGINE NOS.	BUILDER	DATE
1045-64	Derby	1924
1065-84	Derby	1924
1085-104	Derby	1925
1105-14	Derby	1925
1115-34	Horwich	1925-6
1135-59	N.B. Loco. Co.	1925
1160-84	Vulcan Foundry	1925
1185-99	Vulcan Foundry	1927
900-9	Vulcan Foundry	1927
910-24	Vulcan Foundry	1927
925-34	Vulcan Foundry	1927
935-9	Derby	1932

Right *(Plate 138)*: The prominent pipe from the smokebox to the exhaust steam injector distinguished more than a few 'Compounds' and is clearly shown on No. 1010 of the first Deeley series, still with original Type D3 tender, at Cricklewood in 1937. The livery is the very common A5 style of the early and mid-1930s. *A.G. Ellis.*

Left *(Plate 139)*: We have no idea why the bogie 'splash' plates still remained on Carlisle Kingmoor 'Compound' No. 1147 as late as June 10 1936 — some ten years after they had generally vanished from the scene. The livery is Code A7. *Authors' Collection.*

Right *(Plate 140)*: No. 1098, a Leeds Holbeck engine but seen here at Leicester, was a fairly early example of a 'Compound' with elongated front frames. It is also carrying the slightly less common (for the period) 10in numerals, Code A5. The date is October 16 1938 but the insignia are of the pre-1936 black-shaded type. *L. Hanson.*

Above (Plate 141): This splendid broadside view of 'Compound' No. 1111 gives a very clear impression of the characteristics of the most common single tender variant for the class — the Fowler 3500-gallon flush-rivetted type. It also gives a very good guide to the insignia placement with the post-1927 livery, in this instance Code A6. W. Stubbs Collection.

Left (Plate 142): The last of the line, No. 939, pictured here virtually ex-works, new in 1932, not only shows off the Code A7 insignia but also reveals clearly the heavily rivetted nature of both engine and tender. Note also the coal rails and new-style driving wheel balance weights. Authors' Collection.

Turning now to the physical variations within the LMS standard 'Compound' series, the fundamental differences have already been covered and other than livery (below) the most obviously visible single change to the engine portion was probably the gradual substitution of Stanier-pattern chimneys (tall and short) to many examples as the years went by. Since the boilers were completely interchangeable between the MR and LMS series, the above-described tall/short chimney situation could also break down — see Plates 136 & 137. Additionally, exhaust steam injectors (Plates 134 & 138) could also be seen on some examples, both ex-MR and LMS, but we are unable to give comprehensive lists. Further small changes to the engines involved the removal of the bogie 'splash' plates from those so-equipped. This particularly 'Midland' feature was perpetuated on many of the new LMS engines, we believe up to at least part-way through the first Vulcan Foundry, batch. No. 1163 is the highest numbered engine we have personally verified with this feature. Most had been removed by 1926-7, but there were odd exceptions (Plate 139).

The last major change, based, we believe, on experience with Nos. 935-9, was to further strengthen the front frames on many engines by extending them to the buffer plank, as illustrated in Plate 140. This took place over a period of time and, again, we are unable to give comprehensive lists. However, in this matter,

as with all other detail changes, it is our hope that by giving plenty of pictures and also drawing awareness to the problem, we shall help most of our readers to obtain a better overall appreciation of the situation.

The tenders fitted to the LMS 'Compounds' were somewhat more variable than the engines themselves and were regularly changed between engines. Many, but not all of the earlier post-Grouping examples came into traffic with second-hand tenders of one or other of the several Deeley variations already discussed (Plate 130 & 131).

For the most part however, the LMS-built engines when new received the LMS standard Fowler pattern 3,500-gallon tender (Plate 141). Visually rather similar to the Deeley type from which it was derived; however, at 13ft 6in it was some 2ft shorter in wheelbase, thus displaying a more compact visual appearance. Most of the 'Compounds' fitted from new with this type of tender received the flush-rivetted version but, of course, the final five engines (Plate 142): were given the visibly-rivetted tenders of the early Stanier era. These had coal rails from new but additionally and unlike the case of most Class 2P engines, coal rails were also fitted to quite a number of earlier flush-sided Fowler tenders, if attached to 'Compounds'.

The earlier Fowler tenders had a relatively simple 'bulkhead' between coal space and footplate with a permanently 'open'

This page *(Plates 143 to 145):* These three views show examples of the various LMS hybrid tenders fitted to the 'Compounds'. They are not always easy to spot on pictures. No. 1197 (top, Livery Code A6) has a flush-rivetted Fowler tank, No. 927 (above, Livery Code A7) has a similar but visibly rivetted version while No. 1007 (right, Livery Code A5) has a variant type of flush-rivetted hybrid with the top ascending step above the running plate level. All three types had coal rails. *Authors' Collection (2)/ A.G. Ellis.*

aperture at the base from which to shovel the coal. Later examples were fitted with coal doors and earlier examples were sometimes modified to suit. Short of devoting the whole of this book to a blow-by-blow account of every individual tender, it would be impossible to relate the total picture. Furthermore, there were also variations in the positioning of tender ventilation pipes, either inside or outside the coalspace. In general, the ventilation pipes were transferred from within the coalspace to a position behind the rear bulkhead as years went by and it gradually became less common to find a coal-railed tender with ventilation pipes inside the coalspace. Further generalisation is not really possible.

As if this was not complication enough, the LMS also embarked upon a programme of tender rebuilding, utilising what amounted to standard Fowler tanks (designed to fit the 13ft 6in wheelbase LMS standard tender) in replacement of worn-out Deeley-type tanks from otherwise still serviceable longer wheelbase ex-MR tenders. This had the unfortunate effect of producing a quite ghastly looking hybrid type, whose tank length was a quite appalling mis-match with the chassis, leaving an extended platform at the rear. This type has already been encountered with the 'Belpaires', but they were rather more common with the 'Compounds', moreover, there were several sub-species (Plates 143-5). As usual in this situation, we

have devised our own quite unofficial 'shorthand' notation to differentiate the types:

Type F1: Fowler LMS standard flush-sided tender.
Type F2: Fully-rivetted Fowler-type tender (built during the Stanier regime).
Type F3: Hybrid tender, LMS-type tank on MR type chassis - all versions.

Should readers require further refinements, we are inclined to suggest that they figure them out for themselves!! However, we have tried to sort matters out as much as possible in our summaries below, but cannot guarantee we have spotted them all.

There were two quite celebrated examples of special tenders as far as the 'Compounds' were concerned. The earlier of these was the modified Deeley tender fitted to No. 1054 in order that the LMS could 'steal a march' on the LNER in 1928 by giving a 'Compound' enough coal capacity to travel non-stop to Edinburgh from Euston, a day ahead of the much-publicised introduction of corridor tenders on the LNER Gresley 'Pacifics'. This is shown in *Plate 146* and a 'Royal Scot' 4—6—0 was similarly modified for the Glasgow portion (see *Volume 5*). Subsequently, these special tenders, of which a total of three

Above *(Plate 146)*: No. **1054** with its specially modified tender near Kenton circa 1929 in charge of a Euston-Birmingham train whose first five coaches are a particularly neat set of ex-LNWR lavatory non-corridor vehicles. Note the Ramsbottom safety valves and the considerably greater width of the modified coal space. The Livery Code is A5. *W. Stubbs Collection.*

Left *(Plate 147)*: The experimental tender for No. **936** is clearly shown in this view to have been basically a standard Fowler type below the upper horizontal beading with a new top coping added above this level. This tender remained with No. 936 for most of its life, later going to No. 40933. Livery Code A7. *Authors' Collection.*

were modified, were confined to the 'Compounds' and exchanged engines occasionally.

Less obviously valuable from the publicity point of view, but probably of far greater significance in the overall LMS locomotive story, was the specially modified tender attached to No. 936 from 1933 onwards, shown in *Plate 147*. This was a simple, but visually quite dramatic adaptation of the standard Fowler-pattern tender to form a sort of quasi-prototype for the soon to be familiar Stanier-pattern tender, but further discussion of this and other allied matters will have to be held over to *Volume 5*.

So now we come, at last, to the livery of the Midland and

Above *(Plate 148)*: **This lovely picture of No. 1091, resplendent in the pre-1928 crimson livery, could not be bettered as a definitive sample for this period of painting. Note the lined-out cylinders and unpainted 'flutes' to the side rods — see text.** *Stephen Collection, courtesy National Railway Museum.*

Below *(Plate 149)*: **Another 'mint' view, this time of No. 1137 of the North British Locomotive Company series, shows this company's somewhat non-standard treatment of the front buffer plank and the polishing of the smokebox hinges and 'dog' ring.** *Authors' Collection.*

Above: For caption details, see overleaf.

LMS 'Compounds'. Until the Second World War they were always, of course, painted crimson lake — indeed, a derogatory nickname for them on the non-Midland parts of the LMS was 'Crimson Ramblers'. The actual layout of the lining never departed from that introduced by Deeley in 1907 and can be studied at first hand on the restored No. 1000 at the National Railway Museum, York. During LMS days, the lining colour changed from pale to chrome yellow in the mid-1930s and this was a prelude to adopting yellow rather than gold (gilt) insignia in 1937. However, when it comes to analysing the insignia itself, there is a certain degree of complexity.

During the 1923-27 period all was plain sailing, relatively speaking, and every engine up to and including No. 934 carried the 18in figures on the tender but we cannot confirm that every single ex-MR example was given LMS markings before 1928. All the LMS engines carried the company markings and none of them received the earlier individually lettered form. We have only confirmed one ex-MR engine in this configuration (Code A2). This was No. 1012 with a Type D3 tender.

The classic LMS form of the 'Compound' 4—4—0 is shown in *Plate 148*, but within the LMS-built series, there was one group which displayed a not altogether attractive full red front buffer plank — *Plate 149*. We have confirmed all between Nos. 1137 and 1151 as being similar, so the inference must be that the whole of the North British Locomotive Company batch (Nos. 1135-59) was turned out this way. It did not, however, last long and we suspect that even before full repainting the narrow band above the main part of the buffer plank was soon repainted crimson. Thereafter, we have no records of any unorthodox practices in the actual disposition of colour and lining.

There are, however, two interesting minor points to make. In Midland days there had been a degree of uncertainty about the style of lining, if any, to be adopted on the cylinders of the 'Compounds' — they were, after all, the only red engines with outside cylinders inherited from the Midland. There is no doubt that in Midland days, most 'Compounds' in the Deeley form had no cylinder lining during most of the pre-Grouping period

— but as far as we can judge, *all* 'Compounds' in the LMS period had lined cylinder casings with red livery. When MR No. 1000 was first restored by BR it had unlined cylinders but when BR repainted it in 1962, prior to going to Clapham, lining was added and has been retained by the NRM since 1975. This may be incorrect, but a possible explanation is that the MR finally decided to line-out the cylinders shortly before the Grouping, otherwise why would the LMS have done so? It was unheard of for the LMS to enhance the MR livery on any of its red engines, save in the well-recorded case of most non-Midland passenger tanks.

Equally puzzling is the question of the colour of the 'flutes' of the coupling and connecting rods. It was standard MR practice, introduced by Deeley, to paint them black and this was quite regularly copied by the LMS in the case of inside cylinder ex-MR engines. However, we can find no real evidence that black flutes were ever applied to the 'Compounds' in LMS days. The very clear examples in *Plates 148 & 149* seem to confirm this. Yet the MR had regularly painted the flutes of the 'Compounds' exactly as for its other engines with fluted side rods. It is all rather puzzling but we feel that meticulous modellers of 'Compounds' should have lined cylinders and unpainted rods (LMS) and reverse the specification for MR!

Nevertheless, we do not feel it necessary to give a complete list of confirmed pre-1928 liveries save for the ex-MR engines and the right-hand drive LMS series. We cannot confirm all the ex-MR engines as having received LMS markings, whilst in the LMS 1045-84 lists, although all examples received Code A1 livery, the tender variations and exchanges suggest that we are best advised to list only confirmed 'pairings', using the 'shorthand' codification given previously. As far as we are aware, every left-hand drive 'Compound', up to and including No. 934, came into service with Type F1 tenders and in livery Code A1. The slight North British Locomotive Company

Previous page, above & right *(Plates 150 to 152):* **We have already featured quite a number of post-1927 livery variations for the 'Compounds', but make no apology for including these three extra views of what might be called the definitive styles during the post-1927 period when gold insignia with black shading was the customary practice from 1928 until 1937. The engines featured are (previous page) No. 1113 (Code A5), No. 1052 (above) with Type D2 tender (Code A6) and (right) No. 916 (Code A7). All were taken in the mid-1930s when some degree of consistency, numeral size excepted, was present in LMS livery. Note also the exhaust steam injector on No. 1113 (previous page) and the fact that the angle of the light has caused the rivetting detail to show very clearly — a point helpful, perhaps, to modellers.** *G. Coltas/Authors' Collection/H.C. Casserley.*

variation has already been covered. To simplify matters, we shall summarise the pre-1928 situation before going on to the later period.

LIVERY SAMPLES: SUPERHEATED EX-MR AND RH DRIVE LMS COMPOUNDS (1923-7)

The following engines (1000-84 number series) all carried LMS livery code A1 during 1923-7, and were coupled to the tender type indicated in brackets after the engine number/number series. The footnotes regarding oil burners should *not* be regarded as a full list of all engines so fitted:

1000(D1); 1004(D1); 1005(D3); 1009(D3); 1014(D3); 1017(D4); 1027-30(D4); 1036-9(D4); 1041(D4); 1045(D2); 1048-51(D2); 1053(D2); 1055(D4); 1056(F1); 1060(F1); 1065-9(F1); 1070(D1); 1071(F1 *and* D1); 1074(F1); 1076(F1); 1081-3(F1).

Notes: 1. *Of the above-quoted examples the following can also be confirmed as having been equipped for oil burning during 1926: 1000/5/38/41/66.*
2. *Of the LMS LH drive series, the following were noted with oil burning equipment during 1926: Nos. 1104/12/6-7/21/36-7.*

After 1927, the class continued to be given the red livery and it is generally believed that one of these engines, No. 1121, was the first *repainted* engine to be given the new pattern insignia. After 1927, the numeral size used on the 'Compounds' was most commonly the 12in variety but both other heights were employed on many engines, there being strong evidence to indicate that those shopped in Scotland were generally given 14in Midland pattern figures wherever possible. There is also

good evidence that these same 14in figures were used on all the 9XX 'Compounds' after 1927, there being more room for the larger numerals when only three figures were needed *(Plates 150-2).*

The 'Compounds' were especially interesting as being the only red engines regularly shopped at Derby after 1927 and this Works is quite definite that 'Compounds' shopped there had their cab roof top painted crimson — as did all Derby-shopped red engines before 1928. This may seem a little unlikely but in spite of intensive questioning, the view is still held. In fairness to Derby, it must be noted that all pictures of red engines in the elaborate grey livery which Derby used for photographic purposes show the cab roof to have been given the same pale grey paint as for the main engine, rather than the darker shade reserved for the smokebox so it seems probable that Derby *was* unique in this respect. The 'Compounds' were additionally interesting in that they are reported as continuing to have the yellow line round the wheel tyre until they were repainted black in wartime.

Two of these engines, Nos. 1094 and 1099, were selected as 'Guinea Pigs' for the sans-serif insignia. No. 1099 had experimental 12in high block figures of almost pure Gill Sans shape, gold shaded black, with sans-serif 'LMS' on the tender.

Left & below (Plates 153 & 154): Experimental liveries were applied to No. 1099 (left) and No. 1094 (below) in 1935 and 1936 respectively as part of the LMS experiment which led to the 1936 livery. Paradoxically, the proper version of the 1936 Livery was never, as far as we are aware, applied to any of the 'Compounds'. *Authors' Collection.*

Left (Plate 155): Ex-Midland No. 1019, on August 3 1937 coupled to a type F2 tender, was given a new 1936-pattern front numberplate but this picture, taken at Derby, clearly reveals that it kept the traditional livery (Code A6) albeit rather scruffy. *A.G. Ellis.*

This variation was applied in late 1935 as an experimental 'try-out' before finalising the new 1936 style *(Plate 153)*. In 1936 No. 1094 had the distinction of being one of the very few red engines to get the 1936 numerals in black shaded form as a prototype for the new livery. It lost this livery in April 1937 *(Plate 154)*. As far as is known, no other 'Compounds' received block style insignia, although a few did receive the block pattern numberplates *(Plate 155)*. With all red liveries in the 1928-39 period, the 'Compounds' received a narrow crimson band above the front buffer beam below the footplate.

During the mid-1930s, a few 'Compounds' began to appear bearing gold insignia with red countershading and after 1937 red shaded insignia became more widespread. Most of them, however, displayed the newly introduced chrome yellow base colour with plain vermilion shading — see *Plates 156-159*. As with the Class 2P 4—4—0s, some of the tall chimneyed 'Compounds' also received the Northern Division blue prohibition disc including, we believe, Nos. 1049 and 1058. However, we have no pictorial confirmation of this feature which rather seems to have eluded the photographers of the era.

During the war, any repainted 'Compounds' became black, two of the first reported examples being Nos. 1106 and 1166, early in 1940. Standard yellow scroll/serif markings with red shading were the norm, in all three sizes — as illustrated in *Plates 160-162*. The smallest 10in figures seem to have found much favour in Scotland at this time. The plain black livery adopted during the war continued until the end of LMS ownership and, considering the size of the class, very few engines were recorded as still being red after the war. The known post-war red examples are (observation dates in brackets): No. 930 (January 1946, *Plate 158*); No. 1059 (September 1946); No. 1081 (August 1947) and, finally, in September 1951, No. 40934. This latter engine (illustrated in Volume 1, *Plate 345*) was reputedly the last engine in service to display the red LMS livery in pre-preservation days. It was, however, something of a 'cheat' since the red paint was only revealed by a degree of over-enthusiastic removal (in the guise of cleaning!) of the somewhat impermanent first BR black paint. This was done with the full approval of a man who subsequently achieved quite a high position in BR locomotive affairs but who for reasons of prudence had better remain nameless!

After some experimentation and temporary painting styles (*Plates 163 & 164*), the same standard BR lined black livery was adopted for the 'Compounds' for the '2Ps' and, when clean, could look quite smart. There is no doubt that this livery was chosen by the late R.A. Riddles and his former LNWR allegiances were not the least of the reasons for its choice. Thus, the 'Compounds' saw out their days in the colours of their once rival company (*Plates 165-167*). The majority probably had replacement chimneys by this time and coal-railed tenders were the norm, rather than the exception they had been before the war. Other than the preserved No. 1000, the last of the MR examples to be scrapped was No. 41020 (1953) and the last LMS example to survive was No. 41168 (withdrawn in 1961). They had lasted for almost 60 years.

In the following summary, we have again divided the class into the left-hand and right-hand drive series, mainly to simplify the tender variations.

LIVERY SAMPLES 1928-47

EX-MR AND RIGHT-HAND DRIVE LMS 'COMPOUNDS' (NOS. 1000-84):

Letter centre spacing generally 53in. For key to tender types see pages 66 and 75.

TENDER TYPES

LIVERY CODE	D1	D2	D3	D4	F1
A5	1001/3-4	1053	1012	1020/30/4/6/9/54†/ 7†	1007*+/71+/9/9+§
A6	1000/59/72/6	1047-53/64	1007/9/12-3	1016-8/20-1/4/7-9/ 33/6-8/41/3/54†/61†/ 2-3	1013*+/9+§/44+§/ 60+/70/3-5/7/ 8+/82-3
A7	—	—	—	—	1067/9/81-3
A11	1000	—	—	1057†	—
A14	1050	1045	1013	1029/32-3/5/53†	1060+/73+/5+
A15	—	—	—	—	1065
C22	1001/8	—	—	1015/7/29	1050*+/6/76/9/81*
C23	—	—	—	—	1080

+ *Coal Rails to tender*
* *Type F3 tender*
† *Special tender modified from Type D4*
§ *Type F2 tender*

LEFT-HAND DRIVE 'COMPOUNDS' (NOS. 900-39: 1085-1199)

Assume Type F1 tender unless marked in brackets after engine number - for key see pages 66 and 75. Letter spacing 53in. centres generally

LIVERY CODE	EXAMPLES
A5	1094+; 1101+/13/22+/52(D4)/9+/60+/72+/94
A6	1086(D1)/7/9/91/2(D2)/3/3+/5/6(D2)/7(D4); 1100-4/2(D1)/5(D4)/6(F3)/6(D1)/10(D1)/1/ 4-20/33-5/7/9/33/50-2/4/7/8/60+/1-3/4+/ 5-73/85/7-93/5/8/8+/9
A7	900-1/4/6/12/6/9/25/6+/7-8/33-4/5-9†; 1125/7/9/32/6/8-9/42-8/75/9/83-4
A11	1098
A12*	1094/9
A13	917/27; 1133/41(F2)+/75
A14	1088/90+/1+/2(D2)/3+; 1114/9+/58+
A15	926+/30+/3+/4+/8(F2)+; 1130
C21	911/3/22-4; 1099; 1130/49/55/82
C22	1105+/11(D1)/8/22+/54+/65+/6+/70+/2+/86+/ 9+/90+
C23	904/17/25+/6+/7(F2)+/9+/32+

+*Coal Rails:* *Experimental - see text.*
†*All type F2 tender/coal rails - note also that No. 936 had same livery with experimental tender - see text.*

Left *(Plates 156-158):* These three views show the various 'yellow with red shading' insignia styles, as seen on 'Compounds' in the later 1930s. No. 917 (left, upper; Code A13), displays the small numerals quite common in Scotland, No. 1060 (left, centre; Code A14) is showing the most common 12in variant while No. 930 (left, lower; Code A15), is in rather grimy condition, with 14in numerals. However, this was one of the few 'Compounds' to go through the war without being repainted black and this picture, taken at Holbeck, is probably a post-war view. By this time, coal rails on the tender were a commonplace feature. *W. Stubbs Collection/L. Hanson/Authors' Collection.*

Right *(Plate 159):* This detail view of No. 1091 gives a good impression of the 1937 yellow insignia, not to mention much other detail. Note the coal rails on the Type F1 tender and the fact that the front of the bulkhead above the shovelling 'hole' is no longer painted red and lined out as was the case in MR and early LMS days. The livery is Code A14. *A.E. West.*

This page (Plates 160-162): Three black-painted 'Compounds' conclude the LMS livery survey of this complicated class. They are No. 1099 (above, Code C21), with strengthened front frames; No. 1008 (Right Code C22), with Type D1 tender and 1936-pattern numberplate and No. 926 (below, Code C23) with both extended front frames and coal-railed Type F1 tender. Two of them (Nos. 1008 and 926) also have new chimneys. Nos. 1099 and 1008 are pictured during the war and, in 1946; No. 926 in 1948. *W. Stubbs Collection - 2/Authors' Collection.*

Above & Left *(Plates 163 & 164):* By early BR days, the 'Compounds', like many other engines, were becoming rather woe-begone, but by this time they lacked the glamour of the later express types so there was no real incentive to tidy their appearance. None received the 1946 LMS express passenger livery and the vast majority remained plain black for several years, as is well shown by these pictures, both depicting early non-standard BR markings. No. M1162 (above) shows a short-lived, early 1948 style, albeit already using the correct BR-style tender lettering, while No. 41097 (left) shows a very common form of renumbering — with BR number applied in LMS-style figures but accompanied by no other changes. This was the quickest way of putting the new numbers into use, but it did little for the engines' appearance. *Authors' Collection/E. Kearns.*

Left, below *(Plate 165):* During 1948, the former LNWR livery was adopted by BR for many 'second line' passenger and most mixed traffic engines, and vast numbers of ex-LMS machines were so painted, initially with full tender lettering. We must admit that it generally suited most engines to which it was applied - including the 'Compounds'. No. 41103 is seen here at Derby on June 11 1950. The engine, interestingly, has acquired non-fluted plain section coupling rods, as well as coal rails on the tender. *Authors' Collection.*

Top *(Plate 166):* Readers of the appropriate generation may well once have possessed the famous Gauge 'O' Hornby 'Compound' No. 1185. We could not find a decent LMS picture of it, but we thought there might be some nostalgic interest in this view of the engine in standard BR livery, with tender emblem, at Derby on July 27 1954. *R.A. Panting.*

Above *(Plate 167):* Right to the end of the story, tender exchanging continued and we conclude this chapter with a last look at one of the late surviving ex-MR 'Compounds', No. 41038, at Derby in 1950, coupled to yet a further variant of the hybrid 'short tank' LMS/Midland tender — this time without either side-beading or coal rails. The layout of the BR tender lining is, in the circumstances, logical enough, but somehow it doesn't look quite right. The locomotive is commendably clean. *Authors' Collection.*

84

CHAPTER 3:

MIDLAND RAILWAY

PASSENGER TANK CLASSES

ALONE of the English constituents of the LMS, the Midland Railway placed great reliance on the 0—4—4T for much of its passenger tank working. In this it was somewhat reminiscent of the Caledonian Railway in Scotland. However, perhaps to a greater degree than the Caledonian, the Midland also supplemented its 'official' passenger tank fleet by making use to some extent of vacuum brake - fitted 0—6—0Ts, which were otherwise regarded as freight engines. Viewed from the inside therefore, the dominance of the 0—4—4T across the MR system was not quite as noticeable as it might have been.

Moreover, the Midland's one class of 'big' passenger tanks, the Deeley 0—6—4 type, was considerably more numerous than any of the comparable big tank engines of any pre-Grouping LMS constituent, save for the LNWR. Even so the 0—4—4T was the characteristic form of Midland passenger tank.

Pedantically speaking, some of the 4—4—2Ts and all of the 4—6—4Ts designed for the LTSR section were also 'Midland' engines, having been delivered after the LTSR was absorbed in 1912, but these groups of locomotives will be considered in Chapter 8.

KIRTLEY CLASS 1 0-4-4WT (LMS Nos. between 1200-1225; Power Class 1, later 1P

Above (Plate 168): Kirtley 0—4—4WT No. 1200 of the Beyer-Peacock series, in early LMS livery (Code A3). Authors' Collection.

This astonishingly long-lived group of double-framed well tanks dated from 1869-70, well over 50 years before the Grouping, yet the last survivors continued working into the mid-1930s. They clearly had considerable merit. Very much in the typical Kirtley idiom, they had all, naturally, acquired Deeley/Fowler type front-ends by the time the LMS received them and two basic series were represented:

1200-6: Beyer-Peacock, 1869, 'straight-sided' bunkers, no footplate angle iron as such (Plate 168).
1207-26 (not 1212): (Dübs & Co, 1870, bunker sides with top copings and shallow footplate angle iron (Plate 169).

In 1930, the last two survivors of the Beyer-Peacock series (Nos. 1201/3) were renumbered 1212/3 (taking numbers vacated by earlier withdrawals from the Dübs series) in order to allow a few absorbed ex-SDJR 0—4—4Ts of Johnson design to take up the 1200-7 numbers. However, their 'anatomy' clearly revealed their origins — see Plate 170. Some examples were also

Left (Plate 169): The Dübs-built 0—4—4WTs had a shallow footplate angle, top copings below the bunker rails and slightly wider cab footsteps compared with the Beyer-Peacock engines. No. 1207 was photographed circa 1926, also in LMS livery (Code A3). Authors' Collection.

Right *(Plate 170):* 0—4—4WT No. 1212, originally No. 1201 of the Beyer-Peacock series, was re-numbered in 1930, still carrying the pre-1928 red livery (Code A3). The locomotive is pictured here at Derby, on September 15 1930. *W.L. Good.*

Below *(Plate 171):* Condenser fitted No. 1218 pictured at St. Pancras, circa 1927, Livery Code A3. Note the huge 'Cobs' of coal in the well-filled bunker! *National Railway Museum.*

fitted with condensing apparatus for working on to the Metropolitan lines *(Plate 171).*

Not surprisingly, the LMS made few changes to the engines. They were painted red with 14in figures at the Grouping and this livery was retained. Scrapping did not start until 1925 and it is likely that most of them received LMS emblems (Code A3) as shown in *Plates 168-71.* Their structural shape 'forced' the running numbers on to the bunker side in a reversal of 'normal' LMS and MR tank engine practice. Although 25 of the original 26 examples reached the LMS, not much more than a dozen or so survived for long enough after 1927 to be eligible for the revised livery to be applied, and it seems certain that the majority were painted red at withdrawal. However, those which did get the 1928 style again showed a reversal of normal procedure with 'LMS' carried on the bunker and the numbers on the cabside. See *Plate 172.*

Bearing in mind that the last few survivors had limited life expectancy, it would not have been surprising had they bee[n] repainted in plain black livery if repainted at all, but lining [is] visible on sufficient photographs to indicate that Derby, a[s] usual, followed the book correctly — after all, the 'book' ha[s] been written there! It is thought, however, that a few were give[n] lined black with plain (black shaded) insignia during the 1928/[?] period before the introduction of countershaded insignia *(Plat[e] 173).* No. 1219 *(Plate 172)* was the last to go, late in 1935.

LIVERY SAMPLES

CODE A3:	1200-2/7-9/12*/3-6/8/21/4-5
CODE B2/B5:	1218†
CODE B3:	1211/9/25
CODE B7:	1210

*New No. 1212 (old 1212 withdrawn pre-1923).
† Shading detail uncertain

86

Top *(Plate 172):* A quite superb scene. The post-1927 insignia on No. 1219 were countershaded (Code B3) but this is hardly discernible on this picture, save under scrutiny by a magnifying glass. The red lining has similarly almost 'vanished' — but it was there! Note condensing apparatus, detail of particular interest to modellers. *W. Stubbs Collection.*

Above *(Plate 173):* 0—4—4Ts Nos. 1215 (Livery Code A3) and 1210 (Code B7) were undoubtedly photographed at about the time of the livery change of 1928. At this time, it is very likely that No. 1210 was wearing black-shaded characters, the new countershaded style not yet having been introduced. *H.C. Casserley.*

JOHNSON CLASS 1 0-4-4T (LMS Nos between 1226-1430: Power Class 1, later 1P)

With but a very few exceptions, this extensive series of engines came intact to the LMS. The design had originated in 1875 and was built in a whole series of batches until 1900. Three basic variants existed:

1226-35; 1266-1350 — 5ft 4in driving wheels (Nos. 1226-35, notionally 5ft 3in).
1236-65 — 5ft 7in driving wheels.
1351-1430 — 5ft 4in driving wheels but higher boiler pressure.

In practice, there were few significant visual differences, save for the driving wheel size. Four numbers were vacant in 1923, Nos. 1245/81-2 (withdrawn) and 1305 (sold to the SDJR). No. 1305 was given back its old number when re-absorbed in 1930, but is considered with the other SDJR engines in *Chapter 9*. *Plates 174-6* illustrate the three principal ex-MR series in the physical condition in which they reached the LMS.

During the LMS period, driving wheel diameter excluded, there were three principal visual variations to be seen within this class. First, and actually dating back to the mid-1920s was the fitting of Belpaire boilers to a considerable number of engines. This process was brought to a halt in 1928, presumably because, by then, the new generation of standard 2—6—2Ts and 2—6—4Ts was beginning to appear. The Belpaire 0—4—4T rebuilds often emerged with Ramsbottom safety-valves (*Plate 177*) but 'pop' valves were substituted fairly soon (*Plate 178*).

The second common variant in LMS days was the fitting of motor-train control apparatus and this could appear with either the original round-top boiler configuration or with the Belpaire version (*Plates 179 & 180*). Thirdly, quite a number of the engines carried condensing apparatus again including both round-top and Belpaire types (*Plates 181 & 182*). A comprehensive listing of the Belpaire and most of the motor-fitted and condensing versions is carried in *British Locomotive*

Top *(Plate 174):* Johnson 5ft 4in No. 1228 of the very first (1875) series. This picture was taken on June 16 1928 at Derby and shows an early example of the post-1927 lined black livery with un-shaded (black-shaded) characters and 10in figures (Code B5). *Authors' Collection.*

Right: See opposite page, top.

Above & Facing page, lower *(Plates 175 & 176):* These views, from somewhat similar angles show comparative views of the 5ft 7in and 5ft 4in engines, Nos. 1263 and 1347. Apart from the slightly more prominent front coupling rod splasher and the marginally larger front wheel splasher of No. 1263 (facing page), there is little significant visual difference. Both engines are in pre-1928 LMS livery (Code A3). *Authors' Collection/National Railway Museum.*

Left, upper *(Plate 177):* Belpaire-boilered Johnson 0—4—4T No. 1324, with Ramsbottom pattern safety valves pictured circa 1926 — Livery Code A3. At a later stage, the LMS fitted this engine with motor-train control gear. *W.L. Good.*

Left, lower *(Plate 178):* Belpaire-boilered Johnson 0—4—4T No. 1397 with 'pop' safety valves at Bristol on November 10 1935. The livery would have been Code B3, not that the picture reveals this fact! *Authors' Collection.*

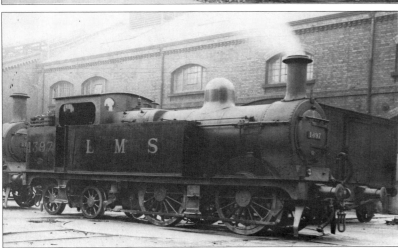

Above & right *(Plates 179-180):* Motor-fitted conversions of 5ft 7in round-top 0—4—4T No. 1246 (above) and 5ft 4in Belpaire engine No. 1424 (right) at Bedford on June 8 1936 and Burton-on-Trent on May 9 1948. The liveries were Code B3 (No. 1246) and C22 (No. 1424), both in decidedly scruffy state. *A.G. Ellis/L. Hanson.*

Left *(Plate 181):* Condenser-fitted round-top 0—4—4T No. 1284 at Kentish Town, on May 6 1923. This engine still carries MR livery — note the works plate on the bunker side (repositioned after LMS emblems were applied), also the polished brass splasher-top beading. The higher capacity bunker is also clearly shown. *A.G. Ellis.*

Catalogue – Vol. 3A (pp. 136-40), but it is not possible to give a full list of the latter two categories. These details are, however, included in the sample summary below.

Lastly, a few engines carried flared-top bunker sides *(Plates 181 & 182)* which increased the coal-carrying capacity. It is tempting to infer that this was associated with the fitting of condensing gear, but photographic evidence *(Plate 190)* disproves the theory for the later-built engines with condensing gear. Engines thought to have had these bunkers are condensing 0—4—4Ts Nos. 1281-5 and 1311-21 but further information would be welcome.

Turning now to livery, the Johnson 0—4—4Ts were always, as far as can be judged, given the officially correct version of whatever livery style was then current. All of them were red with 14in figures in 1923 but it seems unlikely that all were given proper LMS markings before the livery changeover during 1927/8. Interestingly, these engines had not carried the MR emblem on the bunker side *(Plate 181)* so all that may have been done with some of them after the Grouping would have been to obliterate the front MR lettering and add LMS markings. One or two examples received the small 'LMS' (Code A4) *(Plate 183)*, but most confirmed examples with LMS markings were of the conventional arrangement, Code A3 *(Plates 175-7)*.

Lined black, generally with countershaded insignia and 12in numerals, was the normal style after 1927/8 and this suited the engines rather well. Round-cornered lining was normal together

Above *(Plate 182)*: **No. 1315 was a Belpaire-boilered condensing 0—4—4T — also with enlarged bunker and carrying a somewhat degraded lined black livery (Code B3).** *W. Stubbs Collection.*

Above *(Plate 183)*: **Early LMS livery (Code A4) carried by 0—4—4T No. 1402, in 1923. Originally MR No. 691, this locomotive was built at Derby in 1898 and survived until 1949.** *BR(LMR).*

Left *(Plate 184):* This crisp view of No. 1364, at Bristol on April 20 1934, clearly displays the round-cornered lining and countershaded insignia of the post-1927 livery (Code B3). It also gives an idea how, for the shed foreman, keeping the depot yard clear of char and ashes must have been a relentless task. *H.C. Casserley.*

Right, upper & lower *(Plates 185 & 186):* This interesting pair of pictures of No. 1273 in motor-fitted form, taken circa 1934 and 1936 respectively, show the lined black livery in two forms, Codes B3 (upper) and B11 (lower). In neither case is it particularly easy to detect lining or insignia shading. Note the changed position (further forward) of the boiler-side clack valve on the engine in its later state. This valve admits water into the boiler, from the injector. *Authors' Collection.*

with letter spacing at around 40in centres *(Plate 184)*. As usual, the lining and shading did not always register clearly on photographs but there is no valid reason to suppose that Derby ever deviated from the official form *(Plate 185)*.

In 1936 and for a year or so, a few began to appear with sans-serif insignia *(Plate 186)*, and it is likely that any examples repainted during 1938/9 would receive red-shaded yellow insignia with the lined black livery. This type of insignia continued in use during the plain black wartime and post-war periods *(Plate 187)*.

A total of 63 engines reached BR ownership, 62 being re-allocated new BR(LMR) series numbers 58030-91, but not all engines received their new numbers before scrapping. Those which did should have received lined black livery *(Plate 188)*,

but not all did so *(Plate 189)*.

The engines were a familiar sight on the Midland Division throughout the LMS period and into early BR days. It is a shame that no example was preserved - all the more so since No. 1226 (the first of the class) was withdrawn for preservation in 1930. However, it was scrapped in 1932. They were an advanced concept in 1875 and the fact that examples remained in use right through the 1950s meant that their working life spanned some 85 years. The last withdrawal was No. 1424 (as BR No. 58087) in mid-1960 and we conclude our survey of this numerous and widespread class with a few more pictures to show further detail variations *(Plates 190-5)*.

The following tabulated summary attempts to cover most of the significant variations:

LIVERY SAMPLES:

LIVERY STYLE	ROUND TOP BOILER		BELPAIRE BOILER	
	NORMAL CONFIGURATION	MOTOR FITTED	NORMAL CONFIGURATION	MOTOR FITTED
CODE A3	1229/34/59/63/9/85† 1300-1/8-9/13†/7†/ 21†/32/47/63/77*/ 80*/1/90/403-4/20/6-7/9	1273/7-8/302	1288/322/4/8/65/70/ 1*/3*/83/416/21/4/8	—
CODE A4	1293/402	—	—	—
CODE A5	1347	—	—	—
CODE B3	1235/69/92/4/6/300-1 13†/20†/7/9/33-4/ 9/43/64/9-71/4*/6*/ 7*/8*/82*/4*/5*/7/ 9/92/400/4/8/27	1246/73/5-8/85†/ 302-3/30/46/420/6/	1267/86/95/8/315†/ 22/37-8/50/6/73*/5*/ 80*/93/6-7/402-3/11/ 6/21-4/9-30	1272/87/90/7/324/ 40-2/4/57/9/67-8/ 90/425
CODE B5	1228	—	1425	—
CODE B9	1377*/9*	—	1413	—
CODE B11	1389	1273	1429	1428
CODE C22	1382*/404	1278/90	1295	1307/424

† *Condensing apparatus plus flared top bunker*
* *Condensing apparatus only*

Left *(Plate 187)*: Motor-fitted 0—4—4T No. 1278, still with round-top boiler at Millers Dale, on August 9 1947. The livery is the characteristic final LMS plain black (Code C22), with prominent red-shaded yellow insignia, which have been given a 'rub over', probably for this photograph. Note the fire-irons stowed on the tank top, where a 'Y' shaped yoke is provided at the leading end and a peg at the rear, on which the circular handle of the irons were secured. *Authors' Collection.*

Right, upper & lower *(Plate 188 & 189)*: Alternative BR liveries on the motor-fitted and Belpaire-boilered Nos. 58091 (ex-MR/LMS No. 1430) and 58065 (ex-MR/LMS No. 1367). The fully correct BR livery would have been the lining of No. 58091 combined with the insignia of No. 58065. *Authors' Collection/ W. Stubbs Collection.*

Left *(Plate 190)*: 0—4—4T No. 1371 displayed Belpaire boiler, condensing apparatus and normal bunker (compare with *(Plate 182)* and was one of a number of engines to show this particular combination. Livery Code B3. *Authors' Collection.*

Left & above (Plate 191 & 192): Detail views of motor-fitted 0—4—4T No. 1272. The second view reveals (just!) that the engine was lined, with countershaded insignia. Note also the brake and sanding gear details. A.E. West.

Right & below (Plates 193 & 194): Early application of the post-1927 livery is shown on Nos. 1347 (right) and 1425 (below) both with black-shaded 10in figures; however No. 1347 has retained the older red livery — Codes A5 and B5 respectively. Authors' Collection.

Right *(Plate 195):* Many 0—4—4Ts were repainted in plain black livery with yellow/red insignia (Code C22), during the war. However, some examples retained pre-war liveries, as illustrated here by No. 1342 (Code B3). This picture was taken at Derby on September 29 1946 and the 'cleaned-up' insignia reveal (under magnification) the countershaded form which could only have been applied with lining, and certainly no later than 1937/8. Note the new 1936-pattern number-plate. *W.L. Good.*

DEELEY CLASS 3 0-6-4T (LMS Nos 2000-2039; Power Class 3, later 3P)

The so-called 'big' passenger tank did not really come into its own on British metals until the advent of the post-Grouping designs in the 1920s, but the Midland provided an exception in 1907 with the introduction of this class of 40 engines. They were fairly speedily nicknamed 'Flatirons' or 'Hole-in-the-Wall' tanks' because of their distinctive visual lines *(Plate 196)*.

Their basic character scarcely changed save for the extended smokebox/Belpaire fireboxes applied consequent upon superheating *(Plate 197)*. This process began in 1920 and was mostly carried out during the early LMS period. The following engines were received by the LMS in superheated form: Nos. 2002/35/9. The last conversion was in 1927 and we have only

Right *(Plate 196):* Saturated 'Flatiron' 0—6—4T No. 2031 represents the condition in which most of this class reached the LMS, but repainting with LMS insignia was a little unusual in the pre-superheated form, especially in the Code A2 version illustrated. *National Railway Museum.*

confirmed four of them in LMS markings *before* superheating. One of this group (see *Plate 196*) also received the 1923-style bunker lettering. Subsequently, the only significant change was the usual replacement of Ramsbottom type safety valves by the more modern 'pop' variety *(Plates 197 & 198)*.

The red livery was applied exclusively with 18in figures (Code A1) and the lined black usually with the 14in pattern lettering. As usual, it cannot be stated with certainty how many of these engines actually received LMS emblems during the red period but it is highly probable that they were all correctly repainted and marked *after* superheating, in the manner of *Plates 197-8*. In

consequence, several examples probably retained their 'new' red liveries for some time after the livery change of 1927.

After 1927, countershaded insignia were normal for repaints, but there were three known and curious exceptions, Nos. 2018/29/38 *(Plate 199)*, which seemed to have made use of some obsolete 18in transfers. They later received normal markings *(Plate 200)* and by the time of first withdrawals (1935), all 40 engines were similarly and correctly finished. No further livery changes were made and the last survivor was withdrawn bearing conventional livery in 1938 — No. 2012 *(Plate 201)*.

There is a widespread belief, sometimes appearing in print,

Right & below *(Plates 199 & 200):* **No. 2018 received lined black livery with black-shaded LMS and 18in MR-style numerals on the bunker, and was thus photographed (right) at Derby in 1930. Later, it received the conventional (for the class) 14in numerals and LMS markings — Code B4. The shading is barely discernible.** *W. Stubbs' Collection, BR(LMR).*

Right *(Plate 201):* **Deeley 0—6—4T, No. 2012, the last survivor of the Class, withdrawn from traffic and pictured in store at Nottingham Shed, circa 1938. The livery is still Code B3 and the countershading has registered quite well. Note the lining on the tank front — a detail not often visible on pictures of these engines.** *Authors' Collection.*

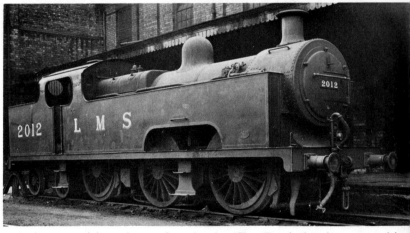

that these engines were less than successful. Certainly, during the mid-LMS period one or two examples gained for the class an undesirable reputation for derailing when running chimney-first with the large wheels leading; this caused a relegation to slower speed freight working. Some shortcomings had undoubtedly been noted in MR days (see *An Illustrated History of Midland Locomotives, Vol. 2, Wild Swan Publications*) but it seems surprising that if this was a real problem it should not have been rectified during the previous 20-25 years! It seems far more likely that they were withdrawn for no more significant reason than that their superheated boilers were 10-15 years old and would be due for renewal anyway. By this time, the new generation of 2—6—4Ts was well established and obviously more efficient, so there was no prima face reason to continue

repairing the ageing 0—6—4Ts. Precisely the same thing happened on the Western Division in regard to the ex-LNWR 4—4—2Ts and 4—6—2Ts, so the contemporary withdrawal of the Deeley 0—6—4Ts does not seem too surprising. Perhaps contemporary observers were taken by surprise that an ex-Midland design should have lasted only 30 years or so!

LIVERY SAMPLES: *Letter spacing 40in centres, post-1927*

CODE A1:	**2002/7/10-11/13-4/7/20-2†/5/9/33-4†/8**
	(all Belpaire and superheated)
CODE A2:	**2031 (round top)**
CODE B4:	**Believed the whole class Belpaire-fitted and superheated**
CODE B5:	**2003**

† *Nos. 2020/1 and 2034 also received LMS markings before rebuilding.*

CHAPTER 4:

MIDLAND RAILWAY

FREIGHT TANK CLASSES

THE Midland Railway was a great freight-handling line as its vast army of 0—6—0 tender engines indicated. To service this traffic in marshalling yards and on transfer/pick-up freight duties the MR naturally employed a considerable number of shunting tank locomotives. Most of these were, not surprisingly, of 0—6—0 wheel arrangement, but there was also a small number of 0—4—0Ts for the lighter duties, or for use in cases where there were curvature/clearance restrictions which inhibited the 0—6—0 form. In this respect, the Midland followed the same policy as most of the larger British systems.

By LMS days, the goods tank engines were concentrated in four broadly homogeneous classes (two 0—4—0 and two 0—6—0 types), plus an assorted rag-bag of elderly 0—6—0Ts. As usual, the following survey is in LMS(MR) number order.

JOHNSON 0-4-0ST (LMS Nos. between 1500-1525; Power Class later 0F)

These rather dainty little engines were visually somewhat different from most of the contemporary 0—4—0STs belonging to other Railways, and dated back to 1883 when a batch of five was built at Derby. They continued to emerge in batches of five over a period of years until 1903 when a total of 30 examples were in service. In 1907, 28 survivors were renumbered and of these, all but Nos. 1501/12/21/6-7 reached the LMS. No. 1506 was renumbered 1509 in 1930 when the SDJR stock was absorbed.

Above *(Plate 202):* **Engine No. 1501, illustrated here, did not quite reach LMS ownership, but its form was wholly typical of the first series of Johnson 0—4—0STs which did work beyond the Grouping of 1923.** *R.S. Carpenter Collection.*

Three separately identified series were built. The first ten examples (LMS survivors Nos. 1500/2-7) are represented by *Plate 202,* the second ten (LMS survivors Nos. 1508-11/3-7) by

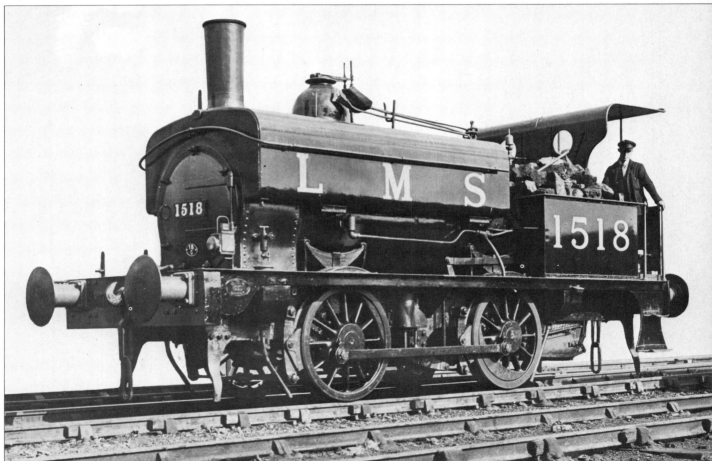

Top *(Plate 203):* **The second series of engines is represented by No. 1514 ex-works in early LMS livery (Code C6) in 1923.** *BR (LMR).*

Above *(Plate 204):* **The third and larger series of 0—4—0STs could most readily be identified by their somewhat deeper saddletanks and modifications to the brake gear between the coupled wheels. The increase in wheelbase was less obvious. No. 1518 is pictured in post-1927 livery (Code C15) and note that the number position did not change in 1927/8 with this Class. Detail of interest to modellers includes the fire-iron stowage arrangements.** *BR(LMR).*

Left (Plate 205): A detail view of the characteristic open-backed cab on No. 1518, in somewhat more scruffy condition than in the previous view. Authors' Collection.

Plate 203 and the last ten engines (LMS survivors Nos. 1518-25) by Plate 204. Effectively, the first two series were all-but alike; but the last ten examples had an extended wheelbase (7ft 6in rather than 7ft) and larger cylinders and tanks. All carried MR Class J or J1 boilers which some sources regard as an alliterative origin of the nickname 'Jinty' for a small shunting tank. As built, they were fitted with open-backed cabs (Plate 205), but the late MR/early LMS period saw most fitted with closed-in cabs — if a single curved sheet from spectacle plate to cab back can thus be distinguished! This modification took some time to implement, several examples were not converted until after the livery change during 1927/8 — see Plate 208 — and some were never modified (such as No. 1516).

Although painted red in pre-1907 MR days, all came to the LMS in standard MR goods engine black, without company markings and carrying 14in figures on the cabside, as shown in Plate 202. The only change, initially, was to add LMS markings after 1923, occasionally in small letters (Plate 203) but usually with the correct red panel (Plate 207). These company markings were placed on the tankside (a reversal of pre-1928 LMS custom) and this insignia placement was retained after the 1927/8 livery change — again somewhat unusual (Plate 208). The 14in figures were often retained but the 12in variety in either plain gold (Plate 209) or, after 1937, red-shaded yellow lettering (Plate 210) was a common alternative.

In terms of detail, an interesting curiosity was the retention by some examples of the original-pattern smokebox door, both before and after the fitting of 'closed' cabs. Plates 206/8-9 show

Above (Plate 206): This interesting contrast shows first series 0—4—0ST No. 1505 (left) with closed-back cab and final series No. 1520 (right) with original cab. The deeper saddle on the later-built engine is best appreciated by looking at the dome height and the position of the front handrail, relative to the tank top. The picture cannot be dated save that it is probably in late Midland days — the letters 'MR' are just visible on the front buffer plank of No. 1505. Authors' Collection.

this feature but we are unable to give a full list.

Withdrawal began in MR days and continued progressively, if only slowly, through the LMS period. Two engines were sold out of service, in 1928 (No. 1511) and 1932 (No. 1524), whilst No. 1509 (ex-1506) lasted in service stock for many years. Three examples reached BR ownership (Nos. 41516/8/23) and No. 41518 was the last survivor, withdrawn in 1958.

The following summary includes only those engines known to have received LMS markings in pre-1928 days and also separates the 'open' and 'closed' cab variants.

LIVERY SAMPLES *'LMS' lettering at 40in centres, post 1927*

	OPEN CAB	CLOSED CAB
CODE C4...	1500/3/15/9/20/2	1511
CODE C6...	1514	—
CODE C13	—	1524
CODE C14	—	1506/9‡
CODE C15	1516*/8	1509‡/10
CODE C22	—	1509‡
CODE C23	—	1523
CODE C25	—	1509‡

‡ Old No. 1506
* with countershaded insignia

Below *(Plate 207)*: **The standard pre-1928 livery (Code C4) is well represented on No. 1511 and the view also shows the somewhat primitive nature of the enclosed cab.** *Authors' Collection.*

Right & opposite page *(Plates 208-210)*: **These three views allow the comparison between the principal post-1927 lettering styles employed on the Johnson 0—4—0STs. The livery Codes are C15, unusually applied in countershaded form to No. 1516 (pictured at Derby, in 1938); C14 (No. 1506) and C22 (No. 1509, pictured at Derby on April 24 1938).** *L. Hanson/Authors' Collection/H.C. Casserley.*

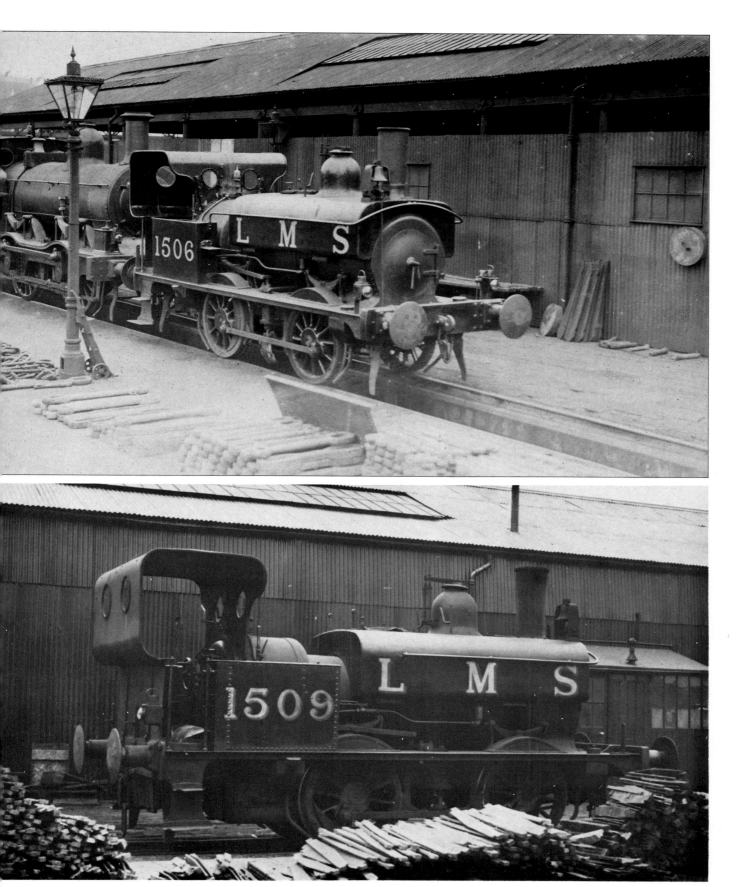

This page: For caption details, see opposite page.

DEELEY 0-4-0T (LMS Nos. 1528-1537; Power Class later 0F)

Right *(Plate 211)*: This view of No. 1536, taken on May 9 1925, shows the Fowler-built version of the Deeley design 0—4—0T, still carrying MR livery without LMS markings. *W.L. Good.*

This small group of ten, rather massively-proportioned 0—4—0Ts emerged in two series. The first five examples appeared in 1907, but the second five were not built until 1921/2, under the Fowler regime, and emerged as 'renewals' of five of the earlier Johnson 0—4—0STs. Like the 0—4—0STs, they had stovepipe chimneys — not a characteristic of the Midland — and the last five had much more heavily rivetted side tanks.

As usual for freight engines, they came to the LMS in plain black livery, without MR emblems, but with 14in figures centred on the tanks *(Plate 211)*. It is likely, but not confirmed, that indication of LMS ownership pre-1928 was to place the red panel midway between the figures and the cabside opening — but we have been unable to find even a single photograph to confirm this supposition. Hopefully, one of our readers might be able to help. After the livery change of 1927-8, the 14in figures continued, but with some indecision as to the placing of the large 'LMS' vis-a-vis the numerals. In *Plates 212 & 213* both versions are given. The 'standard' form was with the 'LMS' at the chimney end — as conventionally-placed as the configuration permitted.

Above & opposite page, top: *(Plates 212-213)*: These views of the genuine Deeley built 0—4—0Ts Nos. 1529 (above) and 1530 (opposite page, top), both show Livery Code C15, but with different placements for the insignia — see text. Note also the much less heavily rivetted construction compared with No. 1536 *(Plate 211)*. *W. Stubbs Collection.*

All ten engines came to BR service with the occasional 'non-standard' repaint numbered among them (*Plate 214*), and even when standard BR livery was applied, there was still some waywardness in the placement of BR marking — see *Plates 215 & 216*. The last two survivors soldiered on until 1966 and were amongst the very last ex-MR engines to remain in service (Nos. 41528/33). Interestingly, these were the pioneer members of each batch of five to be built.

Above *(Plate 214)*: **An early BR repaint, using 10in LMS figures (probably plain yellow) was employed on No. 41533 circa 1948.** *David Gilbert.*

Right & below *(Plates 215 & 216):* The final BR markings displayed on examples of each of the two series of 0—4—0Ts, Nos. 41528 (right) and 41537 (below) reveal that insignia placing was never fully resolved. We believe No. 41537 to be the more typical. *Authors' Collection.*

LIVERY SAMPLES *All are post-1927 examples with 40 in 'LMS' spacing.*

CODE C15:	1528/9†/30/2-3/4*/5-6
CODE C23:	1536

Notes: † *'LMS' at cab end on left hand side of engine, chimney end on right-hand side*
  * *Countershaded insignia*

This small group of ancient 0—6—0 tanks consisted of three principal variants:

LMS Nos. 1605/7: These engines were two surviving Kirtley 0—6—0 well tanks with double frames. Originally MR Nos. 1601/4, they were nominally renumbered in 1923 to make way for ex-NSR engines (See *Volume Two*). Both engines are shown in LMS days in *Plates 217 & 218*, but only No. 1607 received its new number. It was scrapped in 1928.

LMS Nos. 1606/8: These two engines were much rebuilt examples which had started life in the 1880s on the Severn &

Wye Railway. When the LMS received them *(Plate 219)* they were substantially similar to the Johnson Class 1 0—6—0T, but both were withdrawn within two years of the Grouping.

LMS Nos. 1610-9: This was a class of ten engines dating from 1871 and built by Beyer-Peacock to Kirtley's order. All came to the LMS as heavily rebuilt by Johnson, with open-back cabs and new boilers. Built for working over lines with restricted clearances in the London area, none lasted long in LMS days, withdrawal taking place between 1923 and 1927. They came to the LMS in the form shown in *Plates 220 & 221*, but it seems unlikely that any received LMS markings.

This page *(Plates 217 & 218)*: Kirtley 0—6—0WT Nos. 1601 (top) and 1607 (left) were the only two of this kind to reach the LMS No. 1601 (allocated LMS No. 1605) still carried its pre-1907 type brass numerals when seen at Burton on September 10 1923, whereas No. 1607 (ex-MR No. 1604) carried its new LMS number but without apparent sign of company ownership. *R.S. Carpenter Collection/Authors' Collection.*

Left *(Plate 219):* 0—6—0T No. 1606, at one time of the Severn & Wye Railway, was very much in the Johnson idiom when it reached the LMS. This view shows it slightly before the Grouping (Livery Code basically C4) but it is not thought ever to have received LMS markings on the bunker. *Authors' Collection.*

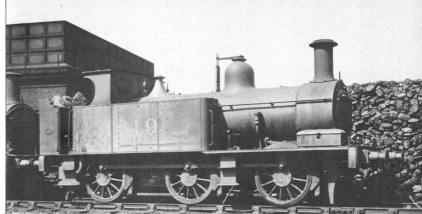

Right & below *(Plates 220 & 221):* Opposite side views of Kirtley's inside-framed 0—6—0Ts Nos. 1619 (right) and 1617 (below) at Kentish Town in 1922 and 1923 respectively. Both are painted black with 14in numerals, but neither received LMS ownership markings. *H.C. Casserley/Authors' Collection.*

This large class of simple-expansion 0—6—0Ts was undoubtedly the archetypal Midland shunting engine during pre-LMS years and like many numerically strong classes, remained well-represented throughout the LMS period and even into BR days. As with most large MR classes, visible variations between individual members were always present and, when the LMS took over, the variety continued to expand.

Essentially, two series of locomotives were represented in structural terms. The first series dated from 1874 and developments thereof were built regularly until 1892 (LMS Nos. 1620-1844). The final continuation (LMS Nos. 1845-99) had a slightly increased wheelbase (7ft 4in + 8ft 2in, rather than 7ft 4in + 7ft 8in) and, originally, a somewhat larger boiler. These rather larger engines dated from 1895-1900, after which construction ceased.

Overlaying this basic difference within the whole series, there was a second obvious division of the shorter wheelbase variant between those with totally enclosed cabs and those with open-back or 'half' cabs. The latter term is not always regarded with approval by some more pedantic observers — but it does form a convenient 'shorthand' way of differentiating the two types. To make matters more confusing, some of the original 'half' cab engines later received the enclosed variation. Additionally, some had lower chimneys and domes (*Plate 231*), some were vacuum-brake fitted and the inevitable MR rebuilding had given them all the Deeley-Fowler front-end 'look' by 1923. Overlay all this with the fact that from circa 1925 onwards, Belpaire firebox replacement boilers began to be fitted to quite a number of them, and it will be appreciated that the visual permutations were numerous, to say the least. *Plates 222-228* endeavour to encompass the majority of the normal variations.

Continued on page 112.

Top *(Plate 222):* 0—6—0T No. 1630 **(Livery Code C6), seen at Peterborough on May 7 1927, was one of the first series to be built and had a closed cab from new. Note the curved top to the rear bunker and the fact that the locomotive was vacuum-brake equipped by this date.** *H.C. Casserley.*

Right *(Plate 223):* 'Half' cab No. 1740 **had a round top boiler and LMS Livery (Code C5) in the pre-1928 period.** *Authors' Collection.*

Right & below *(Plates 224 & 225):* **These two views show 'long wheelbase' variants Nos. 1857 (right) and 1870 (below) of the Class 1 0—6—0T, with round-top and Belpaire boilers respectively. Both engines carry the typical post-1927 livery (Code C13). Note the different cab shapes and proportions. It is tempting to infer that the longer cab was associated with the Belpaire boilers until one examines examples such as** *Plate 227.* *Authors' Collection.*

Below & opposite page, top *(Plates 226 & 227):* **This pair of engines, Nos. 1665 (below) and 1676 (opposite page, top) both displaying Livery Code C13, represent two original 'half' cab engines both now with enclosed cabs; but one of them (No. 1676) also with Belpaire boiler. Again note the cab/bunker variations.** *A.G. Ellis/Authors' Collection.*

Left: For caption details, see opposite page.

Below *(Plate 228)*: No. 1753 (Livery Code C13) retained its 'half' cab when fitted with Belpaire boiler in 1926. This picture was taken some five or six years later. *Authors' Collection.*

Left & overleaf *(Plates 229 & 230)*: Class 1 0—6—0T No. 41748 was a late conversion from round-top to Belpaire in 1953 when it received a second-hand boiler! These views show the engine as a round-top engine (left) in early BR days (with non-standard BR livery) and (overleaf) as finally operating in the period 1953-7), also fitted for working motor-trains. *D.F. Tee/ F.W. Shuttleworth.*

Right: For caption details, see previous page.

Mercifully, from our point of view, *British Locomotive Catalogue – Vol. 3A*, (pp.140-7) gives an engine-by-engine summary of most of these variations so they need not concern us too much more within these pages. The livery summary (below) differentiates the more obvious variations (cab and fireboxes for example) and the following generalised summary should hopefully help to establish the picture a little more clearly as far as the LMS period is concerned:

LMS Nos. 1620-59: Original wheelbase, built with enclosed cabs, and always round-top boilers.

LMS Nos. 1660-1709: Original wheelbase, built with 'half' cab; many later given closed cabs and/or Belpaire boilers.

LMS Nos. 1710-19: As 1600-1709 but shorter chimneys, domes and cabs (originally).

LMS Nos. 1720-4: As 1660-1709.

LMS Nos. 1725-9: Original wheelbase, enclosed cab, vacuum-fitted from new; all later with Belpaire boilers.

LMS Nos. 1730-1804: As 1660-1709.

LMS Nos. 1805-14: As 1710-19 (originally).

LMS Nos. 1815-44: As 1660-1709.

LMS Nos. 1845-49:* Increased wheelbase, enclosed cab.

LMS Nos. 1850-54:* As 1845-9 plus vacuum brake from new.

LMS Nos. 1855-99:* As 1845-9.

* *Many given Belpaire boilers later*

Astonishingly, the Belpaire boiler replacement process went on well into BR days (*Plates 229 & 230*) until the early 1960s, only a few years before the class was extinct. The last survivor, BR No. 41708, was preserved in 'half' cab form with Belapire boiler — in effect its 1926 and subsequent configuration — and was officially withdrawn in 1965. It has now been 'rebuilt' with an enclosed cab, though for what reason, we cannot imagine!

Finally, before turning to the various liveries involved in the LMS period, it should be pointed out that the enclosed cabs fitted to this group of engines tended to display slight variations in both shape and size. We have been quite unable to establish a pattern for this activity so far, but *Plates 222/4-7* clearly show some of the different styles employed.

In livery terms, the Class 1 0—6—0Ts were always painted plain black in LMS days, but as usual, insignia sizes, styles, colours and positioning changed. The 1923-27 'norm' was with 14in numerals and red panel (*Plate 231*) and after 1927, 10in figures were well-nigh universal, along with 'LMS' at 40in spacing (*Plate 232*). The 1928 insignia were almost always in plain gold (or gold with 'invisible' black shading) until circa 1937 when a few examples emerged in the short-lived sans-serif style (*Plate 233*). Thereafter, yellow letters with red shading became the customary style (*Plate 234*) followed after 1948 by BR liveries for the many long-term survivors (*Plates 235 & 236*).

LIVERY SAMPLES *'LMS' at 40in centres, post 1927*				
LIVERY STYLES	**ROUND-TOP BOILER**		**BELPAIRE BOILER**	
	CLOSED CAB	**OPEN CAB**	**CLOSED CAB**	**OPEN CAB**
CODE C4	1624/31/7/46/9/ 77/728/868/86/91	1663/90/805*/8	1778	1772/82/815
CODE C5	1667/9/70/877	1683/719/40	1736	1790
CODE C6	1630/73/861/4/9	1701	—	—
CODE C1	—	—	—	1809
CODE C13	1665/8/9/730†/ 816-7/51/3-4/ 6-7/65/72/6/ 84/95	1671/711/3-5/43/ 6-7/56-8/63/81/9/ 91/3/5/805/7/11/ 27/36/9	1672/4/6/725†/833/ 46/50/2/5/9/70/8/ 90-1	1664/95/708/17/24/ 49/53/88/94/9
CODE C20	1779	1700	1889	1712/54/810
CODE C21	1666/767/79/857/ 71/3-4/85	1748/55/62/835	1725/7/856/60	1661/82/90/9/711/ 80/803/11/42

Notes:
  † *Countershaded insignia*
  * *Still with 'low height' chimney dome*

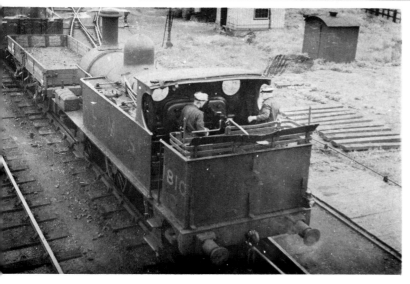

113

Right *(Plate 234):* **This April 9 1949** view at Gloucester shows the final LMS insignia style for many of the Class 1 0—6—0Ts (Code C21). No. 1727 was one of a handful of these engines fitted with enclosed cabs and vacuum brake from new; but by this stage carrying a Belpaire boiler. *Authors' Collection.*

Below & lower *(Plates 235 & 236):* Early and late BR liveries are displayed in these two views of Nos. 41710 and 41712, both still 'half' cab but fitted with Belpaire boilers. No. 41710 is pictured at Derby on July 16 1948 whilst No. 41712 was photographed at Kirkby MPD in August 1964. *Authors' Collection.*

JOHNSON '2441 CLASS' 0-6-0T
LMS Nos. 1900-1959, later 7200-7259; Power Class 3, later 3F)

These larger tank engines were a progressive enlargement of the earlier and numerous Johnson Class 1 series and a total of 60 examples were built between 1899 and 1902, with round-top boilers and enclosed cabs. The inevitable rebuilding gave all of them the Deeley-Fowler front-end look and, starting in 1919, a further rebuild with Belpaire boiler and raised cab roof produced what was effectively the prototype of the LMS standard Class 3F 0—6—0T with the emergence of Nos. 1930/4 (later Nos. 7230/4). In accordance with the note on page 9, this final form will be considered in Chapter 5, along with the LMS continuation of this class but a view of this final configuration is given in *Plate 241*, for the sake of completeness.

The LMS received 56 (of the 60 examples built) in more or less original condition (*Plate 238*), there being at that time only four 'Belpaire' rebuilds (Nos. 1930/3-4/8). Of the 56 round-top engines, a few retained their continuous front hand rails and older smokebox doors (*Plate 237*), but most had the typical later style (*Plate 238*). It should also be mentioned that a slight majority of this series of engines carried condensing apparatus throughout their lives and all 60 were vacuum-braked. The condensing engines were Nos. 1900-29/40-5/7/9/51.

Livery was straightforward and pre-1928 14in figures were universally applied. Thereafter, the 10in figures were adopted

both with the 19XX numbers (*Plate 238*) and also with the 1934 series 72XX numbers which many of them achieved before rebuilding (*Plate 239*). Two at least also achieved the 1936 style, Nos. 7209/58 (*Plate 240*) and, since the final 'Belpaire' rebuild did not take place until 1942 (No. 7259) it is possible that the occasional unrebuilt example might have received the yellow characters (with red shading) for a year or two.

Most engines were rebuilt before the livery change and only a few remained unrebuilt at the 1934 renumbering. For the record, the following information may be helpful:

Engines rebuilt 1928 and later: 1908/9/19/21-2/44/6/53/5-9.

Engines rebuilt after 1934 renumbering: 7208-9/19/21/53/8-9

LIVERY SAMPLES *prior to Belpaire rebuilding only; LMS at 40in spacing, post 1927*

CODE C4:	1907/9/22/36
CODE C13:	1908/53; 7208
CODE C14:	1921
CODE C19:	7258
CODE C20:	7209
CODE C21:	7259

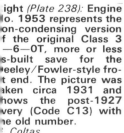

Left (*Plate 237*): The 'large' ex MR shunting tank series, almost as-built, is represented here by No. 1907, carrying early LMS livery (Code C4) — and note that the engine still displays a continuous front handrail. *W.L. Good.*

Right (*Plate 238*): Engine No. 1953 represents the non-condensing version of the original Class 3 0—6—0T, more or less as-built save for the Deeley/Fowler-style front end. The picture was taken circa 1931 and shows the post-1927 livery (Code C13) with the old number. *R. Coltas.*

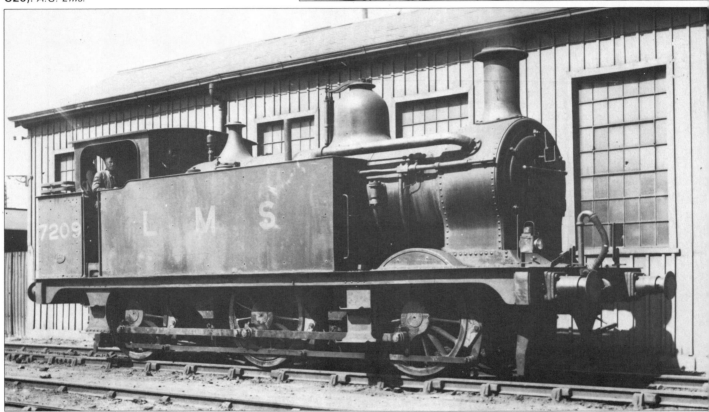

Right *(Plate 239):* Renumbered condensing 0—6—0T No. 7208 (ex-1908) displays the post-1927 livery (Code C13) applied to most of the few remaining unrebuilt engines in the mid-1930s. This picture was taken at Cricklewood on July 24 1937. *A.G. Ellis.*

Below *(Plate 240):* No. 7209 (ex-1909) was photographed on July 3 1937 — the same month as No. 7208 *(Plate 239)* — but carries the 1936 livery (Code C20). *A.G. Ellis.*

Right *(Plate 241):* The final Belpaire rebuilt form of this Class clearly set the style for the later-standard Class 3 0—6—0T, and as such is considered in *Chapter 5.* This picture effectively forms the link and shows No. 1915 in early LMS livery (Code C4). *Authors' Collection.*

116

CHAPTER 5:

THE MIDLAND/LMS
STANDARD CLASS 3 0-6-0T

THE third of the LMS standard classes which developed from a former Midland Railway type was that unsung workhorse of railways the world over, the humble shunting 'tank'. Yet again, the new LMS management must have been mightily pleased with the final Midland version, an account of whose origins formed the final part of the previous chapter, for to the modest total of 60 examples handed over by the Midland, the LMS added a staggering 422 more within the eight years from 1924 to 1931 — and most of these actually appeared before the end of 1928. For a class of such large numerical size, these new engines showed a probably unmatched degree of visual consistency throughout the LMS and, indeed, the ensuing BR period. In fact, there were probably as many or more variations to consider within the small Midland series as there were in the whole of the LMS continuation and it is with the final phase of the evolution of the Midland engines that this review begins.

THE EX-MR CLASS 3 (LATER 3F) 0-6-0T (LMS Nos. 1900-1959, later 7200-7259)

As already stated, there were actually only four 'Belpaire' rebuilds of the Johnson 2441 Class in existence when the LMS was formed and it took some time for the total conversion of the remaining 56 engines to take place — for lists see page 115. When converted, the rounded cabs and new shape boiler/firebox gave a very different visual outline to the class. Two

Above: For caption details, see overleaf.

principal variants were to be seen, with and without condensing apparatus *(Plates 242 & 243)*. In this respect, the split between condensing and non-condensing engines remained precisely the same as in the earlier round-top stage — *see page 115.*

Preceding page & left (Plates 242 & 243): The condensing and non-condensing versions of the ex-MR Class 3F 0—6—0Ts are compared here in the shape of Nos. 1917 (previous page — later No. 7217) and 7254 (left) (formerly No. 1954). The liveries are both post-1927 and are not quite typical. No. 1917 has the somewhat rare (for this class) 12in figures to Code C14; while No. 7254 has a full set of countershaded insignia, not to mention a replacement chimney and dome. W. Stubbs Collection/Authors' Collection.

Below (Plate 244): No. 1951 (later No. 7251) was one of the several Class 3 tanks to be given Ramsbottom safety valves at the time of conversion to Belpaire boiler form. It is also the only example we know of the later pre-1928 livery in this series (Code C5) but we feel there must have been one or two others. A.G. Ellis.

Right (Plate 245): No. 1945 (later No. 7245) was photographed at Kentish Town in 1930, still carrying the first pre-1928 livery style (Code C4). This dates the repaint before mid-1926, but whether or not the replacement 'pop' safety valves were fitted at the same time is not known. G. Coltas.

For the first year or so after the Grouping — possibly until early 1925 — the rebuilt engines emerged with Ramsbottom safety valves (*Plate 244*), but fairly soon, the 'pop' type was fitted and rapidly became standard (*Plate 245*) — although a few examples retained the older type until after the livery change (*Plate 246*). With this change, a virtually standard configuration had been achieved, until the occasional replacement of the original chimneys by a later Stanier pattern began to take place, often accompanied by a flatter-topped dome. Since the original chimneys had no wind guard (capuchon) at the upper front rim, the new chimneys were a much less-obvious departure in appearance from the original item than they were on the tender engines. They could, however, be distinguished by a slightly lesser degree of 'undercut' below the top lip as a comparison of *Plates 242 & 243* should reveal.

Amongst the smaller points of visible detail which distinguished the ex-MR engines from the LMS standard variety were the beaded front wheel splashers, the small reverse curve at the upper edge between tank top and cab opening and the plain vertical back panel of the bunker itself. These features were, of course, retained from their earlier round-top days. Later in their lives, small additional coal-retaining plates were added to the rear of the bunkers (see *Plate 247*) as, indeed they were to many of the LMS standard series too.

In 1934, as part of the comprehensive LMS renumbering scheme (see *Volume 1*) the engines were renumbered 7200-59 at the head of the new series for the 3F tanks. Some, indeed, were not converted until after this renumbering — *see page 120*.

The engines were always painted in plain black livery and generally sported the correct pattern insignia styles, according

Left (*Plate 246*): This picture shows the fairly late retention of Ramsbottom safety valves on No. 1943 (later No. 7243). The date must be 1929 or later since, although superficially wearing Livery Code C13, the 'LMS' is, when examined under a magnifying glass, of the 1929 countershaded form. The figures may have been similar.
W. Stubbs Collection.

Above (*Plate 247*): Former MR 0—6—0Ts Nos. 7221 and M7205 (originally Nos. 1921 and 1905) photographed at Cricklewood on March 11 1948 with coal retaining plates on the bunker rear. The engines have replacement Stanier chimneys and No. 7221 is in late LMS livery (Code C21) whereas No. M7205 is in early non-standard BR style. *E. Kearns.*

Right & below *(Plates 248 & 249)*: **These two views show the definitive post-1927 LMS livery, (Code C13) for the ex-MR Class 3 tanks in both condensing and non-condensing form. The engines are Nos. 7205 (right) pictured at Cricklewood on August 7 1937), and 7238, formerly Nos. 1905 and 1938.** *A.G. Ellis/L. Hanson.*

to period. Any rebuilt before 1928 carried the 14in tankside numerals, mostly with the original bunker panel (Code C4 — see *Plate 245*) but a few engines probably had the later style although we have only confirmed one — see *Plate 244*. By far the most common treatment, however, during LMS days, was the first post-1927 style with 10in figures, (Code C13) very consistently applied whether before or after renumbering *(Plates 248 & 249)*. One or two engines had 12in numerals *(Plate 242)*, although the occasional example received countershaded insignia *(Plate 250)* and a few received the 1936 style of insignia *(Plate 251)*; but the more common later form was with the familiar yellow markings with red shading, introduced in 1937. Being freight engines and therefore repainted less often than passenger types, it seems likely that a fair number ran well into the war years with the plain gold pre-1937 markings. We have no really clear photographs of wartime repaints with yellow/red insignia, so *Plate 247* is the best we can offer. The following summary is nevertheless felt to be a reasonably characteristic cross-section of the LMS period, with the possible exception of the later years when it is likely that proportionally more examples received Code C21 liveries than we have recorded.

After Nationalisation, more chimney replacement was to be seen and, after the first few uncertain months *(Plate 247)*,

Right: **Class 3 0—6—0T No. 7238, pictured at Derby on October 11 1936. See also caption above.** *L. Hanson.*

liveries followed customary BR practice, with 4XXXX numbers and tankside lettering, subsequently superseded by the smaller BR emblem *(Plate 252)*. The last pair of ex-MR 3F tanks was withdrawn in December 1966 (Nos. 47201/2), and although the Midland engines were almost 'lost' amongst the vast array of the LMS standard series, they generally enjoyed a longer lifespan, taking into consideration, their earlier round-top period. None were preserved.

LIVERY SAMPLES:

Letter centre spacing, post-1927, consistently at 40in centres

CODE C4:	1915/25/31/43/5
CODE C5:	1951
CODE C13:	1906/14/20/4/8/35/7/41/3§/8-9/57; 7201/3-6/10/ 2-3/5-8/22/5-6/8-9/31/3-4/6/8-9/43/8-51/6-7
CODE C13‡:	1920; 7205/44/54
CODE C14:	1917/42/7
CODE C19:	7200/14/52
CODE C21:	7207/21/7/37/40/4/50

§ *countershaded 'LMS' see Plate 246.*
‡ *with countershaded insignia.*

Left *(Plate 250):* Not immediately obvious, but discernible under magnification of the original picture, countershaded insignia were used on No. 1920 (later No. 7220) when seen at Cricklewood in 1930. We have no explanation for this and other similar instances of the use of this type of marking on Derby-shopped goods engines. It was clearly against the official rules! *A.G. Ellis.*

Above *(Plate 251):* The **1936 style of painting (Code C19) seen on No. 7214 (formerly No. 1914) at Cricklewood on July 7 1937.** *H.C. Casserley.*

Left *(Plate 252):* **Standard BR livery, with the original smaller tank-side emblem, on No. 47212 at Derby on April 2 1950.** *Authors' Collection.*

Above *(Plate 253):* **The prototype LMS standard Class 3 tank No. 7100 (later No. 7260) newly ex-works in 1924 (Livery Code C4).** *BR(LMR).*

With the benefit of hindsight, it can be seen that the LMS standard Class 3 0—6—0Ts, along with the Class 4 tender engines, were the true harbingers of all that was to become typical of later LMS thinking, for regardless of their precise design, they were the first real manifestations of a 'scrap and build' policy which was well-established long before Stanier took over.

The LMS had inherited a vast array of shunting tanks of all shapes and sizes from its various constituents (especially in England) and many of these engines, particularly on the former LNWR lines, were distinctly venerable — see *Volume 2.* Furthermore, the other large English constituent, the Midland Railway had relatively few large shunting engines and its collection of smaller 0—6—0Ts was also getting a bit 'long in the tooth'. Consequently, it should cause no surprise to discover that an early decision of the LMS focussed on the rationalisation of its shunting activities. This work, which was not revenue-earning in its own right, was vital to the running of the railway and there was every incentive to keep minimise shunting costs.

One very positive way to help in this respect was to have a highly standardised fleet of engines, thus promoting economies in maintenance and spare parts, for example. The fact that the chosen engines were of basically Midland design is less relevant in this context than the philosophy which underlay their building. It is no coincidence either that the marshalling yards of the company were also the first beneficiaries of the diesel takeover in later years, a point which will be explored in more depth in *Volume 5.* Interestingly, the LMS built no more steam shunters after the last of the 3Fs came out in 1931, this large group of engines remaining the mainstay in LMS marshalling yards until well into BR days.

The engines themselves were little more than a 'cleaned-up' version of the 'Belpaire' rebuilds of the Johnson '2441 Class' already described. They had slightly higher boiler pressure and somewhat reduced heating surface compared with the Midland examples, along with a modest increase in water

tank capacity, but their percentage was obvious enough when the first examples appeared in 1924 *(Plate 253).*

Such was the urgency to get them into service, thus allowing the scrapping of many old engines to be pursued without delay, that the LMS went to outside contractors for virtually the whole class and, in the event, only the very last batch of all was constructed in the company workshops. The following table summarises the build and for convenience also includes details of the 1934 renumbering:

FIRST NOS.	1934 NOS.	BUILDER/DATE
7100-19	7260-79	Vulcan Foundry - 1924
7120-34	7280-94	North British Locomotive Company - 1924
7135-49	7295-309	Hunslet - 1924/5
7150-6‡	7310-6	Bagnall - 1929
16400-59	7317-76	North British Locomotive Company - 1926
16460-509	7377-426	Vulcan Foundry - 1926
16510-34	7427-51	Hunslet - 1926/7
16535-49	7452-66	Bagnall - 1926/7
16550-99	7467-516	Vulcan Foundry - 1927/8
16600-24	7517-41	Beardmore - 1928
16625-74	7542-91	Hunslet - 1927-9
16675-84	7592-601	Bagnall - 1928
16685-749	7602-66	Beardmore - 1928/9
16750-64	7667-81	Horwich - 1931

‡ *Built as Nos. 19-25 for the SDJR, taking up the 7150-6 number allocations when absorbed by the LMS in 1930 – see also Chapter 9.*

A brief note about the LMS number allocations will not be out of place, for they were somewhat odd, both before and after the renumbering. The LMS 1923 number allocations had left a gap (7000-199) at the head of the LNWR freight tank series,

Left *(Plate 254):* This view of one of the first batch of 1926 Class 3 tanks, (Livery Code C5) shows the change to 'pop' safety valves and the new position of the rear sandbox filler. This configuration was, in effect, the standard form for the class. No. 16435 became No. 7352 after 1934. *W. Stubbs Collection.*

Right *(Plate 255):* No. 7294, originally No. 7134, has now been fitted with 'pop' safety valves but the tank sides reveal its early origin. The engine is clearly newly ex-shops, probably from Crewe, where the picture was taken. If so, the possibility of pale yellow ('Straw') insignia is quite high. This would make the livery Code C16 — see, however, footnote to 'Livery Samples' on page 131. *L. Hanson.*

thus hinting at the forthcoming new engines, but the Class 3 number series actually started at No. 7100 rather than, as might have been expected, No. 7000. There was no room for more than 40 engines in the ex-MR series without renumbering many ex-MR engines as well, so the choice of the Western Division block was not unexpected. However, from the first number series allocated to the new Class 3 engines, it does rather seem as if the full size of the eventual fleet had not been decided, there being provision for only 100 engines before the LNWR tanks started at No. 7200. Thus, when the eventual decision was made to multiply the type to several hundred examples during the mid-1920s, a new number series had to be found. In the event, the Northern Division freight tank series was chosen, which only involved a modest renumbering of some former Caledonian and GSWR engines — see *Volume 3.* At no time however, did the 'Divisional' numbering of the new engines bear any relationship to their areas of activity.

When in 1934, the LMS decided to renumber all standard engines in the 'below 10000' block, an opportunity to run the '3Fs' upwards from the logical and still vacant No. 7000 was again missed and the new series started from the former LNWR

No. 7200 allocation. This involved rather more transfers of the residual ex-LNWR tanks to the 27XXX duplicate list than would otherwise have been necessary — and the incurring of this sort of expense was rather out of character for the LMS. Finally, the putting of the absorbed ex-SDJR engines into the 71XX series resulted, after 1934, in a small batch of 1929-built engines being in the middle of the main 1925/6-built series.

Turning now to the engines themselves, there was as we have established, an astonishing degree of visual consistency throughout their lives in terms of basic 'anatomy', with only one significant variation. The first 50 engines (see *Plate 253*) carried Ramsbottom safety valves when new and had their rear sandbox fillers on the tank tops, whereas the remainder utilised 'pop' safety valves with the sandbox fillers moved to a more convenient location on the running plate. This resulted in the characteristic 'keyhole' shape at the lower tank side — see *Plate 254*. The Ramsbottom safety valves of the first series were quite quickly replaced by the later type, but the plain side tanks always remained a distinctive feature of this group — as illustrated in *Plate 255*.

Thereafter, few important changes took place. One or two

Left *(Plate 256):* No. **7629** (formerly No. **16712**) had received additional coal rails when fresh from shops at Derby in **1938**. The livery is the post-**1937** standard form for this class — yellow insignia with red shading (Code **C21**). *A.C. Roberts.*

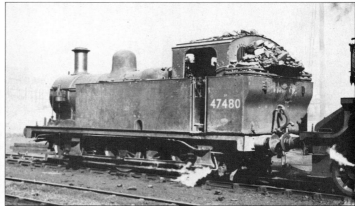

Above, above right & right: *(Plates 257-259):* These three studies of motor-fitted BR No. **47480** show a number of interesting detail points as well as the motor train control gear (adjacent to the smokebox). The close-up of the bunker rear, clearly shows the function of the coal retaining plate, while the left-hand side rear view gives an even better impression of the replacement rear bunker panel. The engine started life as No. **16563**. *All: R.J. Essery.*

Above & left *(Plates 260a & 260b):* **The majority of Class 3 tanks to receive the first version of the pre-1928 livery (Code C4) were the 1924-built engines, all fitted with Ramsbottom safety valves and clearly shown here (above) on No. 7136, later No. 7296. Left: A close-up of the bunker panel of this engine.** *Both: Authors' Collection.*

engines received additional coal rails *(Plate 256)* and there was a handful of motor-fitted conversions *(Plate 257),* but the principal change, as with many of the ex-MR series, was the fitting of coal-retaining plates to the bunker-backs of many examples — see *Plate 258.* This was sometimes accompanied by a complete replacement of the bunker rear panel, readily identifiable by a prominent vertical 'break' in the bunker side panel just ahead of the rear plate — *Plate 259.* There was no identifiable pattern to this modification and we are unable to give comprehensive lists. However, the full replacement of the bunker rear was considerably less common than the fitting of a coal retaining plate and by the end of their lives, virtually all '3Fs' had the latter feature. In these circumstances, it was therefore the shape of the bunker rear which formed one of the relatively few obvious visible distinctions between the LMS and MR series. Other differences were the plain front splashers, the 'straight through' alignment of the upper edge of tank and bunker side and the smokebox front extended forward from its saddle.

In terms of livery, the Class 3 0—6—0Ts could often be as

confusing as their anatomy was simple. However, these problems only began to emerge after first repainting and/or renumbering. Their initial styles can readily be stated. By far the majority came into service in the correct pre-1928 style with 14in figures, including most of those built in 1928. The change from the original bunker panel to the later round-cornered variety was quite early in the series and can be precisely identified from photographic sources as having taken place between the building of Nos. 16414 and 16415. Thereafter, there was no change in livery for new engines until well into the second Hunslet series built 1927-9. These engines were built in two separate Lots, the break being in mid-1928 between Nos. 16649 and 16650. Although we have not confirmed the livery at this precise break in numbers, we are convinced that No. 16649 was the last new Class 3 tank to be given the pre-1928 style. It may well have been the last *new* LMS engine of any type to get a pre-1928 livery — we know of no other contender.

From No. 16650 upwards, all the remaining '3Fs' emerged in correct freight livery, displaying plain gold insignia in the new 1928 style with 10in figures. The three basic 'as new' liveries are given in *Plates 260-2* and the engines to which they applied are summarised as follows:

Code C4: 7100-49; 16400-14
Code C5: 16415-649
Code C13: 16650-764, all with 40in letter centres.

The six ex-SDJR engines were given a handpainted version of livery Code C13 when first absorbed by the LMS, but were plain *blue* for a year or two. One of them is illustrated in *Chapter 9, Plate 437.*

When repainting and renumbering began — and these two developments often coincided — a degree of confusion began to replace the previous tidiness. In part, this was because of the protracted period during which the renumbering took place, combined with an understandable desire not to incur the expense of repainting a humble shunting engine, if this was not strictly necessary. The official edict to use up obsolete pre-1928

Continued on page 128.

Above (Plate 261): No. **16420** (later No. 7337) was one of the first Class 3 0—6—0Ts to receive the later round-cornered bunker panel (Code C5). This picture was taken in June 1926, ex-shops from the North British Locomotive Company, which information certainly gives a fairly precise time for the change in style. *W. Stubbs Collection.*

Right (Plate 262): No. **16697**, along with the next view in *Plate 263*, gives an accurate rendition of the standard 1928-37 style of livery for the Class 3 tanks (Code C13). On this engine, later to become No. 7614, the 'LMS' is spaced a little closer than normal. This sort of thing always happened to some degree but we believe this particular example to be something of an exception. *BR(LMR).*

Below: For caption details, see opposite page.

Left, upper & opposite page, lower *(Plates 263 & 264):* These two views, taken from opposite sides of recently-shopped engines at Derby in 1937, show the change from the plain gold style (Code C13) to the new yellow style characters with red shading (Code C21), which took place towards the end of that year. No. 7277 (opposite page) was formerly No. 7117 and No. 7553 (left) began life as No. 16636. This particular engine was one of two examples (the other being No. 7456) which were transferred to the Northern Counties Committee (Northern Ireland) in 1944 and were, accordingly, re-gauged to 5ft 3in. They became NCC 'Class Y' Nos. 18 and 19, keeping their LMS number order. *W. Stubbs Collection.*

Left, lower *(Plate 265):* Very few Class 3F LMS standard tanks received the short-lived 1936 livery (Code C19) but No. 7313 was one such. It was additionally interesting in that it was one of only seven ex-SDJR examples, formerly SDJR No. 22, first LMS No. 7153. It has also received a new 1936-pattern front numberplate. *L. Hanson.*

Right *(Plate 266):* Almost equally rare — it should in fact have been non-existent according to the official livery 'rule book'(!) — was the use of countershaded insignia on freight engines. Although not fully sharp, this view clearly shows the style in use on No. 7440 (formerly No. 16523) at Leicester on May 27 1937. The picture also reveals that at this stage, coal retaining plates were not in universal use. *Authors' Collection.*

18in numeral transfers, although much more widespread on pre-group LNWR, LYR and Caledonian engines (see *Volumes 2 and 3*) also partly affected the Class 3Fs, and overlaying the whole business was the company's own indecision during 1936/7 of the precise new insignia style to be adopted — a topic already discussed at length in *Volume 1*. Given this state of affairs, it is not at all surprising that a few local variations also made an appearance.

The most common single livery after renumbering was with plain gold insignia (Code C13) while after 1937, Code C21 (yellow insignia, shaded red with 10in figures) was the most usual style as shown in *Plates 263 & 264*, but there was no absolute consistency of approach. The situation defies simple analysis, so rather than try to describe every variation we have identified, we have chosen instead, in *Plates 265-273*, to illustrate as many different styles as we can discover, accompanied by captions of particular detail. As usual, we also provide a tabulated summary of 'codeable' liveries. There are less of these than we would have liked for such a large class, but we feel the coverage is quite reasonably representative.

Above & right (*Plates 267-269*): During the mid-1930s, several contemporary reports of activities began to make mention of some very odd livery practices to be seen amongst the '3Fs'. Using this information and the next group of three pictures, some of the story is explained, as far as we are able.

This first group of views shows the use of 18in figures which would have an odd choice for the Class 3 tanks, even before the livery change. We think that they resulted as a consequence of the official edict to use up old transfer stocks — see *Volume 1 page 214 et seq.* No. 16411 (above) photographed in 1934, was clearly an example of doing just this with the pre-1928 bunker emblem. It resulted in a conventional, if unexpected, Code C2 livery for the engine. This was not unique — see Livery Samples, page 131. What is surprising, however, is the location — Plaistow on the ex-LTSR. Most examples of this practice stemmed from St Rollox, Horwich or Crewe. A depot change without repainting might be the explanation. No. 16411 became No. 7328 in 1936.

What, however, is one to make of the next two pictures (right) both of which show *renumbered* 3Fs with 18in figures and no other obvious signs of company identity? They were taken (upper) at Glasgow (Polmadie) on June 19 1937 (No. 7536, ex-No. 16619) and (lower) on June 21 1938 (No. 7534, ex-No. 16617). In this latter year there was a report that several engines were to be seen operating in Scotland with large 'freehand' figures — look at the '3', for example — but No. 7536 clearly displays Midland-style transfers. Nos. 7334-6 were also similarly quoted as carrying similar insignia but this may have been a mis-print for the same three engines. We think these pictures represent the engines concerned — but what we would really like to know is what insignia did No. 7535 carry at this time?
W. Stubbs Collection/Authors' Collection (2).

This page *(Plates 270-272)*: This group of three pictures, none of which can be precisely dated, shows the use of the 14in standard pattern numerals in the pre-1928 position on the tank side. This was very much a Crewe practice (see *Volume 1 page 214*) and these engines are examples of the Crewe 'hybrid' style being applied, most unusually, to LMS standard designs. This particular variation was not uncommon amongst the pre-group classes — indeed, it was common enough for us to have given it a livery code — reference C12.

The first two pictures show un-renumbered Class 3F 0—6—0Ts Nos. 7149 (top) and 16679 (centre) bearing the Crewe hybrid style with individual letters 'LMS' (barely discernible on No. 7149) on the bunker side (Code C12) exactly as if they were ex-LNWR types! We estimate the pictures as circa 1932/3 and the engines became Nos. 7309 and 7596 a few years later. The third view, however (lower) is a distinct oddity. No. 7475 (originally No. 16558) carries the Crewe-pattern 14in standard numerals — handpainted in 'straw' colour as usual — but retains a round-cornered bunker panel. The engine is not very clean and could not have received its new number much before 1935. We can only presume that it retained its original Code C5 livery for a long time and when renumbered, was not repainted.

An interesting corollary to these observations is that, as far as we are aware, no contemporary recorders observed the use of the Crewe 'hybrid' style on Class 3Fs, but did spot the use of 18in figures in Scotland and elsewhere. Clearly, we cannot guarantee that any of the various oddities we have illustrated were the only ones to be seen and would very much welcome readers' comments. *All: Authors' Collection.*

Right *(Plate 273):* **In 1948, five Class 3Fs, of an original eight examples transferred to the War Department in 1940, were eventually returned to use in Britain. No. 7660, built as No. 16743, was one of these engines and is seen here on return to Derby in 1948. The instructions, in French, on the tank side indicate that the engine is to be consigned via Dunkirk and ferry boat to the workshops at Derby, London 'LITLAND' region! The engine next saw service as BR No. 47660, probably in the same livery as shown in** *Plate 274. W. Stubbs Collection.*

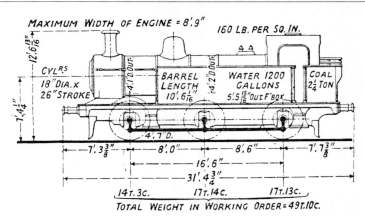

HEATING SURFACE, TUBES—							
LARGE AND SMALL	...	...	...	...	967·5 SQ. FT.
FIREBOX	...	...	...	...	97·0 "
TOTAL	...	...	...	...	...	1,064·5 "
NO SUPERHEATER						

TUBES ... ... 194—1¼ IN. DIA. OUTS. } 10 FT. 10⅝ IN. BET. TUBEPLATES

GRATE AREA ... ... 16·0 SQ. FT.

TRACTIVE EFFORT (AT 85 PER CENT. B.P.) ... ... 20,830 LB.

Recent change not shown on drawing : length of boiler barrel decreased by 1½ in.

" 3F " Class

For caption details, see opposite page.

After Nationalisation, the Class 3 tanks remained a very consistent series and their livery fairly soon settled down to the BR standard form, as illustrated in *Plates 274 & 275*. The last of the LMS Class 3 tanks went for scrap in 1967 but a few are preserved. We will, however, draw a mild veil over the curious livery originally adopted for one of the preserved examples — *Plate 276*.

Readers may have noted that we have avoided use of the popular term 'Jinty' in our analysis of the LMS standard shunting tanks. This is quite deliberate. For one thing, neither of us likes it (!) but, more importantly, it seems to be a latter-day term, applied quite wrongly to this class by enthusiasts. If the name has any validity at all, then it is probably more applicable to the Johnson 0—4—0Ts described in *Chapter 4*.

The Class 3F 0—6—0Ts departed from the scene with almost as little fuss as they had entered it. It is highly unlikely that anyone could compute with any accuracy the amount of work they did, whether it be in the yards, on pick-up freight duties or even, on occasion, storming the 'Northern Heights' of the former GNR main line with a North London passenger train. They were never the best, nor the most glamorous of engines but we reckon they earned their keep better than most. They

survived almost to the end of steam traction on BR metals and when they had gone, it really did seem, more than with many other types, that an era had departed with them.

LIVERY SAMPLES — POST-1927 RE-PAINTED ENGINES ONLY.

1: Letter centre spacing almost always at 40in centres
2: Pre-1934 number batches are quoted ahead of the renumbered engines

CODE C2:	16406/10-1
CODE C12:	7149; 16679/90
CODE C13*:	7100/3/7-9/11/46; 16444/91/5/532/8/41/8/50/60-2/5/8/70/6/82/95/9/639; 7260-1/4/7/77/81/8-9/94/308/27/45/54-5/64-5/7/9/71/3/80/94/405/10/3-4/20/3/46/9/51/61/5/9/74/8-9/81§/2/4/91/520/2/38-9/50/2/69/72/5/80/92/601/8/11-3/24/35/9/49/53/64/8/70-1/9-80
CODE C13‡:	16697/751; 7266/331/440
CODE C14:	7329/33/536
CODE C19:	7313/442
CODE C21:	7331/48/412/27/30-1/4/43/59/63/94/517/41/4/53/622/9/45/9/81

* Some of these, if Crewe-shopped, may have been Code C16 but it is impossible to tell from pictures.
§ Motor fitted. ‡ with countershaded insignia.

Left, upper & opposite page, lower *(Plates 274-275)*: These two views show the common BR livery adopted for the 3F tanks. The change in tankside emblem occurred in 1956. No. 47394 (opposite page) was built as LMS No. 16477 and No. 47517 (left) as LMS No. 16600. The latter engine gives a very clear impression of the bunker detail on these engines. *BR(LMR)*.

Left, lower *(Plate 276)*: As devotees of first-class locomotive restoration, we were lost in admiration for the treatment accorded to No. 16440, (second LMS No. 7357) when it went into private preservation. We were also delighted that such an ordinary 'bread and butter' engine should be preserved — there are few enough in all conscience compared with the more glamorous express passenger locomotives in the private scene. But we cannot endorse the spurious use of the incorrect crimson lake livery (albeit unlined) and the circular LMS emblem, in an attempt to make the engine into something more than it ever was. In the first place, it seems a wholly inappropriate treatment for such an engine; but secondly and more importantly from our point of view as railway historians, however imperfect we may be, it gives wrong information to posterity. This cannot be a good thing - and we say so even at the risk of losing a few friends! Dare we suggest that if the owners really want a red '3F', they do the honest thing and remove the LMS emblem in favour of the name of their own private society? This, at least, would have some historical precedent. Speaking personally, we would prefer to see the coal retaining plate removed and the engine painted in the style of *Plate 254*. It would then be a real piece of living railway history! No. 16440 is pictured here at Derby on October 6 1974. *T.J. Edgington.*

CHAPTER 6:

MIDLAND RAILWAY

FREIGHT TENDER CLASSES

INTRODUCTION

IT is probably safe to say that of all the many groups of engines inherited by the LMS in 1923, the Midland's freight tender locomotives could lay sound claim to be the most bewildering array of them all. All but one — the famous 'Lickey Banker' 0—10—0 — were of the 0—6—0 type, and they represented more than half of the Midland's stock of all locomotives and some 15% of the grand total of all LMS engines at the Grouping — and thereafter overall generalisation ends! At the same time, there were represented several broadly homogeneous groups, so it seems appropriate to give a general review of the evolution of the whole fleet before analysing the different classes in more detail.

Basically, four separate large groups of engines were represented, together with a small residue of some very venerable older designs. The first and oldest of the four groups was that containing the hundreds of survivors from the Kirtley double-framed era, most of which were of the 'curved-top' frame variety, but also including the above-mentioned residue of earlier engines of the 'straight frame' series. There were many small variations within this group but *Plate 277* is wholly typical of the majority, which were dominantly of Power Class 1.

The next group, chronologically, was the even larger series of Class 2 0—6—0s dating from the Johnson era. They all started life as small round-top boiler engines (with two wheel diameters represented) but by LMS days, subsequent modification and rebuilding had imparted to this class the most confusing visual variety. Indeed, by 1923, many had been rebuilt to a form identical with the third group, the Class 3 engines; for simplicity, these are separated out in the subsequent analysis. *Plate 278* is a typical example of a substantially unmodified Class 2 0—6—0 in LMS days.

The third series, the Class 3 engines, originated at the end of the Johnson era with a large round-top boiler enlargement of the basic type, utilising the 'H' boiler. Deeley continued this development and eventually Fowler introduced a Belpaire-boilered version (to which form the Johnson and Deeley examples were eventually rebuilt) and the class was further enlarged by the fitting of this new larger Belpaire boiler to many of the erstwhile Class 2 engines. Since the running numbers (allocated in 1907) never changed in Midland/LMS days, the Class 2 and Class 3 engines were hopelessly 'mixed up' and the running numbers between 3130-3764 did not specifically denote the engine series. *Plate 279* shows a Class 3 engine in its most typical LMS condition.

Finally, superheating was applied to the classic Midland 0—6—0 series to produce the familiar Class 4 type which was

Right *(Plate 277):* **No. 2627 is characteristic of the form in which the bulk of the Kirtley 0—6—0s reached the LMS. The livery code is C4 (with the cab panel somewhat degraded) and the picture gives a very good impression of the rivetted style of Kirtley tender (Type K1).** *Authors' Collection.*

Right *(Plate 278):* This view of No. 3566, taken on October 11, 1936, shows the Johnson Class 2 in what might be called 'closest to original configuration' form. It carries the post-1927 LMS livery, with 14in figures, (Code C15) although it is possible that the transfers might be of the red countershaded variety — a practice not unknown at Derby on plain black engines even though this was not strictly correct. *L. Hanson.*

Left, upper *(Plate 279):* A typical '3F' in typical LMS configuration, with post-1927 livery (Code C13). Engine No. 3565 was one of many examples wich started life as the smaller Class 2 Johnson type. It seems, somewhat unusually to be paired with a smaller than normal tender for the Class — probably 2950-gallon capacity. *Authors' Collection.*

Left, lower *(Plate 280):* The final development of the Midland 0—6—0 was the superheated Class 4, represented here by No. 3934 (Livery Code C13) trailing a rivetted Johnson-pattern tender. *Authors' Collection.*

subsequently adopted as an LMS standard. This version, including LMS-built examples *(Chapter 7)* ultimately totalled 772 engines — the largest series of MR type 0—6—0s both physically and numerically. *Plate 280* shows a Midland example.

Even this brief resumé, shorn of all detail, will reveal the difficulty of analysing these engines. However, when to this is added the possible variations of tender, the problems worsen! It is therefore thought helpful to give an extended note on MR tenders at this point and it should be read as applicable to all 0—6—0s during the LMS period.

MIDLAND TENDERS
ASSOCIATED WITH 0-6-0 GOODS ENGINES

Above (Plate 281): Straight frame Kirtley 0—6—0 No. 2359 survived to become part of the LMS but was withdrawn in late 1923 without being renumbered, or even being allocated a new number — see text. Note the replacement Johnson (first style) tender (Type J1). The locomotive is pictured here alongside the coaling stage at Toton, on July 29 1922. Authors' Collection.

The earliest tenders were of Kirtley 'horseshoe' style, so-named because of the shape of the tank surrounding the coal space. Many were of visibly rivetted construction but a fair number, both low and high-sided, had flush rivetted panels. There were also several further small variations and even the official Midland tender diagram book 'ducks the issue' by stating cryptically that the Kirtley tenders "vary considerably from one another and the dimensions given are only approximate"! In this survey, differentiation is confined to the three readily identifiable styles shown in Plates 277, 285-6.

During LMS times, the surviving Kirtley tenders remained associated purely with Kirtley goods engines but by this stage many of these locomotives had received replacement early Johnson style tenders. Thus, the LMS inherited rather fewer Kirtley tenders than Kirtley engines.

The Johnson tenders came in many varieties, some very difficult to distinguish apart in visual terms. The oldest type to reach the LMS had springs fitted above the running plate in the manner of the Kirtley period, but the shape was rather different — see Plate 281. There was a separate series of these early Johnson tenders (contractor-built) which had 'all round' coal rails of a different type (Plate 287).

Following these was a whole range of what might be described as standard Johnson tenders with springs below the running plate. All shared a common family likeness but no fewer than five principal water capacities were represented, (2,350, 2,750, 2,950, 3,250 and 3,500 gallons). Their dimensional differences were often measured only in inches (height or width) and from photographs it is not always possible to distinguish one from another. However, there was a broad three-fold distinction represented visually by the height of the side panels.

The smallest size had side panels around 3ft 3in high, the intermediate versions (2,750 & 2,950 gallons capacity) had side panels around 3ft 7in to 3ft 8in deep while the highest capacity tenders (3,250 & 3,500 gallons capacity) had side panels varying from some 3ft 11in to 4ft 2in.

It is sometimes possible to make a visual distinction of these three categories from pictures, especially when attached to locomotives of identical 'anatomy'. In this context, Plates 310, 307 & 308 studied in that order, should be of assistance. Plate 310 shows the lowest height with the top horizontal tender beading below the level of the cab cutaway, Plate 307 has this same beading just above the level of the cutaway and Plate 308 shows the same feature some 2-3in higher still. However, given differences in locomotive cab shape, positive identification is not always to simple. Moreover, the more subtle differences are a problem at all times. Additionally, there were variations in bulkhead arrangement and tool box positions for example, which tended to be applied to all the different types. Clearly, from a modelling point of view, the dated photograph is the desired ideal.

Nevertheless, it is possible to make a few generalisations about the overall distribution of tenders through the Class 2 and Class 3 locomotive series. As far as we can deduce from analysing thousands of pictures, it was considerably less common for the Class 3 engines to be paired with anything other than 3,250 or 3,500-gallon tenders. There were, of course, exceptions (including all the ex-Somerset and Dorset Class 3s — see *Chapter 9*) but the above principle holds good for most Class 3 0—6—0s.

Concerning the Class 2 engines, the greatest variety was to be seen in the series which were never involved in rebuilding to Class 3 (Nos. 2900-3129). These engines rarely trailed the 3,250 or 3,500-gallon types. Of the smaller examples used, the medium size (2,750 & 2,950-gallon) were in the ascendancy during LMS days but all of the smaller Johnson types could be seen on some of these engines at times. In the number series 3130-764 which contained both Class 2 and Class 3 engines, most of the Class 2s had the larger type tender — but by no means all. This was because the Midland, unlike the LNWR, tended to keep tenders associated with classes, regardless of rebuilding. Most of this series had been built with at least 2,950-gallon tenders (the majority with 3,250-gallon or larger versions) and the basic *original* distribution was mostly maintained. The 3,250-gallon type was the commonest (at least as far as No. 3764 in the series), but the last group of Class 3 engines (Nos. 3765-834) had 3,500-gallon tenders from new and rarely changed them.

Naturally enough, there was some tender changing, so the best which can be done, short of devoting even more space to this topic(!) is to state which type of tender, according to official records, was normally associated with particular groups.

Unfortunately, the confusion is not yet complete, for even after Johnson's retirement, his final 3,500-gallon design continued to be built almost to the end of the MR period. This later version had a considerable visible array of snap-head rivets and no flat beading. An example is shown in *Plate 280*. The Deeley style high-sided tenders (see also *Chapters 1 & 2*) put in an occasional appearance on 0—6—0s, but since the latter were mostly of the Class 4 variant they are considered in *Chapter 7*.

In summary, the following 'shorthand' will be adopted for the various 0—6—0 tender styles throughout this chapter wherever it seems helpful and where more precise details cannot be given:

K1: Kirtley rivetted style
K2: Kirtley 'flush-panel' style, low-sided
K3: Kirtley 'flush-panel' style, high-sided
J1: Johnson — first type with springs above running plate
J2: Johnson — as J1 but with modified coal rails
J3:* Johnson standard with low sides
J4:* Johnson standard with intermediate height sides
J5:* Johnson type — with 'full' height sides
J6:* Johnson type — rivetted side panels

* *all with springs below the running plate*

It is appreciated that this is a less than 100% precise analysis, but it is hoped that it will assist readers to envisage more of the visual character of Midland goods engines than if no detail at all was offered. Other variations (for example, tender cabs) will be mentioned where relevant, as will any other tender style not covered by the preceding summary and as already indicated, class sections will, where possible, give the officially correct tender style for the individual groups.

KIRTLEY 0-6-0 CLASSES
(LMS Nos. between 2369-2867; Power Class 1/2, later 1F/2F)

The Kirtley double-framed 0—6—0s still existing in 1923 were predominantly of the type represented by *Plate 277*, but also at the head of the list were a handful of survivors of the earlier 'straight frame' series which were in essence lineal decendants of the old MR '240 Class' which had started life as early as 1850. The oldest survivor to pass to the LMS was No. 2382 (ex-MR No. 2303) whose origin could be traced back to 1852!

Above *(Plate 282)*: Pictured at Toton on June 13 1925 is No. 2396 (formerly MR No. 2357), one of very few straight-frame 'Kirtleys' to receive a new LMS-allocated 23XX number. Its livery appears to be Code C4 but there is no sign of company marking; the engine was scrapped in 1925. *Authors' Collection.*

In 1923, of the 21 survivors of this pioneer group, 18 became LMS Nos. 2369/82-98. Four examples (2369/88/93/5) kept

Right *(Plate 283):* 'The one that got away!' No. 421, carrying a very odd version of the pre-1907 MR livery, was actually photographed circa 1928/9 when it was still in existence, as a preserved engine. It became MR 2320 in 1907 and LMS 2385 in 1923 but was scrapped, along with several other old engines, after William Stanier came on the scene in January 1932. *Authors' Collection.*

their former MR Nos. but the remaining 14 engines had formerly been numbered between 2303-66 (which later were wanted for the newly-assimilated North Staffordshire 0—6—0s — see *Volume Two),* and these 14 were allocated Nos. 2382-7/9-92/4/6-8, left vacant by earlier withdrawals from the same class. Most were actually withdrawn before receiving their new LMS numbers (see *Plate 281)* but a few examples did manage to get their new numbers before scrapping — *Plate 282.* One of these venerable engines (No. 2385) was earmarked for preservation in early LMS days, but along with several other pioneering designs, it was eventually scrapped in the early 1930s — *Plate 283.* Other than this engine, the last straight-framed Kirtley 0—6—0 was withdrawn in 1928 (No. 2392, previously MR No. 2354).

Turning now to the 'curved frame' Kirtley 0—6—0s, these must surely represent one of the longest-lived classes in British railway history. Their origins date back to 1863 when the first of many hundreds built subsequently came into service as the pioneer member of what was known as the '480 Class'. This engine received MR No. 2400 in 1907 and lasted until 1932. Its nigh-on 70-year lifespan was not unduly exceptional.

Of course, when the LMS inherited these engines many subsequent changes had taken place. By then, the majority were carrying Johnson cabs, Deeley-Fowler type front ends and standard post-Kirtley boilers *(Plate 284).* They were regarded mostly as Power Class 1, but a few examples were operating with higher pressure boilers and thus regarded as Class 2. Visually they showed no significant differences. There was, however, a third principal variant in this large group of engines. This took the form of fitting a Class 2 boiler and a Fowler type cab — and a

Above *(Plate 284):* Kirtley 0—6—0 No. 2603 was entirely typical of most of this venerable series. It was photographed in 1936, shortly before scrapping (Livery Code C13) although the numeral height is a little difficult to determine. *Photomatic.*

136

quaint ensemble resulted. It came in two forms, with round top and Belpaire boiler respectively — see *Plates 285 & 286*. Some of these were converted after the Grouping.

Although the Kirtley tenders were never fitted to other than Kirtley engines, quite a few of the Kirtley engines themselves were operating with type J1 or J2 Johnson tenders by LMS days — presumably replacing the old (worn out?) 'horseshoe' type — see *Plates 287 & 288*.

Being of Midland origin, the whole group of engines came to the LMS in standard livery — (basically Code C4) but often devoid of company markings *(Plate 289)*. A few examples received the early cabside letters *(Plate 290)* and, later, the proper panel *(Plate 291)*. The livery summary includes only those locomotives with confirmed LMS markings. After the 1927/8 livery change, numeral size varied occasionally, generally following the 'largest which will fit' principle. In practice, this meant that those engines with Johnson cabs received 10in or 12in numerals, but the rounded-cab version of this class could accept the 14in style lettering when only four figures were present, as illustrated by *Plate 288*.

The engines were withdrawn steadily during LMS days but there was still a reasonable number left in 1934 when the LMS duplicate 2XXXX number series was introduced. In general, with five figure numerals, the engines received 10in figures (Johnson cabs) and 12in figures (Fowler cabs). During this

Right & below *(Plates 287 & 288):* These pictures allow comparison between the 'normal' Kirtley and the 'round cab' version. Both engines have replacement early-pattern Johnson tenders — but note the unorthodox coal rails on the Type J2 tender of No. 2579 (right). The livery of No. 2503 (below) cannot be determined (probably C13) but No. 2579 has the 14in figures (Code C15). *Authors' Collection.*

period many engines received crudely painted front numbers rather than new five-figure numberplates — as shown in *Plate 286.*

The very last Kirtley 0—6—0 actually achieved its BR number, 58110 (ex-MR/LMS No. 2630; 2nd LMS No. 22630) and was withdrawn at the end of 1951. A later generation would undoubtedly have saved it for posterity but this was not to be — and the locomotive was scrapped — more's the pity. These curved-frame engines, although of antique appearance, embodied concepts of long-term significance; they established the wheelbase and motion layout of all subsequent MR/LMS 0—6—0s and when it is considered that the last Class 4 0—6—0 did not emerge until 1941, their influence can be appreciated as truly profound. Fortunately, some of their significance is preserved in the surviving Kirtley 2—4—0 (see *Chapter 1*) but it was, after all, the humble 0—6—0 which earned the 'bread and butter' of railways like the Midland, and the National Collection would surely have benefited had a genuine mid-Victorian 0—6—0 survived. *Plates 292 & 293* give further detail views of this significant series of engines.

LIVERY SAMPLES — CURVED FRAME KIRTLEY 0—6—0 ENGINES:-

1. *Tender style is given in brackets after engine number – for key see page 135.*
2. *'LMS' at 40in tender spacing post-1927*

LIVERY STYLE	'NORMAL' CONFIGURATION	ROUNDED CAB CONFIGURATION	
		ROUND TOP BOILER	BELPAIRE BOILER
CODE C4	2424(J1), 2427(J1), 2430(J1), 2443(K2), 2446(K2), 2467(K2), 2469(K2), 2485(K1), 2519(J1), 2520(J1), 2533(J1), 2535(J1), 2572(K2), 2574(J1), 2576(J1), 2582(J1), 2584(K3), 2596(K1), 2614(K1), 2619(K1), 2627(K1), 2647(J1), 2666(K2), 2675(J1), 2692(K2), 2700(K1), 2704(K2), 2710(J1), 2726(K2), 2727(K2), 2732(J1), 2750(K1), 2753(K2), 2755(K1), 2761(K1), 2815(K2), 2836(K1), 2837(K1), 2842(K1), 2856(K1)	2818(K3), 2819(K3)	2567(J1), 2813(K3), 2846(K3), 2853(K3)
CODE C5	2400(J1), 2408(J1), 2414(K2), 2434(J1), 2557(J1), 2559(J1), 2565(J1), 2674(K2), 2709(K1), 2724(K2), 2725(J1)	—	2852(K3), 22852(K3)
CODE C6	2626(K1)	—	2472(J1)
CODE C13	2431(J1), 2435(J1), 2456(J1), 2492(J1), 2497(J1), 2503(J1), 2537(K2), 2538(J1), 2603(K1), 2607(J1), 2613(K1), 2618(K1), 2623(K3), 22630(K3), 2631(J1), 2632(K2), 2662(K2), 2682(K1), 2687(K2), 2692(K2), 2717(K2), 2719(J1), 2721(K3), 2728(K1), 2740(K3), 2763(K1), 2771(K1), 2775(K2), 2783(K2), 2785(K2), 2791(K2), 2807(K1), 2808(K2), 2810(K2), 2811(K3), 2812(K3), 22834(K1), 2838(K2), 2850(K1)	—	—
CODE C14	—	22818(K2)	22567(J1), 22579(J2), 22822(K3), 22846(K3), 22849(K3), 22853(K3)
CODE C15	—	—	2567(J1), 2579(J2), 2846(K3)
CODE C20	—	—	22589(J1), 22863(K2)
CODE C21	22630(K3)	—	—
CODE C22	—	—	22863(K2)
CODE C24	22834(K1)	—	—

Above *(Plate 289):* Kirtley 0—6—0 No. 2645, bearing no company identity to accompany its 14in tender numerals, pictured circa 1924-5. *Authors' Collection.*

Above *(Plate 290):* 'Round cab and Belpaire' Kirtley 0—6—0 No. 2472, with Type J1 tender, was one of only a few of the type to receive the early LMS style painting (Code C6). *Authors' Collection.*

Right, upper *(Plate 291):* The second, round-cornered version of the LMS cab panel, was carried by No. 2557 — Livery Code C5. The picture gives a good impression of the early Type J1 tender. *W.L. Good.*

Right, lower *(Plate 292):* Tender cabs, often of quite monumental proportions, were often fitted to ex-MR 0—6—0s. Kirtley No. 2455 (Livery Code C5) was thus adorned with a particularly ugly example in the mid-1920s. *Authors' Collection.*

Above *(Plate 293):* **No. 22630, the last-surviving Kirtley 0—6—0, which was withdrawn in 1951. It is pictured here in late LMS days.** *Authors' Collection.*

Left *(Plate 293A):* **The spartan cab of No. 22630, in late LMS days, viewed from the tender coalspace. Detail of interest to modellers includes the toolbox on the right, and the layout of the cab fittings — note the single gauge glass to the left of the regulator handle, and also the oilcans on the 'warming shelf' above the firehole. Thick, 'treacly' cylinder oil was thus made less viscous, and easier to pour. The firehole 'flap', used to restrict the amount of cold air drawn into the firebox whilst the main firedoor was open, is lying flat on the cab floor. The fireman 'flicked' the flap into position by means of the securing chain, on the left. The stirrup-shaped handle at the top right hand side of the firehole was used to open and close the firedoor itself, which when opened, lifted horizontally into the firebox. By operating in this way, the door also acted as a 'baffle plate' when opened, ensuring that air drawn into the fire was properly mixed with the flames, which in combination with the effect of the brick arch, minimised emission of smoke and helped promote complete and efficient combustion.** *C.C. Green Collection.*

JOHNSON CLASS 2 0-6-0 DESIGNS
(LMS Nos. 2900-3129 and between 3130-3764; Power Class 2, later 2F)

Top & above *(Plates 294 & 295):* The basic Johnson Class 2 0—6—0 in both wheel sizes is represented by (top) No. 2964 (4ft 10in wheels) and (above) No. 3703 (larger 5ft 3in wheels). The slightly larger splashers were the obvious visual clue. The liveries (both post-1927) are the somewhat unusual (for the type) Code C13 on No. 2964 and Code C15 on No. 3703. Additionally, No. 3703 displays the deeper footplate angle which was confined to engine Nos. 3690-709, whether Class 2 or 3 — see also *Plate 318. W.L. Good/H.C. Casserley.*

The design which in later days was generally referred to as the 'Class 2 freight' can trace its origins back to 1875 when the prototype '1142 Class' 0—6—0 (later MR/LMS 2900), entered service. By 1902, no fewer than 865 broadly similar engines had been produced which for more than a quarter of a century were the Midland's 'standard' goods engines. Their wheelbase and motion layout was a continuation of Kirtley's precepts, but Johnson introduced inside frames and built them in two wheel diameters:

4ft 10in wheels: MR/LMS 2900-3019, 3130-89
5ft 3in wheels: MR/LMS 3020-129; 3190-764

Some sources, including us in *Volume One* of this series, give 4ft 11in for the smaller wheeled version. Practically speaking (given normal type wear in service) there is no significant difference.

Not only did Johnson build this huge group of engines, he also modified the earlier 'Kirtleys' to carry his boiler and cab arrangement. Their cylinders were generally smaller (so they were regarded as Class 1) and their double frames made them visually distinctive, but, in effect, when seen in conjunction with its Kirtley ancestor, the Johnson 0—6—0 represented a formidable line of evolution and almost became 'written into the tablets' as far as Derby was concerned!

However, by the time the LMS received these engines the generally tidy pattern of 1902/3 had been considerably modified and by 1922 the Class 2 0—6—0 group was one of the most confusing series of engines inherited by the LMS. Its only serious rival in this respect was the ex-LNWR 0—8—0 series which has been covered in depth in *Volume Two*. The class was subjected to general upgrading and improvement during the Deeley/Fowler period of the MR (1903-22), and this trend was continued to some extent by the LMS in the earlier years of the Grouping. In general, this upgrading took two forms, both embodying several visual variations.

Firstly, there was a general modification (within the Class 2 power designation) usually manifested by a new Deeley-Fowler style 'front-end' and/or new Belpaire boilers, while secondly there was an uprating to Class 3 by fitting a larger boiler and cylinders — again with/without Belpaire and new cab for example. The uprating process took the engines into the next 'Class' of locomotives — the so-called 'Class 3 freight' — and made them to all intents and purposes identical with the Class 3 engines (proper) which were first introduced (as new engines) in 1903 with a locomotive which became No. 3765. To simplify treatment, the Class 3 rebuilds are incorporated in the next section of this chapter. To add to the confusion, some of the first generation Class 2 — Class 3 rebuilds were, from 1917 onwards, rebuilt yet again with Class 2 Belpaire boilers, thus reverting to their original power group, but in modified form! Thus, in summary, the situation was:

MR/LMS Nos. 2900-3129: Class 2 engines which remained as such, albeit with many post-1902 modifications.
MR/LMS Nos. 3130-764: All originally as Nos. 2900-3129 but many later uprated to Class 3 (but *not* renumbered). The residual Class 2 engines were dealt with exactly as Nos. 2900-3129. Within this group was a small batch of 20 engines (Nos. 3690-709) built by Sharp Stewart, with deeper than normal footplate angle (see *Plates 295 & 318*). It gave them a noticeably different physical appearance.

From this point, attention will be concentrated solely on the Class 2 engines of which the basic Johnson type (small or larger-wheeled) was a round-top boiler engine with inside frames and typical Johnson features. By LMS days, the chimney/smoke-box area showed Deeley-Fowler influence but the overall character of the engines remained much the same. The small and larger-wheeled versions of what might be called the 'basic' configuration are shown in *Plates 294 & 295*.

The next phase, in terms of changed appearance, was the fitting of replacement Belpaire boilers. This process was often accompanied by a slight change in cabside panel treatment, but retaining an otherwise largely unmodified Johnson cab. These variations are shown in *Plates 296 & 297*. Finally came what might be termed the 'full' treatment, when a Fowler-style cab

Left *(Plate 296):* **This picture, and also** *Plate 297 (overleaf),* **illustrate Johnson Class 2 0—6—0s which retained their original cabs when fitted with Belpaire boilers. No. 3592, pictured here at Saltley on August 18 1935, displays the cabside modification carried out in LMS days on many (but not all) the Belpaire rebuilds in order to raise the cabside in the interests of crew safety. This modification did nothing to improve the graceful sweep of the original Johnson cabside panel. The livery is Code C1.** *Bernard Matthews Collection.*

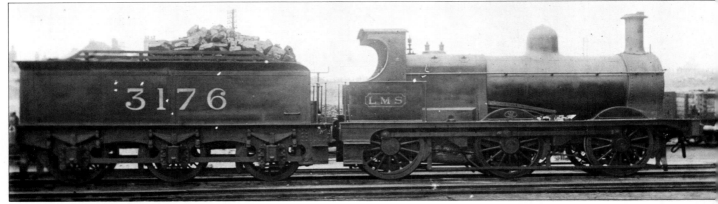

was also incorporated with the new-style Belpaire boiler — see *Plate 299*. Thus, potentially, one could expect to see at least four 'anatomical' variations with either wheel size. The various tender possibilities already described merely added to the complexity.

Another variable detail covering those engines with the rounded eaves Fowler cab was the treatment of the lower cabside panel — the rectangular portion. Most were of quite deep vertical dimensions *(Plate 299)* but a few examples displayed a markedly shallower form *(Plate 300)*. Within the 'deeper' category, quite a considerable number had, additionally, a flat-beading strip below the cab cutaway *(Plates 301 & 302)*.

In terms of livery, plain black was always the 'norm' in the LMS period, as might be expected. Pre-1928 the tender size

Above *(Plate 297)*: Johnson Class 2 No. 3176, still fitted with its original cab (note the unmodified sidesheets) but with Belpaire boiler. Livery Code is C15, with 18in figures indicative of the larger-size Johnson tenders paired with many Class 2 engines; *Plate 311* shows its later cab condition. *Authors' Collection.*

numerals were variable, usually reflecting the tender type *(Plates 296 & 301)* thereafter the 'largest numeral size which will fit' policy was generally adopted with the 1928 livery. This led to a widespread use of 14in cabside figures (see *Plates 298 & 303*) but there were exceptions *(Plates 294 & 302)*. Although gold with black shading (which registered as plain gold on a black engine) was officially correct, there are one or two recorded examples where the red countershaded insignia (officially designated in 1929 for the *lined* black engines) were used as seen

Above *(Plate 298)*: Tender cabs were fitted to many Johnson Class 2s, as seen here on a 2950-gallon Johnson vehicle, coupled to Belpaire rebuild No. 3197 (Livery Code C15). Ramsbottom safety valves are still fitted to No. 3197, pictured here at Cricklewood in 1932. *Photomatic.*

n *Plate 303.* It would seem that even at Derby, things were not lways carried out 'as per the book'!

The short-lived 1936-style sans-serif insignia (sometimes vith red shading) was applied to quite a number of Class 2)—6—0s (see *Plates 304 & 305*) and thereafter the class received he 1937 (and subsequent) yellow insignia with red shading

(Plate 306).

With the advent of new standard LMS engines, quite a number of the lower numbered Class 2 0—6—0s found themselves having 20000 added to their existing MR/LMS numbers after 1934 and, with this change, 12in cabside numerals tended to replace the erstwhile 14in size *(Plate 307),* sometimes with painted front numbers in place of new numberplates (*Plate 308*). This duplication of the old MR/LMS number series did not proceed beyond No. 23018 in LMS days, there being no need to add 20000 until a new standard type emerged. However, after Nationalisation, BR took the opportunity (for the first time since 1903!) to 'sort out' the Class 2 from the Class 3 engines and all the Class 2s (whether in the 2XXXX series or not) were renumbered 'en bloc' into the BR 58XXX number series, thus destroying the 'number identity' which had existed since the MR renumbering of 1907 — *Plate 309*.

The Class 2s were only slowly withdrawn during LMS days and almost 200 reached BR ownership to become Nos. 58114-310. As with other MR classes, it is worth mentioning that an engine by engine summary is to be found in *British Locomotive Catalogue – Vol. 3A* and we conclude this part of our survey with two detailed views (*Plates 310 & 311*) and the usual sample summary.

LIVERY SAMPLES — EX-MR CLASS 2 0—6—0 (INSIDE FRAME)

Preliminary Notes: 1. For simplicity, the summary is divided into two groups, the 'Johnson' cab series and 'Rounded' cab series
2. Assume 'LMS' at 40in centre spacing for post-1927 style
3. For wheel diameter, see page 143.
4. **Tenders** In order to simplify the table, the following assumptions are made - see list of types page 135
 Engine Nos. between 2900-3129:- Tender type J4   *includes references with 2XXXX Nos.*
 Engine Nos. between 3130-3764:- Tender type J5
 Other tender types (Key - page 135) are given in brackets after the engine reference

'JOHNSON' CAB SERIES

LIVERY STYLE	ROUND-TOP BOILER	BELPAIRE BOILER	
		STANDARD CAB	MODIFIED CABSIDE PANEL
CODE C1	3170(J4)*/5(J4)/360/83/407/80*/555/66(J1)/649	3150(J4)/76/220/358/696	—
CODE C2	3133/460/508/707	3227(J4)	—
CODE C3	3537	—	—
CODE C4	2943(J1)/3206(J1)	—	3350(J1)*
CODE C13	2964(J5)	3148/97(J4)*/500	—
CODE C14	22943; 3144	—	3134/64
CODE C15	2916(J1)/3074(J1)/135/8/43/51/7/61/71/5/82/95(J4)/229/55(J4)/62(J4)/4(J4)/80(J4)/310/54/66/82-3/5/417(J4)/22(J4)/34/61/77/80/6/511-2/8/39(J4)/66/90/602/11/32/49/95/703/7	3140/97(J4)*/492(J4)	3134/48(J4)/76/202(J4)/27(J4)/350(J1)*/3/420/38/45/79/85(J4)/85/504(J4)/17/33/5/71/92/617/48/96
CODE C19	3343/554	—	3543
CODE C20	3385	—	3150
CODE C22	—	—	3445
CODE C23	3123/67/230/352/60/83/422(J4)/5/518/54/61/77(J4)	3153/6/489	3150/7/424(J4)/51/73/7/517/27/33/9(J4)/45/51/61/92/691

* Fitted with tender cab

'ROUNDED' CAB SERIES

LIVERY STYLE	'DEEP' CABSIDE PANEL	'DEEP' CABSIDE PANEL (BEADED)	'SHALLOW' CABSIDE PANEL
CODE C1	2976/83/3013/603/9/14(J4)/55(J4)/708/38	—	—
CODE C2	2928/96/3758	—	—
CODE C4	2915(J1)/29(J1)/42(J3)/7(J1)/8(J2)/50(J1)/66(J3)/8(J2)/22969(J3); 2982(J3)/91(J3)	3027(J3)/35(J3)/46(J1)/60(J1)/8(J1)/90(J1)/9(J1)/3103(J1)/12(J1)	—
CODE C5	—	3101(J2)	—
CODE C6	2947/69(J3)	—	—
CODE C13	3004/347(J4)/430	3115	—
CODE C14†	22902/7/12/28/35/9/46(J1)/50/3-5/8/9(J5)/61/8/74(J5)/6/82-4/23001; 3011(J1)/96(J4)/372/732/8	—	22901(J1)/32(J5)/3(J5)/77(J5)/3000
CODE C15	2911/22/57/61/5/78/81/2(J3)/7/9(J1)/92/4/3001/3/7/10(J1)/4/347(J4)/416(J4)/37/78/516/25/36/52*/567(J4)/9(J4)/603/9/66/89/99/704/8/39	3023(J5)/31/9/44-5/7/8(J5)/56(J1)/7/71/5/8(J1)/81/3(J1)/4/94-5/7-8/100(J2)/4(J2)/7(J1)/9/13/6/9/24-5/6(J1)/7	2900/79(J5)/97/3000/6/9(J5)
CODE C19	22966(J3); 3726	—	—
CODE C20	22924/90; 2994	3049	22901
CODE C21	3478	—	—
CODE C22†	22913/26/9/40-1/78/83/3003/14	3035/49	—
CODE C23	3014/564(J4)/725/64	3051/8/62/4/78/99	2999
CODE C25	23008	—	—

* Fitted with tender cab
† In these two categories, with the exception of No. 3011 (Code C14), all references up to and including engine No. 3014 relate to the LMS 2XXXX series.

Right *(Plate 301):* This view of a 5ft 3in Fowler-cab rebuild shows No. 3060 in pre-1928 style (Livery Code C4) at Bedford. Note the early fitting of 'pop' safety valves. *A.G. Ellis.*

Left *(Plate 302):* This view of No. 3035 at Plaistow on August 22 1937 shows an early use of the red-shaded yellow insignia as well as the somewhat less common 12in numerals on a four-figure Class 2 — Livery Code C22. Note the crude 'local' repair to the footplate angle iron just to the rear of the front buffer plank and also the beading strip below the cabside cutaway. *L. Hanson.*

Below *(Plate 303):* The numerals on No. 3517 were undoubtedly countershaded when this picture was taken, possibly suggesting some 'using-up' of old transfer stock at the time of the 1936-7 insignia changes. The picture also gives a very good view of the ugly cabside modification to this belpaire rebuild. *Bernard Matthews Collection.*

Above & right, upper *(Plates 304 & 305):* Derby works seems to have quite liked the 1936 sans-serif insignia and used it on many engines, of both LMS standard and ex-MR origin. The two Class 2 0—6—0 examples shown here are (above) Belpaire rebuild No. 3150 (Code C20) and, very unusually, (right) Code C19 (red-shaded) on round-top 0—6—0 No. 3343. Clearly, transfer stocks were probably high and the 'use up old stock' philosophy was being properly carried out after the abandonment of the short-lived block style. No. 3150 was photographed at Bedford on August 22 1936. *A.G. Ellis/D.J. Montgomery.*

Right, lower *(Plate 306):* No. 3527 received a new 1936-pattern numberplate (as did quite a few ex-MR engines at this time, although there was no distinguishable pattern) but the insignia itself was of the conventional scroll/serif type — by this time in yellow, shaded red — (Code C23) circa 1937. *Authors' Collection.*

Top *(Plate 307)*: **This immaculate works view of No. 22940, at Derby on July 11 1937, shows what must have been one of the first engines to receive the new yellow/red transfers (Code C22). Note the lack of a front numberplate and the medium-height Type J4 tender.** *L. Hanson.*

Above *(Plate 308)*: **No. 22959 (Livery Code C14) pictured as late as August 27 1939, shows the quite common painted front number of the late 1930s. The tender is of Type J5 and makes an effective comparison with** *Plate 307.* **The photograph was taken at Derby.** *Authors' Collection.*

Left *(Plate 309):* Engine No. 58299, photographed at Derby on February 23 1950, represents a typical Class 2 during the early BR period. It was formerly LMS No. 3655 — one of the many Class 2 engines intermixed with the Class 3s until the BR re-numbering created order. *Authors' Collection.*

Above *(Plate 310):* This picture of No. 22969, taken at Derby on May 5 1934, is included here not just to show the new duplicate number applied to the pre-1928 livery (Code C4) but also because it gives an excellent view of the low-sided Johnson standard tender (Type J3) for comparison with *Plates 307 & 308. H.C. Casserley.*

Right *(Plate 311):* An interesting view of cab interior and detail of Belpaire Class 2 rebuilt No. 3176. Close examination of the right-hand cab side-sheet reveals the somewhat crude rivetted extension of this modified type — see also *Plates 297 & 303.* Comparison of the cab floor level and the original height of the side-sheets shows why the modification was judged necessary. *Vic Forster Collection.*

JOHNSON/DEELEY CLASS 3 0-6-0 DESIGNS
(LMS Nos. between 3130-3764, plus Nos. 3765-3834, Power Class 3, later 3F)

The Class 3 0—6—0, conceivably the best of all the family of ex-MR six-coupled goods engines, had its origins in 1903 when Johnson, as one of his last contributions to the scene, introduced a new design employing his large round-top 'H' boiler. This was the pioneer member of the '2736 Class' and later became MR/LMS No. 3765. 40 engines were built and during the production 'run', so to speak, the MR began to fit the same 'H' boiler to many of the older Class 2 engines, thus, in effect, converting them to the new type *(Plate 312)*. Deeley continued to build the new type (Nos. 3805-34) and also continued the upgrading of many more Class 2 engines. The final Deeley period 'H' boiler 0—6—0s, Nos. 3815-34, could be identified by their new style cabs *(Plate 313)*.

A few examples of both types of 'H' boiler-fitted Class 3 came

Above *(Plate 312)*: The original 'H' boiler version of the Class 3 0—6—0 is represented by MR No. 3403 which, rebuilt from a Class 2 in 1904, came to the LMS in this form — the picture was taken at Kentish Town on July 7 1923. It was further converted to the Belpaire pattern in 1926 but with a Class 2 G6 boiler! *A.G. Ellis.*

Left *(Plate 313)*: The Deeley version of the round-top 'H' boiler Class 3 0—6—0 is represented by LMS No. 3567 at Kentish Town in 1925 (Livery Code C1). Once again, the example shown was rebuilt from a small Class 2 Johnson engine (in 1914) and, as with the engine in *Plate 312*, when it received a Belpaire boiler (in 1927) it was of the Class 2 G6 variety, not the larger G7 equivalent, Class 3. *Authors' Collection.*

Above *(Plate 314):* The classic Class 3 (later 3F) Belpaire configuration is represented here by No. 3579, in a works grey version of LMS livery Code C1. This engine (ex-Class 2) acquired this outline in 1919 and remained thus until withdrawn as BR No. 43579, late in 1960. *BR (LMR).*

Above *(Plate 315):* No. 3399 (Livery Code C13) shows a 3F 0—6—0 (with 'pop' safety valves) also displaying the alternative (rivetted) cabside panel. Once again, No. 3399 was an example converted from a Class 2 in 1907 ('H' boiler) and again in 1923 (G7 Belpaire boiler). This form of cabside treatment (see also *Plate 317),* was the later style. *Authors' Collection.*

through to the LMS in this round-top form, but by then the Midland was well embarked on a further upgrading of the Class 3s, utilising a new Belpaire-type boiler and the majority of the Class 3s were in the familiar configuration represented by *Plate 314.* These all carried the Fowler-pattern cab, and during early LMS days the conversion of the final round-top boiler engines was completed. It was some of these which, on losing their 'H' boilers, reverted to Class 2 by receiving the smaller type Belpaire boiler. For the record, the two Belpaire boilers were classified G6 (Class 2) and G7 (Class 3) and again, it is fortuitous that a

comprehensive list is given in *British Locomotive Catalogue Vol. 3A.*

The Class 3 (Belpaire) 0—6—0 became a very standardised machine in terms of appearance during LMS days. Most of them ran with 'standard' Johnson high-capacity tenders (3,250 or 3,500-gallon) and apart from such details like the gradual replacement of Ramsbottom safety valves by the more modern 'pop' type, one of the few more obvious points of difference was the rivetted-style cabside panel, devoid of most of the flat beading which a large number of them displayed *(Plate 315).*

Left *(Plate 316):* Class 3 0—6—0 No. 3333 (with 6ft diameter wheels) at Lancaster Green Ayre on July 7 1923. Note the unique centre splasher. This locomotive was rebuilt conventionally, with 5ft 3in wheels and a G7 Belpaire boiler, in 1924 and lasted thus until withdrawal in 1961 as BR No. 43333. *Authors' Collection.*

These were, essentially, those rebuilt after the Grouping by the LMS.

There were three quite well-known mavericks in this class, Nos. 3326/33/89, one of which came to the LMS *(Plate 316).* These had been given 6ft diameter driving wheels in 1906, for working express fish traffic, but some references also relate the experiment to the forthcoming 0—6—04Ts *(see Chapter 3)* which also had quite large leading wheels. Nos. 3326/33/89 reverted to conventional 5ft 3in wheels in 1922, 1924 and 1918 respectively.

The LMS liveries of the '3Fs' were straightforward. Prior to 1928, the 18in numerals were universal *(Plates 314 & 317).* Thereafter the 10in cabside numerals were favoured, originally in plain gold *(Plate 315)* and from 1937, in yellow with red shading *(Plates 318 & 319).* Between these two styles, a few examples received 1936-type sans-serif markings *(Plate 320).*

Unlike the Class 2 engines, which were totally renumbered as we have already described, Nationalisation saw the Class 3Fs retain their MR/LMS numbers with the addition of 40000 in the normal BR fashion *(Plate 321).* This meant that any ex-MR 0—6—0 in the new BR 43137-834 series was, for the first time since 1907, positively identified as a Class 3, merely from its number. The first of the series (No. 43137) was again renumbered in 1951 (as BR No. 43750) to make way for a new Ivatt Class 4 2—6—0. Like the Class 2 engines, the Class 3 0—6—0s soldiered on into BR days *(Plate 322).* They were good engines and popular both with enginemen and enthusiasts. Many footplatemen would take a Class 3 rather than a Class 4 0—6—0 if given the choice, as one of us can personally vouch! The last examples were withdrawn in 1964.

LIVERY SAMPLES — EX-MR CLASS 3 0—6—0 engines

Preliminary Notes: 1. *Engines are divided into two categories based on cab panel treatment.*
2. *Assume 'LMS' at 40in centre spacing for post-1927 styles.*
3. *For wheel diameter, see page 143*
4. *For ex-Somerset & Dorset Class 3 0-6-0s, see Chapter 13.*
5. **Tenders** *Assume type J5 throughout (usually 3250 gallons for Nos. 3130-764 and 3500 gallons from No. 3765 upwards). Exceptions are given in brackets after the engine reference, key page 135. In case of reference J4, the 2950 gallon type is the more common version with this class.*

LIVERY STYLE	'STANDARD' CAB PANEL	'RIVETTED' CAB PANEL
CODE C1	3246/88*†(J4)/308/10/470†§/556/64†(J4)/7†(J4)/ 79/641†/56(J6)/746†/94/800/9/18	3137(J6)/92(J6)/210/81(J4)/333/69(J6)/70/9/401/ 27/90/523/60/624/33/7/68/70/93/730/62/79/ 802/28
CODE C2	3251/433	3822
CODE C3	3226(J4)	—
CODE C13	3200(J6)/8/43(J4)/5/52/3(J4)/8(J4)/63(J4)/5(J4)/ 7/5/83-4/90/6(J4)/300/6/8/12/5/27/9/32/59/61/ 4/7/86-7/406/29/33/48-9/53/522/9/40/50/ 65(J4)/72/8(J4)/81-2/651/79/715/23-4/7/47/66-7/ 73/82/95/7/812-3/30-1/4	3174(J6)/8(J6)/81/3/212-3/8/47(J4)/61(J4)/73/ 8(J4)/81(J4)/6/313/26/31/55/68/78/81/8/99/ 427/63/4(J6)/74/90/523/83/93-4/608/36(J6)/7/ 65/82/705/10/4/40/55/68/77/80/96/803/6/22
CODE C14	3321	—
CODE C19	3675	3728
CODE C20	3207/26(J4)/317/587	3256
CODE C21	3203(J4)/35/44(J4)/52/98/374/37/448/68/502/ 44/96/660/2/80/760/85/9/825-6	3188/92(J6)/205/22/68/325(J6)/428/35‡/96/ 520-1/48/607/19(J6)/31/57/74/709(J4)/17/34-5/ 63/92/822/7

---

* *Fitted with tender cab*
† *Fitted with 'H' type (round-top) boiler*
§ *Retaining original Johnson style cab*
‡ *Coupled to Deeley pattern high-sided tender, similar to type shown in Chapter 1, Plate 465.*

Above *(Plate 317):* A superb view of Class 3 Belpaire-boilered 0—6—0 No. 3633 (Livery Code C1) at Nottingham in the 1920s. No. 3633 achieved this form in 1923, having had an 'H' boiler from 1911. Note the later pattern cabside treatment. *Stephen Collection (National Railway Museum).*

Right *(Plate 318):* No. 3709 shows the typical latter day 'look' of the Class 3F 0—6—0, in this instance carrying Livery Code C21. This engine became Class 3 ('H' boiler) in 1911 and received its Belpaire boiler in 1923. Additionally, it was one of the Class 3 conversions from the 'deep valance' series — see *Plate 295*. Note also the 1936-style number plate. *C.F. Oldham.*

Left *(Plate 319):* No. 3180 was one of the relatively small number of 3F 0—6—0 conversions displaying the smaller wheel size (Livery Code C21) pictured circa 1947. Note the smaller splashers, devoid of beading (converted 1923). *BR (LMS).*

Left *(Plate 320):* No. 3226, seen here at Derby in 1938, was one of several Class 3Fs to receive the 1936 style lettering — Code C20. *Authors' Collection.*

Below *(Plate 321):* Early BR numbering simply witnessed the addition of the '4' prefix to the former LMS livery, as shown here by very grimy No. 43219. The later style of cabside is clearly shown. *Authors' Collection.*

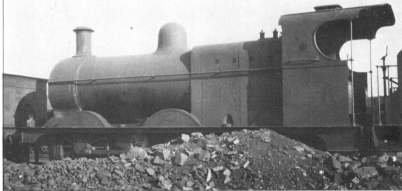

Below *(Plate 322):* The familiar BR condition of the Class 3F is displayed by No. 43586 in the late 1950s, very little different, save for 'pop' safety valves and 'Stanier' type chimney, from the original style Belpaire rebuild shown in *Plate 317.* Note the lining on the splasher beading — conceivably a locally-applied embellishment. *W. Hubert Foster Collection (National Railway Museum).*

FOWLER CLASS 4 0-6-0 (LMS Nos. 3835-4026; Power Class 4, later 4F)

The Class 4 'Big Goods' (Class 3 until 1916) was introduced in 1911 as a superheated Belpaire version of the 'H'-boilered Class 3, using larger cylinders and boiler (classified as G7S) pitched higher to clear the piston valves. This design was adopted 'as it stood' by the LMS as a standard type in 1923, with even fewer modifications than the Class 2 and Compound 4—4—0s or the Class 3 tanks. Like these three classes, the detailed treatment of the Class 4 0—6—0 will be given in *Chapter 7*, but a picture of a typical MR-built example is included in *Plate 323* for completeness.

FOWLER 0-10-0 No. 2290 (Power Class – unclassified)

The celebrated 'Lickey Banker', a four-cylinder ten-coupled locomotive of formidable size — certainly by Midland standards — was built at Derby in 1919 and ran its first trial trip on January 1 1920. It was a locomotive of great power and distinctive appearance of which the MR was justifiably proud.

Originally numbered 2290 by the MR, the 0—10—0 was built specifically for assisting northbound trains up the Lickey Incline from Bromsgrove to Blackwell, which at a ruling gradient of 1 in 37 was the steepest main line gradient in Britain. The theory behind the design of this mighty locomotive was that it could single-handedly take over the banking duties from Bromsgrove previously carried out by pairs of 0—6—0Ts.

The 'Lickey Banker' was the largest locomotive to be built at Derby and weighed 105 tons 2cwt (including tender) in working order, with a tractive effort of more than 43,000lb, so that at the time of its construction, No. 2290 was the most powerful locomotive in the country. It was handed over for traffic to the shed staff at Bromsgrove on January 15 1920 and put to work assisting trains to Blackwell. For a few months during 1921 the engine was equipped to burn oil, but reverted to coal-fired operation until 1926, when as a consequence of the coal and then general strikes oil-burning was resumed for a further limited period.

During 1922, a steam turbine generator was fitted to No. 2290, to power a large headlamp mounted in front of the chimney; the lamp was used to help drivers judge distances when 'buffering up' to stationary trains at night. Doubtless one or two Guards had suffered the effects of heavy impacts by No. 2290! However, some engine crews subsequently refused to use the electric light, as its tell-tale powerful beam made train engine crews aware that No. 2290 was at the rear, leading to the temptation to let the 0—10—0 take more than a fair share of the load. The banker crews, keen to avoid the reprimands which followed if the blame for any delay was laid at their feet, therefore chose to avoid use of the electric light and keep the train crew 'in the dark' as to which locomotive was assisting!

No. 2290 was originally painted by the LMS in standard pre-1928 livery (Code C1), carrying its number in gold on the tender sides, but during the changes of 1927/8 this was moved to the cabsides *(Plate 324)*. From new, the 0—10—0 had displayed MR crests on the cabsides, and photographs show these to have remained *in situ* until 1926. The Midland and later LMS shedplate '4' (Bromsgrove, sub shed to Worcester) was replaced in 1935 by shed plate 21C (sub shed to Saltley) and in 1937 the MR-pattern smokebox numberplate was replaced by a sans-serif style.

No. 2290 generally performed well at its allotted task, and was popular with footplatemen at Bromsgrove, who referred to the machine as 'Big Emma', 'Big Bertha' or simply 'Liz'. One troublesome and unpopular feature of the locomotive was a steam reverser and this was removed and replaced by a more conventional manual version during annual overhaul in September 1938. The engine was maintained by Derby Works, with major overhauls taking place every 11-13 months; in its earlier years No. 2290 went 'dead' to Derby with its motion dismantled, returning to Bromsgrove in the same fashion, accom-

Above *(Plate 324):* **The 'Lickey Banker' 0—10—0 as LMS No. 2290, newly repainted (Livery Code C13) circa 1928/9. Note the outline of the former tenderside numerals, faintly discernible beneath the new paint between the 'L' and 'M'.** *BR (LMR).*

Left *(Plate 324A):* **Known as either 'Big Emma' or 'Big Bertha', the 'Lickey Banker' served out its time in BR days in LNWR-style lined black livery as No. 58100, as illustrated here (and also overleaf). Note that four Ross 'pop' safety valves have replaced the two pairs of Ramsbottom valves originally provided, and that a three link coupling, rather than screw shackle, is provided on the specially-strengthened front bufferbeam. On the upper firebox side, a row of boiler washout plug holes have appeared, compared with** *Plate 324* **(above).** *Authors' Collection.*

panied by commissioning fitters who reassembled the motion and handed the 0—10—0 over for traffic; in later years it ran light to Derby, under its own steam, after assisting a train to Blackwell. Overhauling the 0—10—0 was regarded as a priority by the Works and a second boiler, built in 1922, had helped reduce time spent in Works. The boiler was unique, but shared much in common with that of the large-boilered SDJR 2—8—0s; see *Chapter 9.*

During the Second World War, No. 2290 worked normally, although in 1940 the electric headlamp glass was reduced in size by half and a hood fitted, to reduce the risk of the locomotive being spotted by enemy airmen, and betraying the location of the railway during the blackout. Apart from a short spell in 1924, when No. 2290 was unsuccessfully subjected to trials on coal trains between Toton and Brent, the 0—10—0 spent the entire LMS period working at Bromsgrove. The 1924 trials were unsuccessful as No. 2290 was designed for short periods of hard work, rather than sustained high power output.

The 'Lickey Banker' became part of BR's fleet on January 1 1948, taking the number 58100, this appearing on the cabsides in gilt figures on January 20 1949, this change being accompanied by the addition of a new smokebox numberplate. The tender required no repairs at this time and so retained its LMS lettering until heavy overhaul in May 1950, when the original boiler was refitted and No. 58100 emerged in BR mixed traffic lined black livery *(Plate 325).*

The 0—10—0 was regarded, as originally intended, to be the equal of a pair of Class 3F 0—6—0Ts, though with a saving on coal costs. During 1949, coal consumption per banking trip was estimated by Bromsgrove enginemen as follows: '3F' 0—6—0Ts 5cwt; Beyer Garratt No. 69999 10-12cwt and the 0—10—0 6-7cwt. All told, the Bromsgrove bankers burned approximately 300 tons of coal each week. No. 58100 worked until 1956 when it was withdrawn by BR and transferred to Derby Works. Preservation was mooted but this did not come to pass and the 'Lickey Banker' was scrapped — a sad loss indeed.

Below *(Plate 325):* **A very impressive rear view of No. 58100 hard at work leaving Bromsgrove in 1950, resplendent in the lined black mixed traffic livery applied at Derby on May 3 that year. Tender and cab detail is clearly revealed, including the tender cab provided to protect the enginemen, especially during the frequent tender-first light-engine trips down the 2½-mile line between Blackwell and Bromsgrove. Note also the cab roof ventilator, designed to let air in, and keep rain out! The tender carried four tons of coal and both handbrake and steambrake acted on all six wheels. For short periods in 1921 and 1926 (during the coal and General Strikes) the Lickey Banker had been equipped to burn oil, but when the oil tanks were removed in 1926, the tender sides were lowered, both to facilitate a better view from the cab when running tender-first, and to make hand coaling at Bromsgrove easier.** *Ransome-Wallis Collection/National Railway Museum.*

Right *(Plate 325A):* **No. 58100 at Vigo, running light down the 1 in 37 bank from Blackwell, in August 1955, in readiness for another turn of duty from Bromsgrove. This picture gives a very clear impression of front-end detail, including the large electric headlight fitted in 1922 to assist drivers drawing up to the rear of trains during the hours of darkness. Note however the reduced-size lens, a legacy of the war years (see text). Electricity was supplied by a steam turbine generator. Clearly shown is the '1 in 7' incline of the cylinders, required to ensure that all four connecting rods drove on the middle axle. Because of this steep inclination, the inside cylinders were too close to the smokebox to allow the steamchests to be conventionally placed above the bores, and so steam was fed to the inside cylinders via crossed ports from the steamchests supplying the outside cylinders.** *T.J. Edgington.*

CHAPTER 7:

THE MIDLAND/LMS
STANDARD CLASS 4 0-6-0

WE turn attention now to that most typical of all LMS standard engines, the Class 4 goods, later Class 4F. Love them or loathe them, you could not ignore or avoid them for, when all 772 examples were in service they represented not only the most numerous single type of engine to bear LMS insignia, but the class also represented 'as near as makes no odds', one in ten of everything under steam on the LMS system. Along with the Class 3 tanks (*Chapter 5*) they represented the first 'in bulk' manifestation of the new LMS policy in the 1920s and the reason for their selection for continuation as a standard type was much the same as for the other three 'chosen' Midland designs — there was a continuing need for a medium power goods engine, and taking into account the powerful Midland faction in the LMS Structure, the Class 4 was the natural choice for rapid and unchanged production. In fact, the Class 4 goods was probably the least altered of them all, especially if one ignores what might be called the superficial ephemera.

In *Chapter 6* we traced the development of the Midland 0—6—0 goods engines, from which it can be appreciated that the Class 4 was in every respect the logical superheated continuation of the family. What is somewhat surprising is that having introduced superheating with the first pair to be built (Nos. 3835/6) the Midland took so long before beginning its 'bulk build' of the class. Even so, by the Grouping, there were 197 in existence, 192 on the Midland itself and a further five in the Somerset & Dorset lists — see also *Chapter 9*. These five engines along with 50 of the Midland engines, were built by Armstrong Whitworth and were known as 'Armstrongs' on the S&D'. This made the Class 4, at the Grouping, not only the Midland's most modern freight engine but also the numerically largest of the four MR types to be standardised.

At the same time, although the Class 4 could probably claim to be as good a six-coupled goods engine as any which the LMS inherited, thereby justifying continuation, we must, like other writers, express surprise at the decision to build so many more so very quickly. We have heard the process likened unto the experience of the 'Sorcerer's Apprentice' who, having set the magic spell in operation, did not quite know how to stop it! Even the eventual arrival of Stanier in 1932 could not prevent the well-outmoded Class 4F having a 'final fling' in the emergence of another 45 examples during the 1937-41 period, thus bringing the grand total to 772, a figure only ever exceeded by Stanier's Class 5 4—6—0 and Class 8F 2—8—0 Class. In neither of these cases however did the total number carrying purely LMS colours ever exceed that of the Class 4s.

By any objective criteria, the LMS built far too many Class 4s. The LNWR and LYR had both gone on to use the 0—8—0 wheel arrangement and even the superheated Midland engines could not prevent the wasteful double-heading of coal trains running up the Midland main line. There was a possible alternative in the shape of the 'Somerset & Dorset' 2—8—0, which employed the same boiler as the 'Compound', and the 1924 LMS building programme originally envisaged 100 2—8—0s, presumably based on the 'S&D' type.* In the event, however, the Class 4 was built instead.

The strengths and weaknesses of the Class 4 have been well explored elsewhere, so we will not dwell over-long on turning over this already well-tilled soil. Their 'Achilles heel' was without doubt the poor axlebox design and the not particularly venturesome valve and cylinder events. They were, moreover, rather more difficult to fire than the Class 3 from which they were developed — a point which one of us has explored at some depth in our companion Midland compilation† Given a bit of application in this particular respect, the Class 4 was capable of very good work and the operational needs of many parts of the LMS were by no means beyond its capability.

For example, there were many duties on the LMS — as on many railways — where a simple and robust six-coupled engine could not be bettered and for which the added sophistication of bogies, pony trucks and other more modern complications were hardly relevant. The great number of loose-coupled and non-fitted freight trains, for instance, were ideal jobs for a Class 4, as indeed were the partially-fitted through freights which rarely ran at ultra-high speeds. Express and fully-fitted freights were also regularly handled by the class, though these were less-often seen behind '4Fs' once the Horwich 2—6—0s and Stanier 4—6—0s had appeared on the scene. Holiday excursions and extra passenger trains hardly justified the expense of additional specialised passenger power, but the 5ft 3in diameter driving wheels of the Class 4s gave a mixed traffic capability which often enabled them to take adequate care of much of this 40—60 mph traffic. The LMS certainly found plenty of use for the Class 4s all over the system, and they surely earned their keep.

It has already been said that the Class 4 was the least-changed of any of the perpetuated Midland designs after the Grouping, save for much ephemeral detail which rarely made much difference to performance. However, since it is so rarely recorded in most books, it is just this sort of detail on which we have elected to concentrate in these surveys; by this yardstick, there was plenty of visual variety to be observed, even within what was a very homogeneous group of engines. So much was this the case with the Class 4s that it should be made plain from the outset that there is no way in which an engine-by-engine review can be given, as in the case of the numerically smaller types. The best which can be done is to try and identify all the possible variations, give as broad a spectrum of examples as we can and hopefully, by drawing attention to all the finer details, point readers in the right direction to carry out their own further investigation should they so wish. We have little doubt that we may well have probably missed out a few and if so, there is even less doubt that someone, somewhere will write and tell us — they usually do, thank goodness! As usual, in our coverage of the MR/LMS standards, the review which follows is divided separately into the Midland and the LMS-built examples.

Engines of the LMS built 1923-51 - P. Rowledge, OPC, 1975
† *An illustrated Review of Midland Locomotives, Vol. 1* — Wild Swan, 1984

The Class 4 0—6—0 was introduced by Fowler in 1911 as a development of the Class 3 0—6—0, using a superheated version of the G7 Belpaire boiler first fitted to 4—4—0s in 1909. The new 0—6—0s also had slightly larger cylinders than those of the Class 3. The superior power of the first two new engines of the Class (Nos. 3835/6) prompted the Midland to build many more in the final few years of its independent existence, after the First World War, and all examples embodied the familiar and by this stage almost conventional 'Deeley-cum-Fowler' visual lines — see Plate 326. All had right-hand drive and when absorbed by the new company, were all coupled to Johnson-style tenders, wherein existed the first observable variations.

Some of these engines — mostly the earlier examples — used second-hand genuine Johnson tenders, with flush-rivetted side panels and flat beading. Two main varieties were to be seen, with and without the vertical centre bead and these are compared in Plates 327 & 328. Within the second of these two broad divisions (that without the vertical centre bead), a third variety was occasionally to be seen which displayed much visible rivetting — see Plate 326. However, this type should not be confused with the fourth variety of Johnson-styled tender (actually built by Fowler) which had much visible rivetting but no beading. These were widely used behind the Midland Class 4 goods engines — as shown in Plate 329.

As far as the precise distribution of these four types amongst

Above (Plate 326): The classic Midland Class 4 goods 0—6—0 in the condition in which all examples reached the LMS is represented by this striking view of No. 3915. The tender is of the third variety with flared top, mentioned in the text. The tender rivetting is very clearly seen but it needs a second look to establish that there is also beading below the flare and above the running plate. *W. Stubbs Collection.*

the engines is concerned, any reasonably tidy pattern which may once have existed was somewhat diluted by subsequent tender changes before the LMS inherited them. In general, the first three varieties were confined to the first 80 or so locomotives, the fully-beaded first type being particularly common amongst the very lowest numbered Class 4s, while the fourth and most common style was almost universal from No. 3920 upwards and probably slightly earlier in the consecutive number sequence. Certainly, the Armstrong Whitworth batch (Nos. 3937-86 plus the five SDJR engines, and all subsequent Derby-built engines up to No. 4026, had these tenders when new and none seem to have changed them, as far as we can judge, until well into LMS days. Many engines kept this type of tender throughout. Some of these final-style tenders were, however, to be seen running behind earlier engines in LMS days. The summary at the end of this section includes these tender differences.

Turning now to the engines themselves, only one minor change took place and this was almost at the time of the

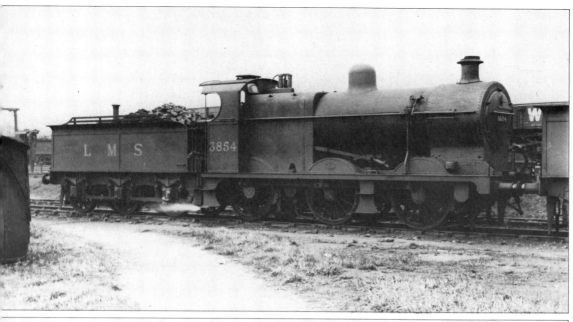

Left, upper & lower (Plates 327 & 328): These two views, taken from somewhat similar angles, allow comparison between the two flush-panelled varieties of tender fitted to the earlier examples of the Midland Class 4 series. No. 3854 (upper) has the smaller type with vertical centre beading, while No. 3883 (lower) has the larger version, without centre beading. Both pictures were taken at Hasland in May 1932 and show very late retention of Ramsbottom safety valves. The livery on both engines is the normal post-1927 (Code C13) style but note the wider centre-to-centre letter spacing on the larger tender. Both: W.L. Good.

Above (Plate 329): Obviously fresh-from-shops No. 3976 (Livery Code C13) is seen here coupled to the most common single type of tender associated with the Midland-built Class 4Fs, the 3500-gallon flared-top rivetted type, without beading. Although of patently Johnson shape, these tenders were actually built during the Fowler regime. Note also the presence of an exhaust steam injector, revealed by the pipe from smokebox side to running plate and again, the retention of Ramsbottom safety valves after the livery change. Authors' Collection.

Grouping, when the last 15 MR examples (Nos. 4012-26) were put into service with simplified cab-side beading and without the characteristic Midland splasher-edge beading (*Plate 330*). All the Midland engines carried Ramsbottom safety valves when built, and many kept them for ten years or more after the Grouping — see *Plates 327-30* — long after the majority had been replaced by the 'pop' variety (*Plate 331*).

After the Grouping, the ex-MR Class 4s could usually continue to be recognised by their various flared-top tenders and, save for Nos. 4012-26, by their spasher beading but in due course, some of them began to receive the LMS pattern flat-sided tenders (*Plate 332*). This was not particularly common, however, until BR days. Another characteristic change, as with most ex-MR engines, was a gradual replacement of the original Fowler chimneys and dome covers by those to the later Fowler and/or Stanier LMS standard patterns, regularly, but not exclusively, of the new lower height — *Plates 333/334*. Some of them received exhaust steam injectors (*Plate 330*), and well before the end of their days, all had lost the characteristic valve spindle tail-rod housings above and between the front buffers — *Plate 334*. Finally, amongst the more obvious structural variations, tender cabs began to appear on a few examples during the mid-1930s — as shown in *Plate 335*. This way by no

means a new idea, for the Midland had used tender cabs from an early date, but as far as the Class 4s were concerned, it was not until later LMS and during BR days that their use became more common and were particularly associated with the Settle - Carlisle line. Even so, tender cabs were never as widespread as, say, on the ex-LNWR 0—8—0s which also began to get tender cabs at much the same time — see *Volume 2*.

As far as the livery of the ex-MR Class 4s is concerned, there was, as might be expected, considerable consistency of appearance, especially before 1928. All came to the LMS with 18in figures on the tender sides, MR heraldic emblems on the cabsides and in plain black livery. We are absolutely certain that all that happened in many cases, was the obliteration of the MR markings in favour of the LMS version, but other engines were fully repainted. However, we cannot say whether all engines

Below (Plate 330): **This picture shows No. 4024, one of the final 15 ex-MR Class 4Fs at Leeds Holbeck on August 26 1934, yet again still with original safety valves. The lack of splasher beading and the modified cabside panelling are quite clear. This engine also had an exhaust steam injector.** *W.L. Good.*

Right (Plate 331): **By contrast with the previous views, Class 4 No. 3921 had received 'pop' safety valves when seen at Derby on June 26 1932. It is interesting in still having the pre-1928 livery — but the type of cabside panel is impossible to distinguish under the grime.** *H. Hall.*

Right *(Plate 332):* **It was not very usual for ex-MR 4Fs to receive replacement high-sided tenders until, BR days, generally speaking, but No. 3874 had received one as early as November 23 1929 when photographed at Blackwell. The livery is a somewhat grimy Code C13.** *W. Stubbs Collection.*

Above & left *(Plates 333 & 334):* **These two pictures show replacement 'short' pattern chimneys and new-style flatter dome covers on ex-MR Class 4Fs. No. 4004 (above) (Livery Code C13) has a Fowler pattern chimney while the early BR picture of No. 43884 (left) shows the Stanier-pattern version. The tall replacement Stanier chimney on an ex-MR Class 4 can be seen in** *Plate 338.* **Note also the different types of tender and that, compared with No. 4004, No. 43884 has lost its valve tail rods and their front covers, on the upper edge of the front bufferbeam.** *Authors' Collection/A.G. Ellis.*

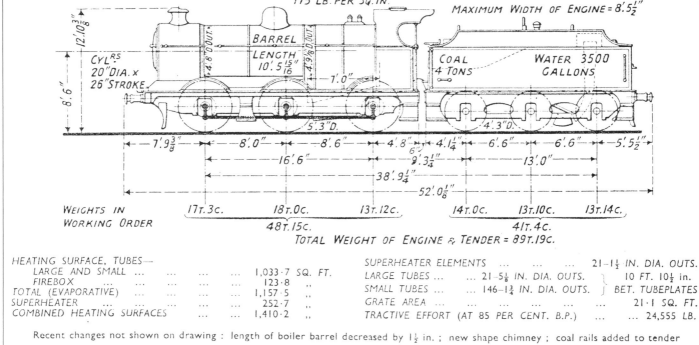

175 LB. PER SQ. IN.

MAXIMUM WIDTH OF ENGINE = 8'.5½"

CYL^RS 20" DIA. x 26" STROKE

BARREL LENGTH 10'.5 15/16"

12'.10 3/8"

8'.6"

COAL 4 TONS   WATER 3500 GALLONS

4'.8" D. OUT.   4'.9" D. OUT.

7'.0"

5'.3" D.

4'.3" D.

7'.9 3/8" — 8'.0" — 8'.6" — 4'.8" 6" — 4'.1 1/4" — 6'.6" — 6'.6" — 5'.5 1/2"

16'.6"   9'.3 1/4"   13'.0"

38'.9 1/4"

52'.0 1/8"

WEIGHTS IN WORKING ORDER

17T.3C.   18T.0C.   13T.12C.   14T.0C.   13T.10C.   13T.14C.

48T.15C.   41T.4C.

TOTAL WEIGHT OF ENGINE & TENDER = 89T.19C.

HEATING SURFACE, TUBES—							SUPERHEATER ELEMENTS ... ... 21–1½ IN. DIA. OUTS.
LARGE AND SMALL ...	...	...	...	1,033·7	SQ. FT.		LARGE TUBES ... ... 21–5⅛ IN. DIA. OUTS. } 10 FT. 10½ in.
FIREBOX ...	...	...	...	123·8	,,		SMALL TUBES ... 146–1¾ IN. DIA. OUTS. } BET. TUBEPLATES
TOTAL (EVAPORATIVE) ...	...	...	...	1,157·5	,,		GRATE AREA ... ... 21·1 SQ. FT.
SUPERHEATER ...	...	...	...	252·7	,,		TRACTIVE EFFORT (AT 85 PER CENT. B.P.) ... ... 24,555 LB.
COMBINED HEATING SURFACES ...	...	...	1,410·2	,,			

Recent changes not shown on drawing : length of boiler barrel decreased by 1½ in. ; new shape chimney ; coal rails added to tender

"4F" Class

Top (Plate 335): **No. 3999 had lost its valve tail rods, acquired a tender cab and was fitted with 'pop' valves when seen at Crewe on August 14 1938 — Livery Code C13.** L. Hanson.

carried LMS ownership markings (as shown in *Plate 336*) during this early stage, or what kind of cabside panel was employed. The following summary only gives confirmed examples. Interestingly, unlike the ex-MR 4—4—0s, for instance, we have been unable to find a single example, amongst literally thousands of pictures, which shows the individual cab letters 'LMS' on a Class 4 freight engine. We wonder if there were any.

After the livery change during 1927/8, the classification became '4F' with the 'F' simply added to the existing raised brass cabside numeral and the '4Fs' settled down to another fairly consistent paint scheme for a few years, this time with plain gold insignia, employing 10in numerals absolutely exclusively as far as we can determine (Code C13). However, there were some variations in tender letter spacing; with the centre-beaded Johnson tenders, the spacing was at 40in centre

Left (Plate 336): This view of No. 3922 not only gives a good view of the pre-1928 livery, Code C1, but also shows much detail of the 3500 gallon rivetted tender. Authors' Collection.

Right (Plate 337): Taken at Derby in July 1947, this photograph shows former Somerset & Dorset Class 4F No. 4561, probably after an intermediate repair. Only the smokebox and cab appear to have received any new paint but under magnification, the insignia can be seen to be newly-applied transfers of the red-shaded variety (Code C21). Note the lack of valve tail rods and the replacement Stanier chimney and dome. Authors' Collection.

Left (Plate 338): This view of No. 3847 at Derby on October 16 1938, with small Johnson tender gives a much clearer impression of the insignia (Code C21) used from 1937 onwards. The disposition of the 'LMS' in relation to the tender beading is quite clearly seen. Note also the 'tall' Stanier-type replacement chimney. A.C. Roberts.

with the 'M' always placed to the rear of the centre beading (see Plate 338) but with all other flared-top tenders, the lettering was centred on the side panel and at a somewhat wider centre spacing which we believe to have been the 'standard' 53in value. There may have been a few minor variations, of course. From 1930 the ex-SDJR engines gradually assumed normal LMS liveries on repainting (see Plate 337) but see also Chapter 9.

As far as we can ascertain, none of the ex-MR Class 4F 0—6—0s received the 1936 pattern sans-serif insignia, but from 1937/8 onwards, the usual change to yellow insignia took place, almost always with plain vermilion shading, retaining the same dimensions and letter spacings as before — (Code C21), see Plate 338. However, at this time the war intervened, engines got very dirty, and especially in the case of goods engines, it becomes very difficult to be precise. There would be a residue of pre-1937 plain gold insignia to be seen, while some engines would undoubtedly receive 'local' refurbishment, probably in plain yellow paint. If any were shopped at Crewe, they would almost certainly have been given the 'straw'-coloured painted insignia (see *Volume 1, page 214*) and all three variations would be all-but indistinguishable in service. All we can do is give a 'best estimate' in our summaries.

The ex-MR Class 4Fs were passed on to BR as an intact class, in 1948, and in *Plates 339 & 340* we give typical late vintage views. One example is preserved, No. 3924, while the final withdrawal from active service was No. 43953 in 1965.

LIVERY SAMPLES:

Preliminary Note on tenders: **These engines almost always carried flared-top 'Johnson'-styled tenders** *(see main text).* **In this table, assume final type (rivetted and non-beaded) with 53in letter centre spacing (post-1927), unless annotated in brackets as follows:**

T1:	First type, fully beaded — i.e. with central vertical beading — 'LMS' at 40in centres (post-1927).
T2:	Second type, fully beaded without central vertical beading and 'LMS' at 53in centres (post-1927).
T3:	Third type, as T2 but visibly rivetted.
F:	Fowler flat-sided LMS standard tender, 53in letter centre spacing
CODE C1:	3836(T1)/50(T1)/9(T1)/61(T1)/88(T2)/95(T1)/922/ 31/82/4011/24
CODE C2:	3897(T2)/902(T2)/42
CODE C13:	3835/42(T2)/4(T2)/52(T1)/4(T1)/6(T1)/66(T1)/ 71(T1)/4(F)/83(T2)/8(T2)/909(T3)/10(T2)/21/8/ 32-4/7/46/9/54/6/66-7/9/72/6-7/80-1/92/8/ 9†/4001/4/7†/8†/9†/24-5
CODE C21:	3840(T2)/5(T2)/7(T1)/58(T1)/60(T1)/70(T1)/2/ 5(T1)/8(T2)/9(T2)/80(T2)/5(T2)/93(T2)†/5(T1)/ 905(T2)/35/49/62/7-8/79/88-9/93(T2)/4023; 4560-1
CODE C24*:	3851(T1)/4000†

† *Fitted with tender cab*
* *Wartime examples, possibly degraded (retouched) version of Code C21.*

Below *(Plate 339):* **Class 4F 0—6—0 No. 43875, paired with an original Johnson beaded tender and fitted with a replacement tall Stanier chimney and reduced-height dome cover.** *Photomatic.*

Right *(Plate 340):* **No. 44025, one of the last of the Midland series, in very grimy condition at Gorton shed on July 9 1964. Note the lack of splasher beading, the later high-sided tender and the full set of replacement reduced-height boiler fittings.** *Authors' Collection.*

166

THE LMS STANDARD CLASS 4 (LATER 4F) 0-6-0 (See text for number lists)

Above (Plate 341): **Class 4 No. 4153 was one of the first Crewe-built engines of this class and is entirely typical of the LMS standard version with new style tender (Livery Code C1).** *Authors' Collection.*

The LMS commenced its own massive build of Class 4 engines by repeating the final Midland version with but few minor changes to the design. These included a reversion to the original cabside beading style of Nos. 3835-4011, the substitution of 'pop' safety valves in place of the Midland Ramsbottom variety and the reduction in height of the boiler mountings so as to come within the LMS 'composite' loading gauge. However, these fittings remained utterly Midland in basic shape. The most obvious visible change was the new style of flat-sided tender to which they were attached — and even that was not 100% consistent in the first post-Grouping batch of 30

examples from Derby, which included ten engines (Nos. 4037-46) paired with second-hand beaded Johnson tenders. The normal form is shown in *Plate 341* and the 'maverick' version in *Plate 342*. At a later stage, a few of the first ten also received second-hand Johnson tenders — *Plate 343*.

After this initial 'hiccup', things soon settled down and the LMS placed orders with a variety of contractors for the building

Above (Plate 342): **No. 4045, of the first post-Grouping Derby batch, was one of ten Class 4s which entered service accompanied by second-hand Johnson beaded tenders, thus giving the whole ensemble a more Midland-like appearance. The livery is Code C1.** *Authors' Collection.*

Right *(Plate 343):* By April 15 1939, when this picture was taken, Class 4F No. 4028 had not only lost its original tender but had also acquired tall boiler mountings (both chimney and dome) in succession to its original shorter ones. The location is Walsall shed and the livery is a fairly newly received Code C21. Note also the removal of the tail rod housings. *Authors' Collection.*

Below *(Plate 344):* One of the late-built right-hand drive engines, No. 4307, at Stoke in 1933, repainted in post-1927 style livery (Code C13). It had probably been shopped at Derby, hence the 53in letter centre-spacing; later it was repainted again at Crewe with 'straw' insignia and 40in letter spacing — see *Plate 361.* This is one of those rare cases were photographic evidence of a particular engine clearly confirms the differences in paintshop practice analysed on pages 163-166. *Photomatic.*

of its new freight engines. The only variation to the design implemented during this period was a change to left-hand drive for most of the engines from No. 4207 upwards. However, there was one higher-numbered batch of right-hand drive engines, Nos. 4302-11, *(Plate 344).* These were built to an earlier Lot number issued to Crewe Works which, in the event, received higher running numbers than the higher Lot number issued to Derby Works for the first left-hand drive series! Theoretically, we suppose, the Crewe engines should have arrived first on the scene but such was the speed with which the orders were fulfilled that the '4Fs' were arriving 'thick and fast' during the 1924-8 period, from what must have seemed to be all corners of the kingdom! Moreover, Crewe Works was in the throes of reconstruction which would affect its normal speed of output — see *Volume 2.* However, by 1928 Crewe was back in full swing, so to speak, and produced 50 examples in fairly short order during that year (Nos. 4507-56). For the record, this initial and massive first post-Grouping build is summarised here:

LMS NUMBERS	BUILDER/DATE
4027-56*	Derby - 1924/5
4057-81*	North British Locomotive Company - 1925
4082-106*	Kerr Stuart - 1925
4107-76*	Crewe - 1924-6
4177-206*	St. Rollox - 1924/5
4207-301	Derby - 1925-7
4302-11*	Crewe - 1926
4312-31	St. Rollox - 1927/8
4332-56	Kerr Stuart - 1926/7
4357-81	Andrew Barclay - 1926/7
4382-406	North British Locomotive Company - 1926/7
4407-36	Derby - 1927
4437-56	Crewe - 1927/8
4457-66	Horwich - 1928
4467-76	St. Rollox - 1928
4477-506	North British Locomotive Company - 1927
4507-56	Crewe - 1928

* Right-hand drive, remainder left-hand drive.

To this list were added in 1930 the five ex-SDJR Class 4Fs, all of them built to the Midland design already described. These 'S&D' engines were numbered in immediate succession to the LMS-built series as Nos. 4557-61. It would clearly have caused far too much trouble to number them with the ex-MR series.

This concluded the building of the '4Fs' for almost ten years, by which time it must have seemed unlikely that Stanier, of all people, would countenance a further perpetuation of a by now obsolete design. Yet he did. The general view, which we accept as plausible if not altogether convincing, is that the need for more goods engines in the Class 4 category could most cheaply be met by constructing further '4Fs', rather than a new design of engine which it is known was under consideration. This is a complex situation which we shall examine in detail in *Volume 5*. This was one area where the Stanier team could not quite make up its mind as to the most appropriate type and, in the event, the

envisaged design replacement for the ubiquitous 4F never appeared during Stanier's reign. It was subsequently left to Ivatt to fill the gap, right at the end of the LMS period, late in 1947, with the first of his Class 4 2—6—0s — see *Volume 5*.

So it was that the dear old Class 4F underwent what amounted to a third incarnation, after the MR and early LMS series. Unlike the Stanier-built versions of the Class 2 and 'Compound' 4—4—0s however, *(Chapter 2)* there was precious little evidence of the 'new order' in the final batch of Class 4s. Very much the same mixture as before, the only immediately obvious changes were the addition of coal rails on the tenders from the outset, Stanier pattern chimneys (which, somewhat interestingly, were of the 'tall' variety), a change to plain rather than fluted section side rods and a lack of valve spindle tail rods — see *Plates 345 & 346*. The building of the last 45 engines was somewhat protracted between 1937 and 1941 and shared

Left, upper & lower *(Plates 345 & 346)*: Engines No. 4565 (upper) and No. 4584 (lower) show opposite side views of the final Stanier series of left-hand drive Class 4Fs and were built at Crewe and Derby respectively. Note the plain side rods, tall chimneys and coal-railed tenders, also the 1936-style numberplate on No. 4584. No. 4565 is wearing the Crewe-style livery (Code C16) unusually with 53in letter centre-spacing, whereas No. 4584 is carrying the officially specified, red-shaded yellow insignia (Code C21). The shading is unclear and we are by no means certain that all the final Derby-built Class 4Fs received this shaded style. *Authors' Collection.*

This page (Plates 347 - 349): These three pictures show various replacement chimney and dome combinations, together with an assortment of other changes, on two left-hand drive '4Fs' at Bedford in 1937 (Nos. 4228 and 4237) and a right-hand drive example, No. 4049, at York in 1948, Livery Codes C13, C13 and C21 respectively. No. 4228 (top) has a tall Stanier type replacement chimney and tall dome cover, No. 4237 (centre) has the tall Fowler chimney but original short dome; while No. 4049 (below) has a short version of both. It also has an exhaust steam injector. Note the tail rod housings still in place on No. 4237, but absent from the other two locomotives). No. 4228 was pictured on March 29 1937, and No. 4237 on August 1 of the same year. *A.G. Ellis (2)/ A.C. Roberts.*

Above *(Plate 350):* **No. 44596 was built with a Fowler-pattern tender and tall Stanier chimney (see text) but in BR days it was operating as shown here, with one of the curious flat-sided Stanier tenders and a new short chimney. The livery is the characteristic BR black with small-size tender emblem — first version.** *A.C. Roberts.*

between Crewe and Derby as follows:

Nos. 4562-76: Crewe - 1937.
Nos. 4577-606: Derby - 1939-41.

All told, there were 772 of them in service by this stage, of which 575 were the LMS standard version, and we shall now consider the detailed variations within this group.

All engines had the plain splashers of the final Midland batch and most of them, save for the above-mentioned Stanier series, had the reduced-height boiler fittings. Inevitably, over the years, some 'chopping and changing' took place which *Plates 347-349* attempt to portray. As with the Midland series, exhaust steam injectors were a quite common addition *(Plate 349)* and tail rod housings were gradually removed after the decision to dispense with the valve spindle tail rods themselves; in the course of time these were found to be wholly superfluous.

As already mentioned, some (but not many) of the LMS series received replacement flared-coping tenders while a few of the late-built engines were paired with flat-sided Stanier tenders originally coupled to Class 5XP 'Jubilee' 4—6—0s — see *Plate 350*. Like the Midland series, tender cabs also made an appearance during the later 1930s *(Plate 351)*, but auxiliary coal

Left *(Plate 351):* **This BR view of No. 44390 shows the characteristic tender cab style adopted with the Fowler-pattern tender on many Class 4Fs. This development dated from the late 1930s but was more widespread after the war. Note the coalrails — certainly needed for the large quantity of coal carried on this occasion. It appears to be of appalling quality!** *A.G. Ellisl.*

Right *(Plate 352)*: No. **4453**, probably recently 'out of shops' on February 26 1939, and with coal rails on the tender. The picture was taken at Crewe and the insignia strongly suggest the 'straw' colour, characteristic of this works (Code C16). However, the letter spacing is the 53in centre-to-centre dimension and it seems to suggest (along with *Plate 345)* that Crewe had finally adopted standard letter spacing for standard engines by the late 1930s. However, we doubt if it was really that simple and would welcome more information. *W.L. Good.*

rails on the Fowler tenders were somewhat rare on the pre-1937 built '4Fs' until quite late in LMS days *(Plate 352)*. Later — and particularly in the BR period — coal rails, with or without coal doors, and tender cabs became rather more commonplace.

All told however, the Class 4Fs of the LMS series retained a great degree of visual consistency for some 10-15 years after first building, but this was not quite so true in the case of their liveries, even 'as built'. We believe the following analysis to be correct but would welcome additional information should any reader be able to help.

The new LMS engines did not begin to appear until the correct pre-1928 liveries had been established, so none of them appeared with individual cabside 'LMS' markings. There is, however, some uncertainty as to the exact breaks in two

particular respects, firstly the change in cab panel style (Code C1 to Code C2) and secondly the precise change-over point to the new 1928 pattern insignia.

As far as the cab panel is concerned, the first style *(Plate 341)* was applied to all engines up to and including No. 4216 — the last of the 1925 Derby batch. The change took place during the big 1926 Derby batch and the new emblem was in use when No. 4248 was built. This was some half-way through the Derby build for that year, so we reckon it could have been one of the first examples to use the new-style cab panel. Thereafter, all Class 4Fs which received the pre-1928 livery, did so in Code C2 form — see *Plate 353*. The numerical sequence then ran unbroken to No. 4429, which was taken out of the 1927 Derby batch to form the prototype for the new livery *(Plate 354)* but it

Above *(Plate 353)*: The Class 4 0—6—0s were rarely as 'spick and span' as this beautifully turned out example, No. 4259, at Kentish Town in 1926, showing the second style of pre-1928 cab side panel (Livery Code C2). This is a definitive view of the left-hand drive Class 4s in original condition. *A.C. Roberts.*

Above (Plate 354): The official view of the first engine of any kind to carry the new '1928' livery, Class 4 No. 4429. The style was actually decided upon late in 1927 and in this prototype of the Code C13 version, we are not sure whether the insignia were transfers or hand-painted. BR (LMR).

Left (Plate 355): This view, taken at Annan in 1927, shows a brand new North British-built Class 4, No. 4491, on its delivery trip — note the lack of any shed plate on the smokebox door. The paintwork is so shiny as to obscure the tenderside figures, but the cab panel is just visible — Livery Code C2. Authors' Collection.

is believed that the remainder of this Derby series, up to and including No. 4436, received the old-type livery.

Crewe began to use the new insignia layout with No. 4437, and for many years we believed that from this point onwards the new livery was universal. We had, however, overlooked the 'joker' in the pack — the North British Locomotive Company batch of 1927, Nos. 4477-506 (Plate 355). We have now confirmed at least three of these engines in Code C2 livery and there is no good reason to believe the others were any different, so we now believe that the highest numbered Class 4 to carry an authentic pre-1928 livery was No. 4506, not No. 4436 as we have previously stated. Thus, in summary, we consider the 'as built' styles to have been:

Nos. 4027-216	Code C1
Nos. 4217-47	Code C1 or C2, C1 being more probable in most cases
Nos. 4248-428	Code C2
No. 4429	Prototype 1928 livery
Nos. 4430-6	Code C2
Nos. 4437-76	1928 livery, see below
Nos. 4477-506	Code C2
Nos. 4507-606	1928 livery, see below (excluding Nos. 4557-61, ex-SDJR)

It can thus be seen that the majority of Class 4s (some 429 out of 575 to be precise) emerged in the pre-1928 style and many of them undoubtedly retained this insignia well into the 1930s. Most were virtually brand new when the livery was changed and there would be less cause to repaint a freight engine than a passenger one, so it is at least possible that the pre-1928 form was conceivably the most common single decorative style for these engines at any time during LMS ownership, especially if one adds the ex-MR engines to the list. The many varieties in the 1928 style, both in terms of individual works variations (at all times) added to the more general changes which began in the mid-1930s, probably prevented the '4Fs' from ever becoming as consistently liveried again until BR days.

As far as the 1928 livery for the '4Fs' is concerned, we believe that the 'as new' version for those engines in the No. 4437-556 series to which it was applied was exclusively with 10in figures as illustrated in *Plates 356 & 357*. However, there is some doubt in our minds as to which insignia colour was used. Those engines built at St Rollox and Horwich are virtually certain to have been given gold (gilt) insignia in accordance with official company policy — gold transfers, shaded black — as soon as new transfer stocks were available but it is quite likely that some examples came into service before this point with hand-applied insignia — precise colour unknown, but probably still gilt. On the other hand, the Crewe-built engines from No. 4437 onwards may all have had the familiar hand-painted 'straw' coloured markings

Above *(Plates 356 & 357):* **These two views amplify the remarks in the text regarding the post-1927 livery for some of the Class 4Fs. No. 4457 (upper) the first of only ten Class 4s built at Horwich, almost certainly carries gold insignia (Code C13) while No. 4547 (lower) one of the large Crewe batch built in 1928, bears the typical straw-coloured variety, (Code C16). The centre-to-centre letter spacing is, we believe, the basic clue as to the differentiation between these two very similar styles, 40in at Crewe, 53in elsewhere. The similar angle of view helps emphasise the difference.** *Photomatic/BR (LMR).*

ince much freight engine painting at Crewe took place in the recting shop, where transfers were rarely used at the time in question. Furthermore, it seems that the Crewe-painted Class Fs normally displayed their tender lettering at 40in centres, whereas the others had the more usual 53in centre spacing. If ur supposition is correct, the 40in letter spacing would enerally infer 'straw' insignia (Crewe Works) while the 53in pacing would strongly suggest gold insignia (remaining Works). Our summaries are based on this assumption, but urther information would be welcome.

The final build of Class 4Fs emerged after the changes to insignia colour in 1937. We do not think this affected the Crewe atch (Nos. 4562-76) which were, it is believed, all given the sual 'straw' paint (Plate 345), but the Derby engines came out during the difficult 1939-41, period and there is some degree of ncertainty here. It is thought all engines received red-shaded ellow characters when new, as would be expected, but there nay have been some exceptions — see for example Plate 346. As lways, however, the numeral height given to the new engines emained at the normal 10in for this class. In summary, herefore, the 'as built' liveries for the 1928 and subsequent eries are thought to have been:

Nos. 4437-56 ... Code C16, generally with 40in letter spacing
Nos. 4457-76 ... Code C13, generally with 53in letter spacing
Nos. 4507-56 ... Code C16 as Nos. 4437-56.
Nos. 4562-76 ... Code C16 but some (all?) with 53in spacing — see Plate 345
Nos. 4577-606 . Code C21, generally with 53in letter spacing

Repainted Class 4Fs generally followed the accepted custom of the Works in which they were shopped, entering the usual *caveat* regarding the differentiation between 'straw' and unshaded gold insignia. As might be expected, there were one or two 'hiccups' at the transition between the pre-1928 and the 1928-style liveries, but these were few and far between, given the size of the class. The only two examples known to us are Nos. 4248 and 4374, both of which were observed with Code C13 cabside numerals but with their 18in pre-1928 tender numerals still in place. Unfortunately, the photographic evidence of this state of affairs is too poor for reproduction.

When the 1928 style began to be applied more widely to repainted engines from the LMS standard series, the tidy pattern of exclusively 10in cabside figures (adopted for those engines built new with the 1928 livery) began to break down. There was an official company instruction in force after 1927 to use the largest size of new numerals which would fit the cabside of any repainted engine and this was quite often interpreted meticulously 'north of the border.' This resulted — we think

Left (Plate 360): **For many years we had supposed that the 1936-style insignia, quite commonplace on many types, had totally missed the Class 4Fs. Eventually we discovered two examples only, of which No. 4153 was one. It carried the somewhat more uncommon black shaded version, (Code C20). The picture was taken at Derby in 1937.** Authors Collection.

Right & below (Plates 361 & 362): **These typical and reasonably clean repainted engines in the immediate pre- and post-war period show No. 4307 (right) in 1938 at Stoke, carrying the Crewe-style livery with 40in letter spacing (Code C16 — see also** Plate 344**) and No. 4232 (below) at Rowsley on February 27 1949 with the Code C21 style. How it came to be so clean at this date is something of a mystery — it is certainly a pleasing picture.** Authors' Collection.

niquely at St. Rollox Works — in quite a number of 4Fs being repainted with 12in numerals (Code C14) and at least one with 4in numerals — see *Plates 358 & 359*. The experimental 1936-style hardly affected them and we know of only two examples so finished, one Code C19 and one Code C20 (*Plate 360*). Some, however, did get the block-style front numberplates, including most, if not all, of the final Derby-built engines — see *Plate 346*.

After the 1936 experiments, repainting generally moved to the use of the new red-shaded yellow characters, with 10in figures once again almost exclusively employed — including in Scotland — but Crewe continued its distinctively different ways! *Plates 361 & 362* sum up this period, during which time things got grimier and grimier, the Class 4s probably suffering more than most by virtue of their unglamorous duties.

The class went intact to BR ownership in 1948 and the next few years witnessed a continuation of the gradual replacement of the various original boiler fittings which had begun in LMS days. This process probably resulted in the majority of engines not carrying their original chimneys and domes when withdrawn. Other variations also took place, some of which are shown in *Plates 363 & 364*. Perhaps the most common new feature was the addition of an extra rainstrip at the join of cabside and roof. Like the addition of coal rails, this modification was introduced just before the war, but became very much more prevalent in post-LMS days. However, this BR period is really beyond our detailed remit.

Above *(Plate 363)*: A few Class 4Fs were converted to oil burning in 1947, all reverting to coal firing in 1948. This view shows No. 4585 at Derby in October 1947 (Livery Code C21) with clearly only the insignia having received any cleaning attention. The red shading is not very clear, but it is there. Note too the extra rainstrip added at the top of the cab side — a feature of several Class 4Fs in later years and also visible in several other later period pictures in this survey. *Authors' Collection.*

Left *(Plate 364)*: Some '4Fs' were used with snowploughs and in these instances a sliding cover was fitted over the tender coalspace, as illustrated here by No. 44142, pictured here at Derby on November 13 1949, bearing its new BR number in LMS-style figures. *Authors' Collection.*

By the time most 4Fs were scrapped they were finished as shown in *Plate 366*, with the small tender emblem, but a few examples did receive the larger version — see *Plate 365*. Scrapping did not begin until 1959 but the carnage was swift, all but 11 examples having disappeared before the end of 1965 and the rest the following year. Three examples are preserved, the official example in the National Railway Museum collection being the first of the LMS series. No. 4027. Also preserved are No. 4123 (Bristol Suburban Railway) and 4422 (North Staffordshire Railway).

As usual, we conclude our review of the class with some livery samples for the LMS period, but for *repainted* engines in the post-1927 period only. The original liveries are given on pages 173 and 175.

LIVERY SAMPLES:

Notes:

1. Assume Fowler LMS standard tender without coal rails unless indicated as follows:
   + Johnson pattern tender — first style with vertical centre bead — see main text
   $ Stanier flat-sided tender.
   § Coal rails to Fowler pattern tender (for engine Nos. 4027-556 only); Nos. 4562-606 always had coal rails.
   † Tender Cab fitted.
2. Other annotations as follows:
   * With pre-1928 numerals (18in.) on tender instead of 'LMS'.
   ø Possibly C16 — see *Plate 352*
   ‡ 40in. letter centre spacing where 53in. might be expected — see also Note 3 (below).

* This is a 'best guess' livery. It could be a degraded Code C21 or even Code C16 at 53in. letter spacing.
3. Letter spacing should be assumed at 53in. centres except for Johnson pattern tenders and livery Code C16 (both generally 40in. — see text).
4. As well as being confined to repainted post-1927 liveries, this table is further limited to the recording of styles only where they differ from the 'as built' version. Clearly, if an engine was repainted precisely as built, it would be impossible for it to be distinguished from its original state as far as pictorial evidence is concerned.

CODE C16:	4032/57/9/102/53/66/75/82/203/24/61/78/83/303/7/12/42/52/61/86/90-1/432
CODE C19:	4417
CODE C20:	4153
CODE C21:	4028+/31/49+/90/6/100-2/6/11/38/57-8/60/8/80/4‡/7/202/10/32/5/56/61‡/95/9/346§/420/45§/7§/522/78‡$/94$/604$
CODE C24*:	4115/90§/9/490/516§/84/8†

CODE C13:	4027/9/35/40+/67§/77§/86/8/94/8/105/22/7-8/39/41/55-6/8/72/8/200/8/14/20/2/6/8/33-4/7/43/8*/9/55/93/7-8/307/12/8/33/6-7/41/4/74*/97/404/6/9/13/19/36/40/3-4/9/53§ø/78/91/524-6/8/32/5/46/53/5
CODE C14:	4178/84/6/254/60/314/24-6
CODE C15:	4113

Above *(Plate 365):* The large BR tender emblem was a rarity on the Class 4Fs, as indeed were the larger BR cabside numerals, but both were sported by No. 44159 on this occasion — date unknown but probably early in the 1950s. It was a Scottish engine and even in BR days, Scotland's interpretation of standard livery practice did not always match the English equivalent. *A.G. Ellis.*

Right *(Plate 366):* By 1962, more than 100 Class 4Fs had been withdrawn but some examples, including No. 44139, were still being given full overhauls. This picture was taken at Derby on October 14 1962 and shows the final style of BR painting with the second version of the tender emblem. Comparison with *Plate 341* will show how little these rugged old workhorses had changed in any really fundamental sense during the intervening years. *Authors' Collection.*

CHAPTER 8:

LONDON TILBURY & SOUTHEND
AND
STRATFORD UPON AVON &
MIDLAND JUNCTION RAILWAYS

ALL CLASSES

THE LONDON TILBURY & SOUTHEND RAILWAY

T does not need a profound knowledge of railway geography to realise that the presence of the former LTSR lines in the MS system was rather odd, surrounded as they were by LNER (ex-GER) routes. Literally, of course, the legal reason was because of the purchase of the LTSR in 1912 by the Midland Railway but this, in itself, was also surprising. Prior to 1880, the Great Eastern Railway had been the supplier of locomotives for the Tilbury system, after which time, the 'Tilbury' itself had assumed responsibility and maintained a fierce independence against any blandishments from other companies, particularly the GER.

This independence remained strong for more than 30 years, but eventually the final MR offer proved too tempting and the 'Tilbury' lost its independent status. However, it always worked as a semi-independent outpost of both the MR and, later, the MS. In fact, its locomotive fleet remained highly individual and also distinctive until the mid-1930s, when the big Stanier 4—6—4Ts began to arrive.

The LTSR had an accurately descriptive title and, long after it became absorbed by the Midland, its old name carried on in popular useage, usually abbreviated to 'Tilbury' or some such and we shall continue this policy here.

By 1923, the locomotives of the 'Tilbury' were beginning to show signs of Midland influence — particularly in terms of boiler fittings and livery, but they nevertheless remained recognisably apart from the pure Derby breed and remained thus throughout their lives with the LMS. With two exceptions, they were all tank engines and predominantly of the 4—4—2 wheel arrangement. Indeed, so suited was this type to the duties involved that both MR and LMS added further examples of the third series of 4—4—2Ts until as late as 1930 — a rare privilege for a 'non-Derby' locomotive at this point in MR/LMS history. Apart from this large family of engines, the only other Tilbury contribution were small groups of 0—6—2Ts and 4—6—4Ts, plus a pair of 0—6—0 tender engines. However, the expression 'Tilbury Tank' generally implied the 4—4—2 type and it is with these engines that we start our survey.

THE 'TILBURY' 4-4-2 TANKS (See text for number lists)

These celebrated engines came in three principal series, each the last two being a progressive development of the original 1880 design. However, before analysing each of the three series in turn, it is essential to discuss the whole group, particularly their numbering. They were a quite confusing set of engines, but easier to comprehend if the basic sequence is sketched-out first.

The type originated in 1880 with the 'No. 1 Class' 4—4—2T designed by William Adams (GER and later LSWR) in the days before full 'Tilbury' independence. Many sources attribute them to Thomas Whitelegg — who was indeed the LTSR locomotive chief — but there is no doubt that the *design* was pure Adams, even if their introduction to service and supervision was under Whitelegg's control. They had 6ft 1in diameter driving wheels and by the time the LMS received them, several visual variations existed of which *Plate 367* is possibly the most typical. They were placed in Power Class 1 during MR/LMS days.

Following on from the 6ft 1in wheeled engines, Whitelegg himself introduced the next series, the '37 Class' of 1897, with 6ft 6in wheels — but all of these were rebuilt during the 1905-11 period to form, in effect, the third type of 'Tilbury Tank' in terms of the MR/LMS inheritance, discussed later in this section.

The second oldest series of 'Tilbury tanks', as far as the LMS was concerned, was the '51 Class' Whitelegg design of 1900. These were a somewhat larger-boilered version of the original 6ft 6in '37 Class' and came through to the Grouping largely as-built, save for the inevitable MR detail fittings — see *Plate 368*. These engines were placed in Power Class 2.

The third series of tanks represented in the LMS lists originated with the first '37 Class' rebuild of 1905 which, in effect, was a still further enlargement of the 6ft 6in type to produce an even bigger engine than the '51 Class' of 1900 (*Plate 369*). Most readily distinguished by their 'rounded' cabs, 16 of these ultimate developments were in existence at the end of the independent 'Tilbury' period — all 12 '37 Class' rebuilds plus four built new in 1909, slightly modified. This latter quartet included the preserved No. 80 *Thundersley*, today based at Bressingham. It was the final type, in its modified (1909) version, which formed the basis of subsequent MR/LMS ordering (*Plate 370*) and ultimately it became the most numerous of the three series. Originally, and also during early LMS days, this series was placed in Power Class 2 but the LMS eventually put them into Class 3 and from hence forward, we

This page (Plates 367-369): Three views, all from similar angles, showing the progression of the 'Tilbury tanks' as they existed in 1923. Above: No. 2123 (later No. 2213 then No. 2090) is a Class 1 engine with 6ft 1in diameter driving wheels, short smokebox and early LMS livery (Code A3). It is pictured at Derby, on May 20 1924. Right, upper: No. 2095 (originally No. 2161) is a Class 2 engine with 6ft 6in driving wheels and still with original length smokebox and Ramsbottom safety valves, shortly after renumbering (circa 1929) and painted in the new livery (Code B3). Right, lower: Tilbury Class 3 No. 2157 (later No. 2146) in the first LMS livery (Code A3) but with LMS emblem ahead of the cab opening. This was a rebuild from the '37 Class' type and set the basic pattern for the MR/LMS continuation of the type. Note the short smokebox — believed to be the only example left of this configuration on this series of engines at the start of the LMS period. *Authors' Collection.*

Above (Plate 370): This picture shows one of the Nasmyth Wilson quintet of Class 3 4—4—2Ts, No. 2124, painted in the first LMS livery (Code A3) with the company emblem on the bunker. Note the deeper tank and bunker sides and the absence of the slight panel recess above the driving wheels compared with the '37 Class' rebuilds (Plate 369). This slight anatomical change was introduced with the last four Tilbury 4—4—2Ts built new in 1909 (see Plate 385). Authors' Collection.

shall differentiate the three series by their final LMS Power Class groups.

Turning now to the numbers built and the LMS numbering of the whole series, these engines can lay strong claim to having the most bewildering number changes of any group of engines in LMS ownership. At various times, some had three numbers, some two and others never changed. The confusion is made worse because each renumbering was more of a 'reshuffle' within broadly the same number block. However, in a survey such as this, matters of identification of type are important, so it is necessary first to consider this complex numbering before proceeding with the detailed analysis.

The first renumbering was almost immediate in 1923, Class 1 engines Nos. 2110-9 becoming 2200-9 to make room for the first ten LMS-built Class 3 engines, which then became the second Nos. 2110-9. Then, in 1925, the LMS built five more Class 3s (Nos. 2120-4), and the original Class 1 Nos. 2120-4 became 2210-4. In 1927, ten more new Class 3s caused the original Class 1 Nos. 2125-34 to become 2190-9, so that the new Class 3 engines could have the numbers 2125-34. The original Class 1 Nos. 2135-45 were then renumbered 2056-66 and the recently renumbered series 2190-2214 were renumbered for the second time as 2067-91, having run for only a few years with their second numbers!

The next to suffer in 1927-8 were the original 2146-79 group — the Class 2 and Tilbury-built Class 3s. The Class 3 engines (Nos. 2146-57 and 2176-9) became the second 2135-50 in the same order while the Class 2 engines (Nos. 2158-75) became Nos. 2092-2109. This of course invaded the 2100-9 number series for the first time and caused the renumbering of the ex-LTSR 4—6—4Ts — see page 193. The bulk of this renumbering took place before the livery change but finally, in 1930, the LMS built ten more engines and, fortunately, simply

added them on at the end of the Class 3 types as Nos. 2151-60. Thus, the 'Tilbury tank' number series eventually ran consecutively from 2056-2160.

FINAL LMS NUMBER	REMARKS
2056-66:	Original 2135-45, LTSR built Class 1 engines
2067-76:	Original 2125-34, later 2190-9, LTSR built Class 1 engines
2077-91:	Original 2110-24, later 2200-14, LTSR built Class 1 engines
2092-2109:	Original 2158-75, LTSR built Class 2 engines
2110-2134:	LMS-built Class 3 engines
2135-2146:	Original 2146-57, LTSR built Class 3 engines (in fact, rebuilds from the original '37 Class' engines)
2147-2150:	Original 2176-79, LTSR built Class 3 engines (built new as such)
2151-2160:	LMS built Class 3 engines

The 'P' suffix to the Power Class was added from 1928 onwards.

As can be seen, the final number sequence was eminently logical, progressing through the power groups, whilst in decorative terms, the renumbering only really affected the pre-1928 liveries. Nos. 2151-60 were not built until after the livery change anyway. To complete the record, it should be mentioned that although the Class 1 engines were all withdrawn in the early 1930s, the Class 2 and 3 engines were again renumbered after Nationalisation to make room for Fairburn 2—6—4Ts. This scheme was as follows, although not all the Class 2 engines received their allotted BR numbers:

2092-2104 }
2106-2109 } allotted BR Nos. 41910-41926
2110-2160   became BR Nos. 41928-41978.

Concluding this preliminary note, a few general comments about the LMS livery of the 'Tilbury tanks' also seems helpful. All were painted crimson lake in the pre-1928 period, and most had 14in numerals but the 18in variety was also used, but confined to the LMS-built examples. However, a complicating feature at this time was the placing of the LMS Coat of Arms on the Class 1, 2 and Tilbury-built (rebuilt) Class 3 engines. This was often sited ahead of the cabside opening and not on the bunker side. In consequence, the running number was in these cases placed midway between the Coat of Arms and the tank front. Pictures of the Class 3 engines built in the LMS period indicate that the Coat of Arms was correctly placed on the bunker on this particular series — compare, for example, *Plates 369 & 370.*

Another interesting feature of all these engines was the fact that the footplate angle was generally lined, along with the step plates, cylinders and other sundry details below the footplate. While this was normal for nearly all pre-group tank engines with the red livery, it was not usual on ex-MR tank engines. Moreover the footplate angle itself was usually lined at both top and bottom edges with the red livery on the Tilbury-built engines, but *not* generally on the later LMS-built

examples. The black bordering to panels was also rather wide on the LTSR series.

After the livery change of 1927/8, most of these engines were given the intermediate livery — generally with 12in number and 40in letter spacing — while during the war, most of them became plain black. One or two carried the crimson livery for a short time with the 1928 insignia (usually hand-painted) but how long these engines ran like this is not known. The last LMS batch never carried the red livery. With the intermediate livery, the 'Tilbury tanks' had a lined lower edge to the footplate angle — again unlike most other ex-MR passenger tank engines.

Livery samples are divided into classes and will be found after the detailed analyses which follow.

CLASS 1 4-4-2T (Final LMS Nos. 2056-2091)

The Class 1 4—4—2Ts with 6ft 1in diameter driving wheels were essentially the William Adams design of 1880. By the time the LMS inherited the engines, all had received MR style fittings and the majority displayed extended smokeboxes — see *Plate 371.* Within the class, however, were four engines of markedly different appearance. These were Nos. 2059/74/9/83 (ex-LTSR Nos. 3, 7, 23 and 29). Early in the century, they had been given condensers and shorter chimneys for working to Whitechapel (on the Metropolitan District lines) and by 1904 they had also received rounded cabs because of restricted tunnel clearances. By LMS days, only the latter feature remained but could be associated with either smokebox length — *Plate 372 & 373.* It was this cab modification which set the style for the cabs of all the Class 3 engines, starting with the 1905 '37 Class' rebuilds.

In terms of livery, all examples were painted red and many (probably most) received LMS markings before the livery change. The emblem was more commonly applied ahead of the cab opening in the manner of *Plate 371,* but some engines had them on the bunker, as in *Plate 367.* Engines from the series

Above *(Plate 371):* **This fine view of Class 1 No. 2136 (later 2057) clearly shows the extended smokebox and Midland-style 'front end' characteristic of most of this series in LMS days. The Livery Code is A3 — but note the insignia placement compared with** *Plate 367.* **No. 2136 displayed the somewhat more typical arrangement for this particular class.** *W. Beckerlegge.*

which were fairly rapidly renumbered in 1923 frequently went back to traffic circa 1923/4 with no company markings at all — as in *Plate 372* — but at all times the pre-1928 livery was applied with 14in figures, Code A3.

One or two of the Class 1 engines just managed to receive the 1928 livery before final renumbering into the 20XX series, but the majority received their ultimate numbers before (or more probably at) the time of their assumption of lined black. With this livery, 12in figures and 40in letter spacing was universally adopted and *Plates 374-6* show examples thus finished.

Scrapping of the whole class took place between 1930 and 1935, and it is likely that a few were still in red livery when withdrawn.

Left, upper & lower *(Plates 372 & 373):* The 'round cab' variant of the Class 1 4—4—2T is represented here (upper) by (right) No. 2206 (ex-No. 2116, later No. 2083) with short smokebox (Livery Code A3) and (lower) No. 2059 (ex-No. 2138) with extended smokebox (Livery Code probably B3). The upper picture was taken at Plaistow in 1925. No. 2206 is not displaying any LMS markings, while 4—6—4T No. 2107 is still carrying a MR Coat of Arms on the cabside. *Authors' Collection.*

Right *(Plate 374):* During LMS days, 'pop' safety valves replaced the older type and this modification shows well on Class 1 No. 2076 (ex-Nos. 2134, 2199) at Plaistow in 1930 (Livery Code B3). *G. Coltas.*

Above *(Plate 375):* No. 2056 (formerly No. 2135) was the pioneer 'Tilbury tank' of 1880 and still retained Ramsbottom safety valves on August 22 1931, when photographed at Tilbury in lined black livery (Code B3). It was scrapped a year later. *Authors' Collection.*

Above *(Plate 376):* This detailed rear view of No. 2083 (see also *Plate 372*) gives a good impression of the rounded cab shape later to become familiar on the Class 3 4—4—2Ts. The livery is Code B3, and the picture was taken at Tilbury on October 21 1933. *Authors' Collection.*

CLASS 2 4-4-2T (Final LMS Nos. 2092-2109)

Left *(Plate 377)*: Class 2 4—4—2T No. 2168 (later No. 2102) with short smokebox and first LMS livery (Code A3) at Shoeburyness on August 24 1929. By this time, the engine should have received its new number. *H.C. Casserley.*

This relatively small group of engines, numbering 18 examples, had 6ft 6in diameter driving wheels and was actually the third series of 4—4—2Ts to be built by the 'Tilbury'. Visually, they were an enlarged version of the Class 1 series and they dated from 1900. Inevitably, the MR had applied detail changes between 1912 and 1922, but their rather handsome proportions were not to any significant degree affected whether with their original length smokebox *(Plate 377)* or, the much more common extended version *(Plate 378)*.

Unlike the Class 1 and Class 3 engines, the renumbering operations within the 4—4—2T series were quite simple with this group. They entered the LMS with their ex-MR series numbers 2158-75 and the change to 2092-109 was virtually coincident with the 1927-8 livery alteration. All the examples we

Above *(Plate 378)*: This late LMS view of No. 2103 (formerly No. 2169) shows the extended smokebox and 'pop' safety valves which characterised most of these engines during much of the LMS period. The livery is wartime plain black (Code C22). *Authors' Collection.*

have positively confirmed show the pre-1928 livery exclusively with the first series numbers and the post-1927 style almost equally exclusively with the later number series.

The typical pre-1928 livery form was with 14in numerals and crest positioned ahead of the cab cut-away *(Plate 379)* while the post-1927 lined black form employed 12in numerals and 40in letter centre spacing. As with some of the other classes at this time, some of the 12in transfers seem to have been supplied in the Midland rather than the LMS standard shape but not very often, it is thought. *(Plate 380)*.

There was one particularly interesting example from this group of engines, which not only exhibited several unorthodox liveries at the 1927-8 changeover but also displayed a quick succession of visible anatomical variations. This was No. 2175, (later 2109) and is shown in *Plates 381-3*.

All engines of this series except No. 2105 (withdrawn 1947) survived to reach BR, by which time, many (if not most examples) were probably carrying plain black livery in the style of *Plate 378*, but there are not many positively-confirmed examples. Allocated BR Nos. 41910-26, only three engines (Nos. 41922-3/5, ex-2104/6/8) actually received them, and No. 41922 was the last to be withdrawn, in 1953.

Right *(Plate 380)*: **4—4—2T No. 2095 migrated to Sheffield in LMS days, as illustrated here. Compared with** *Plate 368,* **the locomotive has an extended smokebox and Midland-pattern figures (note particularly the '9' and '5') but the basic livery is still the same — Code B3.** *A.G. Ellis.*

Above *(Plate 379)*: **This view clearly shows the characteristic 'Tilbury' variation of the pre-1928 LMS livery, with emblem ahead of cab opening. The engine is Class 2 No. 2168 again (see also** *Plate 377)* **but, although the picture was taken earlier than the previous view, the engine has an extended smokebox!** *A.G. Ellis.*

LIVERY SAMPLES:

LIVERY STYLE	NORMAL SMOKEBOX	EXTENDED SMOKEBOX
CODE A3†	2161/8/70	2166/73
CODE A5	2175	—
CODE A6	—	2109
CODE B3	2095/9	2092-102/4-5/7-9*
CODE C21	—	2097
CODE C22	—	2103

† *All with crest ahead of cab*
* *No. 2109 also with top feed dome and this livery*

This page *(Plates 381-383):* This interesting group of views, though not all of the best quality, trace some of the developments of Class 2 4—4—2T No. 2175, later No. 2109. The first view (left, top) shows short smokebox and red livery with post-1927 insignia, (Code A5) while the second view (left, lower) reveals extended smokebox with the engine still carrying red livery (Code A6) shortly after renumbering. The last view (below) shows the curious second 'top feed' dome fitted in the early 1930s along with 'pop' safety valves. By this stage, the livery was lined black (Code B3) but two versions of the non-entitled post-1927 livery must be considered unusual, if not unique. *Authors' Collection.*

CLASS 3 4-4-2T (Final LMS Nos. 2110-2160)

This series, the most characteristic form of 'Tilbury Tank' — at least to more modern day observers — originated in 1905 with the rebuilding of the first 6ft 6in driving wheel 4—4—2T (ex-LTSR No. 37) with a much larger boiler and the rounded-style cab first used on four of the 6ft 1in engines — *See page 179*. All 12 were thus rebuilt, and by the time the LMS received them, they were in the form of *Plates 369 or 384*, depending on whether or not the smokebox had been extended. All, of course, had MR-type detail fittings and this group came to the LMS as Nos. 2146-57 (later 2135-46).

The next four (LMS Nos. 2176-9, later Nos. 2147-50) originated in 1909 as new engines to the 1905-rebuild style but with deeper tanks and bunkers *(Plate 385)*. These included, as mentioned above, No. 2177 (later No. 2148) originally LTSR No. 80 *Thundersley*, now happily preserved as part of the National Collection.

The Midland 'adopted' this slightly modified design for new

Above *(Plate 384)*: **'37 Class' rebuild No. 2148 (later No. 2137) with extended smokebox, the normal form for this type in LMS days. The livery is Code A3 with the 'Tilbury'-style insignia placing.** *Authors' Collection.*

construction and at the time of the Grouping, more were on order. These came into service in 1923 as Nos. 2110-9 of which all but the last two carried MR insignia, despite the Grouping — see *Plate 386*. This was unusual in any case since most MR passenger tanks did not carry the company heraldic markings — see *Chapter 3*. They also had 18in numerals, rather than the previous 14in height characters. The last two examples of this series carried LMS markings (one of them in Code A2 form) on the *bunker (Plate 387)*, but all ten still displayed the double lining on the footplate valance of the pre-group series, although the black bordering to the panels became somewhat narrower.

The next five engines (Nos. 2120-4) appeared in 1925, still

Right *(Plate 385)*: **This view shows one of the four 'new build' LTSR engines of this class, No. 2178 (later No. 2149). Note the tank/bunker modifications, subsequently copied in the MR/LMS continuation.** *Authors' Collection.*

with double lining on the footplate angle, this time with the proper LMS crest correctly on the bunker but showing a reversion to 14in numerals — see *Plate 370*. They also had 'pop' safety-valves from new, and were built by Nasmyth Wilson — which probably explains the livery differences.

In 1927, another ten were built by the LMS (Nos. 2125-34) still painted in pre-1928 colours but with more 'standardised' footplate angle and panel lining, and a return to the 18in number

Top *(Plate 386):* 4—4—2T No. 2117 was the last of the series to be delivered in MR livery, albeit in 1923. *Bernard Matthews' Collection.*

Above *(Plate 387):* No. 2118, the first 'Tilbury Tank' to carry LMS markings, is thought to have been the only example to be given the early 1923 LMS livery (Code A2) which it received when built. No. 2119 may well have been similar when new, but the only confirmed record we possess shows it with LMS emblem on the bunkerside, and this may well have been its 'ex-works' condition. *Authors' Collection.*

Above *(Plate 388):* LMS-built 4—4—2T No. 2125 is painted in a somewhat more conventional layout of the pre-1928 LMS livery (Code A1) with narrower black borders to the panel areas and lining at the lower edge only of the footplate angle — compare this picture with *Plate 384.* Note the upper cabside Power Class markings, later changed to 3/3P. *BR (LMR).*

Right *(Plate 389):* Although the engine is not very clean, the lining on the Westinghouse pump reveals that No. 2154 of the final series carries the post-1927 livery (Code B3). *Authors' Collection.*

Left *(Plate 390):* No. 2113 is now branded Class 3, but is still clearly painted red and bears hand-painted insignia (Code A5). Note the retention of the double footplate lining and wider black borders to the panels — indicating that the engine was probably re-lettered rather than fully re-painted. *Authors' Collection.*

Left *(Plate 391):* **This picture shows No. 2113 again, in the later 1930s, now with 'pop' safety valves and transfer insignia of the countershaded variety with 12in numerals. It should be in lined black livery, (Code B3) but under magnification the step plates and cylinders are revealed to be lined-out, a very unusual refinement with this livery.** *Authors' Collection.*

Above *(Plate 392):* **This broadside view of No. 2112 at Plaistow in June 1934 gives a very clear indication of the insignia layout on the lined black Class 3 'Tilbury Tanks' (Code B3).** *A.G. Ellis.*

size — *Plate 388.* The building of this series more or less prompted the rationalisation of numbering described earlier in this chapter, in consequence of which the original pre-group Class 3s became Nos. 2135-50. Finally, in 1930, the LMS built the last ten examples (Nos. 2151-60), and put them in to service with lined black livery from the outset — *Plate 389.*

At the time of the formal livery change from red to black, which also coincided broadly with the renumbering of the ex-LTSR engines, a few of the class retained their red liveries with the new style insignia for a while, initially employing hand-painted characters — *Plate 390.* At least four engines are thus confirmed (Code A5) — see following summary — and there may have been more. After this, lined black with 12in figures (Code B3) became the predominant style, re-painting often coinciding with, or occurring quite close to the change to pop valves for those not built with such features — *Plates 391 & 392.* There were also a few with 14in figures *(Plate 393)* but not many, it is thought.

During and after the Second World War, plain black livery became the norm but there are not very many positively confirmed examples. They were probably mostly Code C22.

The class was passed intact to BR, becoming Nos. 41928-78 in the same order, and in *Plates 394 & 395* are given typical BR views of these characteristics locomotives, little changed in essentials from the original 1905 concept.

LIVERY SAMPLES:

The 'as built' liveries of the LMS series were:

Nos. 2110-7 ...	Code A1 (with MR markings as *Plate 386*)
No. 2118	Code A2 *(Plate 387)*
No. 2119	Code A1 (not positively confirmed — see *Plate 387*)
Nos. 2120-4 ...	Code A3 *(as Plate 370)*
Nos. 2125-34 .	Code A1 (with footplate lining as *Plate 388*)
Nos. 2151-60 .	Code B3 (with 40in letter centre spacing as *Plate 389*)

}All with double-lined footplate angle

Other than these, the sample recorded liveries are as follows, all post-1927 style having 40in letter centre spacing:

CODE A1 ...... 2111/22
*CODE A3 ..... 2111/5-6/46/8/53-4/7/76-8, all with crest ahead of cab opening
=CODE A5 ..... 2112/3/37/47
CODE B3 ...... 2111-21/4-6/9/31-2/4/8-41/3-4/6
CODE B4 ...... 2151/8
CODE C21 2110
CODE C22 2111

* *In this category, ex-LTSR examples (those between 2146-57 and 2176-9) were bearing first series numbers*
= *In the case of No. 2147 this was the second 2147, originally No. 2176. The reference was right at the time of changeover.*

Above *(Plate 393):* **A very interesting scene at Plaistow in the early 1930s, showing No. 2158 (left), displaying 14in numerals (Code B4). The two engines beyond are Nos. 2154/2.** *G.R. Grigs.*

Right *(Plate 394):* **This view shows an original '37 Class' 4—4—2T rebuild bearing its BR series number 41958 in LMS characters, circa 1948-9. It was originally No. 2151, later No. 2140 during LMS days. The recess above the running plate and below the tankside was one of the identifying features of the original Class 3 engines rebuilt from older machines — see also** *Plate 369. R. Petter.*

Left *(Plate 395):* **BR lined black livery, as carried here by No. 41978, represented the final decorative style for the surviving 'Tilbury tanks'. Coincidentally, the picture is actually of the last engine to be built, ex-LMS No. 2160.** *Photomatic.*

In 1910, Robert Harben Whitelegg succeeded his father Thomas as Locomotive Superintendent of the 'Tilbury', by which time, apart from a little residual rebuilding of 4—4—2Ts, the development of this famous breed had all but finished. The younger Whitelegg therefore turned his attention to something altogether more impressive, a 4—6—4T. One hesitates to call it a development of the 4—4—2 type, more of a 'new broom' approach, but Robert Whitelegg was destined to be frustrated. His new giants had hardly been ordered when the LTSR succumbed to Midland Railway blandishments, the 'Tilbury' was taken over and Whitelegg was in effect out of a job — or at the very least playing a very muted 'second fiddle' to Derby.

Built by Beyer-Peacock with Schmidt superheaters, the 4—6—4Ts were delivered in 1912, with MR series numbers and livery. By all accounts, the Midland was not particularly impressed and tried to sell the engines, — to no avail — and they

came into book stock in 1913. Few changes had been made when the LMS received them in 1923 and *Plates 396 & 397* give opposite side views of the type in full crimson livery, Code A1.

The complex renumbering of the 4—4—2Ts described earlier in this chapter caused the 4—6—4Ts also to be renumbered circa 1928/9, by which time No. 2100 had been scrapped and the seven survivors became Nos. 2193-9. This renumbering took place at the livery change, which could result either in old livery with new number *(Plate 398)* or new livery with old number *(Plate 399)*. Interestingly, the latter example retained the red livery.

With the pre-1928 red livery there were two insignia layouts. Marginally more common was the arrangement as shown in *Plate 396 & 397*, with the number centrally placed between the tank front and cab opening, but three examples, including the renumbered 2195 *(Plate 398)*, had their numbers applied

Top & left *(Plates 396 & 397):* **Opposite-side views of 4—6—4Ts Nos. 2100 (top) and 2102 (left) both showing the pre-1928 livery (Code A1) with insignia arrayed in the rather more common style for this class. The rear view of No. 2102 shows well the distinctive cabside cab window design, the lined splashers over the rear bogie wheels, and coal trimmed in the textbook style — with large lumps placed carefully around the edge to hold smaller pieces safely in place. This picture was taken at Shoeburyness, on August 24 1929.** *Authors' Collection/H.C. Casserley.*

Right (Plate 398): No. 2195 (formerly No. 2103) shows the alternative pre-1928 insignia placement — see text. Note also the change to 'pop' safety valves. The picture was taken at St. Albans, circa 1929, probably when the LMS was experimenting with alternative uses for these not very popular machines. They were even tried on the Midland main line coal trains! A.G. Ellis.

Left (Plate 399): This official view of 4—6—4T No. 2106 is principally of interest in showing the old number with the post-1927 red livery (Code A5) to which the engine was strictly not entitled. BR (LMR).

midway between tank front and cab front — see also *Volume One, Plate 104.* These three engines were Nos. 2103-5 (plus No. 2195 ex-2103). The other five were all as *Plate 396.*

Lined black livery was the official style after 1927/8 but it is certain that most were scrapped before repainting. Apart from No. 2100, Nos. 2193-5/9 had all gone by the end of 1930 and we only have records of two (Nos. 2196/8 — *Plate 400)* in the 1928 livery, both Code B4. No. 2197 may have been similar.

The Whitelegg 'Baltics' were unloved from the first. The Midland didn't really want them, the LMS couldn't really use them and they were rapidly outdated by later designs. They had

Above (Plate 400): For all their lack of success, the 4—6—4Ts had a pleasing simplicity of line and the 'balanced' look characteristic of many designs to this wheel arrangement. No. 2198 (ex-No. 2106 — *Plate 399)* illustrates this rather well at St. Albans in the early 1930s when the locomotive was carrying lined black livery (Code B4). A.G. Ellis.

a massive and simple dignity but this was not enough to save them. Whitelegg, of course, took his frustrations off to the GSWR in 1918 but with not much happier results. This time it was the Grouping which intervened; but as we have seen (see *Volume Three Chapters 5/6)* this was probably just as well!

'69 CLASS' 0-6-2T (LMS Nos. — see text; Power Class 3, later 3F)

This class of 16 rather good-looking and very successful engines originated in 1903 when Beyer-Peacock built six examples to Thomas Whitelegg's design. Four more were added in 1908 and another four in 1912 after the Midland takeover. They carried Nos. 2180-93 in the MR lists but were immediately given LMS Nos. 2220-33 in 1923, only to revert to 2180-93 in 1939! In 1947 they were again renumbered in the series 1980-93, which they retained (with the addition of 40000) after Nationalisation.

For some 50 years or so, as with the Class 3 4—4—2Ts, this small class of non-standard engines survived all the pre-group carnage of many other non-Midland designs and helped retain the individuality of the Tilbury section well into BR days. Their

appearance scarcely changed, save for such small details as the substitution of 'pop' safety-valves and the (eventual) removal of the Westinghouse brake pumps, and they performed their mainly humdrum duties without fuss and with considerable competence.

Always painted plain black, their pre-1928 livery was probably always with 14in figures *(Plate 401)* but there are few confirmed examples. Thereafter, plain gold characters with 12in figures were normal until the late 1930s *(Plate 402)* but a few managed to receive the red countershaded insignia *(Plate 403)*. Slightly before the 1939 renumbering, yellow characters with red shading took over *(Plate 404)* and this continued to the end of the LMS period *(Plate 405)*. Interestingly, the 1939

Left (Plate 401): Although not of the highest quality, this is one of the very few pictures which shows an ex-LTSR 0—6—2T in pre-1928 LMS livery. It is the somewhat less-common version with rounded LMS bunkerside panel, (Code C5). We cannot state if this was the typical form, but it is the only version so far confirmed. Engine No. 2225 was subsequently renumbered 2185 and then 1985. *Authors' Collection.*

Above (Plate 402): The well-proportioned nature of the Tilbury 0—6—2Ts is illustrated here by No. 2220 (later Nos. 2180/1980) in the early 1930s (Livery Code C14). Note the change from Ramsbottom to 'pop' safety valves. *Authors' Collection.*

Above (Plate 403): Occasionally, but to no set pattern, gold insignia with red countershading was used on freight engines instead of the black-shaded variety. This happened particularly with the North London 0—6—0Ts (see *Volume Two*) and sometimes with the Tilbury 0—6—2Ts One clear example of this variation is seen on No. 2229 (later Nos. 2189 & 1989). The numbers are the 12in standard variety but we have no coded the variation which was strictly non-standard. *Authors' Collection.*

renumbering was accompanied by the exclusive use of the 1936 pattern sans-serif numberplates, which at that time had been obsolete for three years.

Scrapping commenced as late as 1958, yet all but one had gone by early 1959; No. 41981 lingered on in solitary state until mid-1962. They were, by a long way, the last pure 'Tilbury' engines to disappear and can make one small claim to fame in that not a single example was scrapped until well after all other LTSR designs had totally disappeared, save for the preserved *Thundersley.*

LIVERY SAMPLES:

Letter centres, post-1927 at 40in spacing

CODE C5 2224-5
CODE C14 .... 2220-1/3/6/31-3 plus 2229/30 with countershaded characters
CODE C21 1987
CODE C22 .... 2221/3; 2183/6/8; 1982/5
CODE C24 1989

Above (Plate 404): Red-shaded insignia on freight engines did not officially appear until the advent of the red-shaded chrome yellow transfers in 1937. No. 2223 (later Nos. 2183/1983) showed this new style (Code C22) quite clearly during the later LMS period. *Authors' Collection*

'49 CLASS' 0-6-0 (LMS Nos. 2898-2999; Power Class 2, later 2F)

Above (Plate 406): No. 2898 was the first of the two '49 Class' 0—6—0s (see text overleaf) and is seen here at Plaistow on August 8 1925, still carrying the MR crest on the cab, with 14in tender numerals. Whether it retained these or received the 18in numerals later, like No. 2899, is not known. H.C. Casserley.

In 1898, the Ottoman Railway (in Turkey) cancelled an order with Sharp Stewart for two 0—6—0 engines which had already been built. For some reason the 'Tilbury' stepped in and bought them and they became the only tender engines ever owned by the LTSR. They must have been quite sound purchases, for the MR fitted new Belpaire boilers (plus the usual Derby fittings) and the LMS saw fit to keep them in service until both were 35 years old — a rare privilege for a class of just two members. *Plates 406-7* give a good impression of No. 2898, while No. 2899

(as No. 22899) was illustrated in *Volume One, Plate 108*. LMS liveries were straightforward. No. 2899 was given 18in figures (Code C1) after the Grouping (the other may have been the same — but see *Plate 406*) and both received the post-1927 style with 12in figures (Code C14). In 1935, the sole survivor (No. 2899) was put on the duplicate list and received 10in cabside figures (Code C13) which we inadvertently described as C14 in *Volume One, Plate 108*. Letter spacing of the 'LMS' lettering was at 40in centres and set just above the horizontal row of rivets.

Above *(Plate 407):* **A rear view of No. 2898 again (see also page 197), this time in post-1927 style (Livery Code C14) pictured on October 21, 1933, just prior to withdrawal. Note the modified design of the tender front and cab windows, doubtless required because of the LTSR climate, which was very different to the Mediterranean conditions for which the locomotive was originally designed.** *Authors' Collection.*

THE STRATFORD UPON AVON & MIDLAND JUNCTION RAILWAY

The SMJR was one of those small systems, much beloved of railway enthusiasts, which tended to get utterly lost against the huge backcloth of the amalgamated LMS system. Essentially it consisted of one primary east-west artery, linking the various Midland, LNWR, GCR and GWR north-south routes between Olney (MR) via Roade (LNWR), Woodford and Hinton (GCR), Fenny Compton (GWR), Stratford-upon-Avon (GWR) and Broom Junction (MR).

It was constituted as the 'SMJ' by an act of 1908 as an amalgamation of several even smaller and financially bankrupt concerns and has recently been the subject of a fine and definitive history by Arthur Jordan *(Published by OPC – 1982)* to which we would refer our readers who wish to know more.

In locomotive terms, the 'SMJ' contributed one 2—4—0 and 12 0—6—0s to the LMS fleet. Hardly surprisingly, the new LMS was not wildly impressed with any of these engines, but it did allocate them systematic numbers (290; 2300-11) under the standard system and most engines received them before scrapping.

It seems to have been axiomatic in British railway history that the smaller the fleet, the greater (proportionally) the variety of traction and the 'SMJ' was no exception. Therefore, like the Wirral and Knott End Railways for example *(Volume Two)* the best way to deal with the collection is to review the locomotives (in LMS number order) by means of extended picture captions.

Below *(Plate 408)*: 2—4—0 No. 290 (EX-SMJR No. 13); Built in 1903 by Beyer-Peacock, this locomotive was based on a design supplied to the Hull & Barnsley Railway in 1885. Allocated its LMS number in 1923, it was scrapped in 1924 (without renumbering) to recover useable parts for other locomotives. This picture was taken just prior to withdrawal. *BR (LMR)*.

Above *(Plate 409)*: 0—6—0 No. 2300 (EX-SMJR No. 2); This engine was a much rebuilt Beyer-Peacock machine dating originally from 1880, with 4ft 6in diameter driving wheels. It is shown in this view carrying LMS livery (Code C4) immediately before withdrawal in April 1926. *Authors' Collection.*

Below *(Plate 410):* 0—6—0 Nos. 2301-2 (EX-SMJR Nos. 3-4); The next two 0—6—0s were similar to No. 2300, but had smaller boilers and 5ft driving wheels and dated from 1881 and 1885 respectively. This official view shows SMJR No. 3 as withdrawn (without renumbering) in 1924. No. 4 became LMS No. 2302 (Livery Code C5) and differed by having a round-topped boiler. It lasted long enough to become No. 2397 (also Code C5) in 1927 before withdrawal and scrapping in 1929. *BR (LMR).*

Right *(Plate 411):* 0—6—0 No. 2303 (EX-SMJR No. 7); This engine was bought from the LBSCR (whereon it had carried No. 428) in 1920, having been built as early as 1884 to a Stroudley design. It is shown here at Stratford in September 1923, bearing LMS livery (Code C4) — still pure 'Brighton' save for its Midland chimney — now there's an idea for modellers! *Authors' Collection.*

Above & left *(Plates 412 & 413)*: 0—6—0s No. 2304-6 (EX-SMJR Nos. 10-12); These engines, dating between 1895 and 1900 were a quasi-development, with higher boiler pressure, of Nos. 2301-2 but all with round-top boilers. The two views show (above) SMJR No. 10 (never renumbered by the LMS) and (left) LMS No. 2305, the first ex-SMJR engine to receive an LMS number. It also had a Midland chimney and buffers, plus a substantial safety-valve support. The Livery Code was C4 and the engine lasted long enough to become No. 2398 in 1927 before withdrawal and scrapping in 1930. The third engine of this group had the anatomical details of No. 10 but its LMS livery is not known. However, it too lasted until 1930, becoming No. 2399 in 1927. Almost certainly its livery would have been Code C5. *Authors' Collection.*

Left *(Plate 415)*: SMJ 0—6—0 No. 15, allocated LMS No. 2307, built in November 1904 by Beyer Peacock and withdrawn in 1925. See also overleaf. *Authors' Collection.*

Right, upper & previous page, lower *(Plates 414 & 415):* 0—6—0s Nos. 2307-9 (EX-SMJR Nos. 14-16); Beyer-Peacock 0—6—0s Nos. 14-16 were delivered in 1903-6 as a straight-frame variant, with 4ft 9in wheels and higher boiler pressure, of the previous SMJ types. Reversion to Belpaire boiler was made and all examples are believed to have been renumbered, with the possible exception of No. 2308 (withdrawn 1924). The other two disappeared in 1926 and we illustrated No. 2307 as SMJR No. 14 in *Volume One, Plate 114.* These two views show (previous page) SMJR No. 15 (allocated LMS No. 2308) and (right, upper) LMS No. 2309 (ex-SMJR No. 16, Livery Code C4). Note the MR chimney and smokebox on No. 2309. *Authors' Collection.*

Right, lower & below *(Plates 416 & 417):* 0—6—0s NOS. 2310-11 (EX-SMJR Nos. 17-18); The final SMJ 0—6—0s were another pair from Beyer-Peacock, still with the 4ft 9in wheels and Belpaire boilers of the previous type, but with yet higher boiler pressure. Although relatively modern in date of origin (1908), they only lasted until 1925 and 1927 respectively. The pictures show No. 2310 (right) in LMS (Livery Code C4) still with SMJ lining, and SMJ No. 18 (below) which as LMS No. 2311 received the 'proper' Code C4 style when renumbered. *Authors' Collection.*

CHAPTER 9:

THE ABSORPTION OF THE SOMERSET & DORSET FLEET

THE Somerset & Dorset Joint Railway retained its independent title for seven years after the Grouping, until 1930, at which time its locomotives were transferred to the LMS at the same time as the rolling stock went to the Southern Railway. It had enjoyed joint line status for 55 years, mostly under Midland and LSWR ownership, but latterly changing to LMS and SR control.

The railway itself dated back before 1875 (the date of incorporation as a joint system), tracing the geographical elements of its title to an amalgamation between the Somerset Central and the Dorset Central in 1862. The Somerset Central started life in 1852 as a broad gauge system, while the Dorset Central traced its origins back to 1856. Even the enlarged amalgamated system did not serve any major centres of population, so originating traffic was relatively modest. When the Midland reached Bath in 1869, the logical development was to try to extend the 'S&D' northwards to meet the Midland, thus linking the standard gauge Midland and LSWR networks by a route cutting through the heart of broad gauge territory, thus giving 'through route' prospects to the line. To this end, an act of 1871 authorised the linking of Bath (MR) to Evercreech ('S&D'). Completed in 1874, even this extra boost to revenue could not balance the books until the MR and LSWR, having out-manoeuvred the GWR, purchased the 'S&D' thus initiating the SDJR in 1875. This did give rise to a considerable upsurge of traffic, once the Midland and LSWR had more positive control of affairs.

Although jointly owned, the SDJR always maintained a distinctive character for most of its life, including a famous and noteworthy blue livery which was neither MR or LSWR in origin. This distinctiveness extended to locomotive matters too. Although nominally under Midland ownership in the persons of Johnson, Deeley *et al*, the SDJR always had its own Locomotive Superintendent, based at Highbridge, and this post was no titular sinecure. 'Somerset & Dorset' engines may indeed have been mostly designed at Derby and strongly reminiscent of the domestic Midland product, but the local man at Highbridge was

Above: Standing outside the Midland Railway locomotive shed at Bath on August 7 1950 are SDJR 2—8—0s Nos. 53805 (left) of the small-boilered 1914 Derby-built series, and No. 53806 of the 1925 large-boilered series, built in 1925 by Robert Stephenson & Company Ltd. Both engines are carrying BR cabside numbers utilising LMS-style transfers. With a tractive of 35,932lb they were the most powerful 2—8—0s in the country, when they first appeared, in 1914. *Ivo Peters.*

frequently instrumental in putting his own contribution into the equation, thus giving rise to several classes of engines which were similar to, but never quite straight copies of, the MR style.

It was only in later years (late Midland and early LMS) that some dilution was made in the form of pure MR or LMS designs, rather than distinctively different products. Some of these were to pure MR/LMS 'standard' designs, adopted as such by the newly-formed LMS in 1923. These have been considered in detail in previous chapters, in like manner to those of the same type(s) which came from the MR. Even during this period, however, there was one new 2—8—0 design which had no counterpart on the MR and was designed specifically for the joint line in 1914. It was repeated (slightly modified) as late as 1925, during LMS superintendency.

When the 'S&D' locomotive fleet was acquired by the LMS in 1930, it consisted of 80 engines of which exactly one quarter (eight 4—4—0s, seven 0—6—0Ts and five 0—6—0s) could be considered LMS standard types. The engines were not always given a consecutive LMS number series in the manner of many pre-group systems but were frequently fitted into appropriate gaps in the existing system (usually the ex-MR series) created by withdrawn engines of the same wheel arrangement.

As usual in our survey, the detailed treatment of classes follows the normal LMS sequence of types.

SDJR '5ft 9in' 4-4-0 (LMS Nos. 300-303; Power Class 2P)

Right *(Plate 418):* Blue-liveried 4—4—0 No. 301 (ex-SDJR No. 15) was the only 5ft 9in engine to receive LMS markings while retaining its 'H' boiler. Note the 'forward' position of the dome and the old-type smokebox door. It was scrapped in 1931. The livery can conveniently be coded A9 and it seems possible that the numerals are genuine black-shaded LMS transfers. The 'LMS' is clearly hand lettered and unshaded. *H.C. Casserley.*

These engines originated in 1891 as what might be called a miniaturised version (with 5ft 9in diameter driving wheels) of the characteristic slim-boilered Johnson MR 4—4—0. Eight examples were built down to 1897 of which four reached the LMS. By this time, all had received new, larger boilers, two of them being the round top 'H' pattern *(Plate 418)* while Nos. 302/3 had Belpaire boilers *(Plate 419)*. No. 300 did not receive its LMS number before scrapping and all had gone by the end of 1932.

All four engines trailed the SDJR variant of the J1 type Midland low-sided tender *(see page 135)*. This was essentially of normal MR pattern but with upward extensions of the side sheets between top horizontal beading and flared coping. It is particularly well illustrated on the picture of '6ft' 4—4—0 No. 320 *(Plate 420)* and this modification enhanced its water capacity to 2,60 gallons.

The LMS livery of these engines — as was the case with almost all SDJR engines for a year or two after their absorption — was distinctive. Essentially, the original SDJR livery (frequently blue) was retained to which was applied hand-painted LMS insignia in creamy-yellow paint. Some sources say pure white but this is not thought very likely, although more information would be welcome. These new insignia closely followed the 1928 standard patterns but were not an exact copy and were readily distinguishable from the genuine LMS transfer insignia. However, letter and numeral heights, together with spacing, followed 'the book', so to speak. Moreover, the lining on the blue engines was applied according to pure MR/LMS layout. Consequently, it is possible to use our livery coding system for many ex-SDJR engines, even in this early phase, remembering to interpret the 'ground' colour as blue in the case of engines not painted black.

Given this preliminary comment, the three renumbered 5ft 9in 4—4—0s carried LMS liveries essentially Code A9 (Nos. 301/3) and Code B9 (No. 302), but devoid of insignia shading and all with letter spacing at 40in centres. The lined black example arose not because of LMS repainting but as a result of the SDJR having contemplated changing to black with red lining in 1929, starting with this particular engine. The experiment was not, as far as is known, repeated.

Left *(Plate 419):* This engine is believed to have been the only ex-SDJR passenger locomotive to come to the LMS in lined black. No. 302 represents the Belpaire form of the 5ft 9in 4—4—0 and was formerly SDJR No. 17. Note the cab alterations compared with *Plate 418.* The livery is essentially Code B9 and once again, the cab numerals are apparently LMS transfers, even though the tender lettering is handpainted. *Bernard Matthews Collection.*

SDJR '6ft' 4-4-0 (LMS Nos. 320-321; Power Class 2P)

These two extremely well-proportioned engines were survivors (built 1908) of a group of five engines originally introduced in 1903, bearing 'H' boilers from new. When received by the LMS, they carried Belpaire boilers (*Plates 420 & 421*). Both were painted in lined blue (essentially Code A9) with unshaded insignia and 40in letter spacing. Both had the distinctive 2,600-gallon tenders. No. 320 was withdrawn in this configuration but No. 321 lasted until 1938, by which time it had received a standard MR 2,950-gallon tender and orthodox LMS lined black livery (Code B4) — See *Plate 422*. It was the only non-standard ex-SDJR 4—4—0 to be given a full and correct LMS repaint.

Below *(Plate 420):* This excellent rear view of 6ft 4—4—0 No. 320 (ex-SDJR No. 77) on June 6 1930 clearly shows the lined blue livery with handpainted LMS characters in Code A9 arrangement. The characteristic SDJR variant of the basically Midland tender is clearly apparent. *H.C. Casserley.*

Left *(Plate 421):* 4—4—0 No. 321 (ex-SDJR No. 78) was also in blue livery on reaching the LMS and this picture, taken at Bath, probably shows it thus finished, although it is hard to be certain. The cabside numerals seem to be rendered in 12in transfers but the 'LMS' appears to be handpainted. *Bernard Matthews Collection.*

Right *(Plate 422)*: **This picture shows No. 321, paired with a MR tender and painted in standard LMS lined black livery (Code B5). Note the retention of Ramsbottom safety valves.** *Authors' Collection.*

SDJR '7ft' & '6ft 9in' 4-4-0 (LMS Nos. 322-326 & 623-625; Power Class 2P)

Above *(Plate 423)*: **Midland design 4—4—0 No. 323 (ex-SDJR No. 40) was one of five '483 Class' engines supplied to the SDJR. It is seen here with lined blue livery and handpainted LMS markings shortly after acquisition by the LMS.** *Authors' Collection.*

These eight engines were identical to the MR/LMS standard Class 2P types. Nos. 322-6 were to the ex-MR '483 Class' pattern and Nos. 633-5 had actually been built as Nos. 575/6/80 (in the LMS Class 2P continuation) before being sold to the SDJR in 1928. For completeness, two pictures (one of each Class) are given of these engines in the immediate post-1930 livery of blue with LMS markings *(Plates 423 & 424)* but more detailed coverage of the Class is in *Chapter 2*.

Above *(Plate 424):* **A splendid photograph of LMS standard Class 2P No. 635 (ex-SDJR No. 46) in lined blue livery, as running circa 1930-31. This engine had started life as LMS No. 580 prior to being sold to the Joint Line.** *Authors' Collection.*

SDJR 0-4-4T (LMS Nos. 1200-1207/ 1230-1232/ 1305; Power Class 1P)

Left *(Plate 425):* **MR design 0—4—4T No. 1305 (ex-SDJR No. 54) in lined blue livery with LMS markings — effectively Code A8. Note the motor train control gear attached to the smokebox.** *Authors' Collection.*

Prior to the introduction of 4—4—0s in the 1890s, the 'Somerset & Dorset' had used 0—4—4Ts for its passenger workings, Johnson having persuaded his SDJR colleagues as early as 1877 that this type would be appropriate. He was obviously correct because the last one did not disappear until 1946! Nevertheless, the SDJR 0—4—4Ts, although very like those on the Midland, were not (with one well-known exception; No. 1305 — see next paragraph) quite the same. They were nominally one inch smaller in driving wheel diameter (5ft 3in rather than 5ft 4in) as if it mattered (!) and had a somewhat longer bogie wheelbase which may have been of some significance.

In terms of LMS numbers, Nos. 1200-7/30 dated from 1877, Nos. 1231/2 from 1885, and No. 1305 from 1884. The 12XX numbers given in 1930 were taken from withdrawn ex-MR 0—4—4Ts (mostly of the Kirtley type), but No. 1305 was a genuine ex-MR engine, purchased by the SDJR in 1921 and given its old number back when the LMS took over. Interestingly, one of the original 1877 engines (No. 1230) became the last survivor of the Class.

By LMS days, considerable visual variety existed in what was supposedly a homogeneous group. In this respect, the SDJR was not exempted from Derby's well-known propensity for rebuilding anything it laid its hands upon! The classic MR shape, with dome-mounted Salter safety valves and graceful brass casing over the firebox, was confined to No. 1305 (the genuine MR engine — *Plate 425),* whereas the SDJR round-top boilers (by LMS days) had a normal dome and much more

Above *(Plate 426)*: **SDJR-type round top boiler 0—4—4T No. 1201 (ex-SDJR No. 11) still in well-kept blue livery, during 1930. The handpainted front number was characteristic of most ex-SDJR engines at this time. Compare the boiler mountings with** *Plate 425.* *H.C. Casserley.*

substantial firebox-mounted safety valve housing *(Plate 426)*. Three examples had Belpaire boilers (Nos. 1230-2 — *Plate 427*) and five, including two of the 'Belpaires', were motor-fitted *(Plate 428)*. These were Nos. 1206-7/30/2/1305. Two of them failed to receive LMS numbers (Nos. 1200/4) and all except No. 1230 were withdrawn during 1930-2.

A consequence of this rapid withdrawal of the Class was that the LMS never bothered to repaint any examples, save No. 1230. They came to the LMS in blue livery and we have

confirmed at least seven thus finished with LMS insignia — essentially Code A8, with unshaded characters. These were Nos. 1201-3/5/7/32/1305 and a particularly good impression of the hand-painted characters is given in *Plate 429*. No. 1230 is likely to have carried the same style during 1930-31, but is known to have had at least two fully correct LMS lined black repaints, including one in the 1936 style — *Plates 430 & 431*. By this time it had left the 'S&D' system for a new home in the Midlands.

Right *(Plate 427)*: **Belpaire boilered 0—4—4T No. 1232 (ex-SDJR No. 55), motor-fitted and in blue livery — a colour it probably kept until withdrawal and scrapping in 1932.** *Bernard Matthews Collection.*

Above (Plate 428): Motor-fitted round-top 0—4—4T No. 1207 (ex-SDJR No. 31A) is generally similar to No. 1201 in *Plate 426*, but carries a flared-top chimney of rather attractive aspect. The picture was taken at Highbridge on July 5 1930. Once again the livery is lined blue. *H.C. Casserley.*

Above (Plate 429): This close-up view of 0—4—4T No. 1205 (ex-SDJR No. 29A) gives a very clear indication of the 1930 style re-marking of ex-SDJR engines. Note the simple obliteration of the old pre-1930 insignia without a full repaint. The engine is painted blue. *Authors' Collection.*

Above (Plates 430 & 431): **These two pictures of motor-fitted, Belpaire-boilered 0—4—4T No. 1230 (ex-SDJR No. 32) show the two LMS standard liveries carried by the 'one that got away'. The liveries are Code B3 and B11 respectively. Note the change to 'pop' safety valves between the two pictures, both taken circa 1936-8. In spite of apparent appearances, both liveries carried red-shaded insignia.** A.G. Ellis/ Authors' Collection.

SDJR FOX WALKER 0-6-0ST (LMS 1500-1507; Power Class 2F)

These engines were the only survivors to the LMS of a type whose origins went back prior to the formation of the Joint Committee, having first appeared in 1874. Building continued until 1876 and eight of the original nine examples reached the LMS in 1923.

Built as banking engines (for the Evercreech — Bath line) most were life-expired when they reached the LMS, and relegated to shunting duties. Nevertheless, all save Nos. 1501/3 received LMS markings in the typical hand-painted style — essentially Code C16, with 40in letter spacing. We have confirmed all of them in the style typified by *Plates 432-4*.

In so far as a heavy 0—6—0ST can be considered good-looking, then these 'Somerset & Dorset' engines probably qualify. They were distinctly well-proportioned with more than normally handsome boiler fittings, including a distinctly jaunty chimney. Although five examples had gone by early 1931, Nos. 1504-6 lasted until late in 1934. It is not known whether any of these received conventional LMS pattern transfer insignia but all three certainly received new front numberplates.

Top & left *(Plates 432 & 433):* Fox-Walker 0—6—0STs Nos. 1500 (top) and 1502 (left) (ex-SDJR Nos. 1 & 3) give a clear impression of the LMS livery of these solidly-built engines — essentially Code C16. Note the cabside of the Sentinel 0—4—0T No. 7190 in the background, behind No. 1500. Modelling detail of interest includes the footstep and handrail on the tankside to facilitate access to the tank filler lid, and the 'lugs' used to remove the saddletank during repairs. *H.C. Casserley.*

Right *(Plate 434):* **0—6—0ST No. 1507 (ex-SDJR No. 9) was one of three survivors of a later series of four of these engines delivered during the early Joint Line period (LMS Nos. 1505-7). Note the variation of cab front treatment.** *Authors' Collection.*

SDJR GEARED SENTINEL 0-4-0T (LMS Nos. 7190-7191; Power Class — unclassified)

In 1929, as replacements for elderly 0—4—0Ts at Radstock, the SDJR ordered two chain-driven 100hp Sentinel locomotives of highly distinctive beetle-like, shape *(Plate 435)*. They survived throughout the LMS period and were not withdrawn until quite late in the BR period (1961 and 1959 respectively). Always painted plain black, such details as we have of their insignia are given in the captions to *Plates 435-437*. Part of No. 7190 may also be seen in the right background of *Plate 432*, bearing hand-painted characters.

Below *(Plate 435):* **Geared Sentinel 0—4—0T No. 7191, soon after acquisition by the LMS. The picture is poor but the characteristic handpainted insignia can be faintly discerned on the cabside. Insignia placing remained in this style throughout LMS days.** *Authors' Collection.*

Left (Plate 436): On the original print, the BR 'lion & wheel' emblem is very faintly discernible above the number of BR No. 47191. R.C. Riley.

Right (Plate 437): BR No. 47190 shows the early post-nationalisation form of marking used on these curious and quite long-lived engines. Ivo Peters.

SDJR FOWLER 0-6-0T (LMS Nos. 7150-7156; Power Class 3F)

In 1929, the SDJR took delivery of seven LMS standard 0—6—0 Class 3F tanks. These are covered in more detail in Chapter 5, but, for completeness, a picture is given in Plate 438, showing one of them carrying early hand-painted LMS insignia.

They reached the LMS in plain blue livery, having been delivered thus to the SDJR only a year before the LMS take-over; they became Nos. 7310-6 as a result of the 1934 renumbering scheme.

Left (Plate 438): All seven LMS standard 0—6—0Ts were delivered to the SDJR in plain blue livery. This was retained for a year or so after 1930 and No. 7155 (ex-SDJR No. 24, later LMS No. 7315) is seen here in 1933 at Plaistow(!) almost certainly still in plain blue livery with LMS insignia. Authors' Collection.

SDJR JOHNSON 0-6-0 (LMS Nos. 2880-2890; Power Class 2F)

Top *(Plate 439):* Johnson 0—6—0 No. 2887 (ex-SDJR No. 68) carrying handpainted LMS characters (essentially Code C18) and a flared-top chimney — altogether an attractive looking ensemble. *H.C. Casserley.*

Above *(Plate 440):* The alternative round-top boiler arrangement was carried by 0—6—0s Nos. 2888 & 2890. Note the forward position of the injector clack valve above the leading splasher on this view of No. 2890 (ex-SDJR No. 71) in LMS livery (Code C18, with handpainted characters). No. 2888 (ex-SDJR No. 69) had the normal injector position, as illustrated by *Plate 439. H.C. Casserley.*

These engines, known on the SDJR as 'Scotties', were the last 11 survivors of what had been the largest class of engines on the system. Introduced in 1878, in all essentials they were a 4ft 6in driving wheel diameter version of Johnson's standard Midland goods engines. Their nickname derived from the Scottish origin (Neilson & Co.) of the first examples built. Originally 28 in number, their building took place in small batches between 1878 and 1890. Most LMS survivors were from the later series, as might be expected, but No. 2886 dated from 1879.

The LMS gave the 'Scotties' a new series of numbers between the Kirtley and Johnson ex-MR 0—6—0s — a logical enough place — but none lasted beyond 1932. In a sense this was surprising, considering they were no older than many of their ex-MR relatives. However, their somewhat smaller wheel size and other departures from the 'standard' Midland form probably explains their short LMS life.

Needless to say, visual variety in both engine and tenders was apparent by 1930. The nearest to original form were the round-top examples with typical Johnson boiler mountings (*Plate 439*). These were, by 1930, Nos. 2885-7/9. Two other round-tops (Nos. 2888/90) had second-hand boilers with 'normal' domes and large safety valve casings (*Plate 440*). The Belpaire variant

Left *(Plate 441)*: This picture of No. 2884, (formerly SDJR No. 38) illustrates the third variant of the 4ft 6in 0—6—0, with Belpaire boiler. The locomotive again displays the typical 'S&D' livery of the 1930-31 period and was photographed at Templecombe on June 7 1930. *H.C. Casserley.*

Below *(Plate 442)*: Belpaire boilered 0—6—0 No. 2881 (ex-SDJR No. 35) with 'S&D' type 2600 gallon tender. The Livery Code is C18, with handpainted lettering. *Bernard Matthews Collection.*

Right *(Plate 443)*: No. 2889 (ex-SDJR No. 70) was given proper 14in transfers as shown here, soon after reaching LMS ownership (Code C15). It was probably the only example so treated. *Authors' Collection.*

(Nos. 2880-4) is represented by *Plate 441* of which Nos. 2880/1 were paired with the unique SDJR tender — see *(Plate 442)*.

As far as we can verify, all were painted black and most received hand-painted insignia during 1930 in the form illustrated by *Plates 439-442* (essentially Code C18) with 40in letter spacing. All save Nos. 2882/6/9 are thus confirmed and, except for No. 2889, these too are likely to have been similar. The 'odd man out' *(Plate 443)* seems to have been the only engine of this series to receive 'correct' LMS livery before scrapping.

MIDLAND CLASS 3 0-6-0 (LMS Nos. between 3194-3260; Power Class 3F)

Right *(Plate 444)*: Class 3F 0—6—0 No. 3216 (ex-SDJR No. 72) bearing handpainted characters (Code C16) in the early 1930s. *Bernard Matthews Collection*

In 1896 and 1902, the SDJR had taken delivery of ten standard Midland goods engines (five in each year) with 5ft 3in diameter driving wheels. The final five were actually diverted from a Midland Railway order and were in red livery on arrival. By LMS days, the 'Bulldogs', as they were known on the SDJR, had all been rebuilt to the standard Class 3 Belpaire form and, as such, were almost indistinguishable from those of the parent system, already covered in *Chapter 6*. However the leading sandbox indicated their SDJR origin. All had 2,750-gallon MR pattern tenders (Type J4).

Somewhat unusually, although there were undoubtedly plenty of appropriate and hitherto unused numbers in the LMS lists (e.g. 2868-79, 91-7) all ten of these engines took up random numbers of withdrawn engines in the former Midland 0—6—0 lists. This was not without its logic but meant that the ex-SDJR No. 3211 was, in fact the second engine of the same type to bear the particular LMS number in question. The numbers re-used were: Nos. 3194/8/201/4/11/6/8/28/48/60.

When the LMS inherited these locomotives, renumbering was rapid and executed in the usual hand-painted style. Most examples were painted plain black and given 10in figures (essentially Code C16) with 40in letter spacing *(Plate 444)*. There was, additionally, one blue example, No. 3218 *(Plate 445)*. Thereafter, the normal LMS livery for the type (Code C13) became the standard style *(Plate 446)* plus, presumably, the wartime continuation with red-shaded yellow characters. All save No. 3198 reached BR ownership and received their 4XXXX numbers *(Plate 447)*. No. 43216 was the last to be withdrawn, in 1962. As far as we can ascertain, they retained their (relatively) small tenders throughout their lives.

```
LIVERY SAMPLES:

*CODE A8:   3218 (in blue with unshaded characters)
 CODE C13:  3194/201/4/11/48
*CODE C16:  3204/16/28/48/60
 CODE C21:  3201/28/60

* Hand-painted characters – see text.
```

Left *(Plate 445)*: By LMS days, most of the ex-SDJR 0—6—0s had received plain black livery, applied from 1921 onwards, but No. 3218 (ex-SDJR No. 73) was clearly an exception and ran for a year or two in lined blue, as seen here at Highbridge on July 5 1930. *H.C. Casserley.*

Above & right *(Plates 446 & 447)*: These two views of Class 3F 0—6—0 No. 3194 (ex-SDJR No. 62) show the typical LMS (above) and BR (right) painting schemes for this class. The LMS style is Code C13 and the engine survived until the end of 1960. Note the forward sandboxes, a feature of the SDJR locomotives not to be found on the MR machines. *Bernard Matthews Collection/ Authors' Collection.*

FOWLER (MR DESIGN) 0-6-0 (LMS Nos. 4557-4561; Power Class 4F)

Right *(Plate 448):* Class 4F 0—6—0 No. 4557 (ex-SDJR No. 57) in LMS days, livery not clear but probably Code C13. By pure coincidence, the LMS numbers of this essentially 'standard' group of five engines perpetuated the old SDJR numbers in the last two digits of each number. *D.S. Field Collection.*

Just as in the case of the 4—4—0s and, later the 0—6—0Ts, the SDJR purchased five standard MR superheated Class 4 0—6—0s in 1922. They are covered in *Chapter 7*, but *Plate 448* is included here for completeness. Oddly enough, we have no pictures of any of this series carrying the early (1930-1) hand-painted characters but they did receive them. They were known as 'Armstrongs' on the SDJR as they had been built by Armstrong Whitworth & Co. Ltd.

FOWLER 2-8-0 (LMS Nos. 9670-9680, later 13800-13810; Power Class 7F)

The last Derby design built purely for the SDJR was not even a modification of an existing Midland type, but represented the first real attempt to produce a big engine for the formidably difficult Bath — Bournemouth route. A new 2—8—0 chassis was designed, with outside Walschaerts valve gear which could accept the same type of superheaded boiler being fitted fo the Midland 'Compounds' and '990 Class' 4—4—0s. An effective locomotive was produced, albeit spoiled by the normal Midland

Above *(Plate 449):* Small-boilered Class 7F 2—8—0 No. 9672 (ex-SDJR No. 82, later LMS No. 13802) bearing handpainted insignia, pictured circa 1930, (Livery Code C16). *Bernard Matthews Collection.*

design detail weaknesses, particularly axleboxes.

Nevertheless, the 2—8—0s made a startling contribution to SDJR operations. Six examples were built in 1914 under Midland auspices at Derby *(Plate 449)* and the LMS authorised

Above (Plate 451): No. 13807 (ex-SDJR No. 87, first LMS No. 9677) is seen here tolerably clean, carrying standard LMS livery Code C13. The original boilers of this second series of 2—8—0s were non-standard but had close affinity with that of the 'Lickey Banker' 0—10—0 — see pages 156-158. It was not until BR days and in the interests of standardisation of repairs, that the whole 2—8—0 series was modified to take the smaller boiler and No. 13807 (as BR No. 53807) was thus reboiled in 1954 — see also Plates 453 & 454. Bernard Matthews Collection.

a further five, with larger boilers and left-hand drive, from Robert Stephenson & Co. in 1925 (Plate 450). These later engines were paired with LMS standard tenders whereas the first batch had trailed Deeley-type MR tenders. Interestingly, it is one of these Deeley tenders which is now paired with the restored Midland 'Compound' at the National Railway Museum, York. The 11 engines were initially numbered 9670-80 when the LMS took over, in the logical series after the LMS Class 7F 0—8—0s.

The building of more of these LMS standard 0—8—0s in 1932 (see Volume Five) raised a conflict with the original LMS numbers allocated to the 2—8—0s, resulting in the 'S&D'

engines being put into the 138XX series — just two years after they had been given their first LMS numbers, following absorption of the 'S&D' fleet in 1930. By this time, two of the large-boilered engines (Nos. 9679/80) had received replacement small boilers (see Volume One, Plate 113) but it was not until BR days (during 1953-5) that the other three large-boilered engines received replacement smaller units.

It has always been a source of some surprise that neither the Midland nor the LMS saw fit to build this type for the parent system. They would have been far more effective than many of the engines built for freight duties in the pre-Stanier period and their long survival until almost the end of the 'S&D' route in

Above *(Plate 451):* This rather pleasant view of 2—8—0s Nos. 53801 and 13807, taken at Bath shed in 1949, clearly shows the difference between the original small-boilered and the later large-boilered 2—8—0s of the former Somerset & Dorset Joint Railway. The LMS livery of No. 13807 cannot be precisely determined — probably Code C21 — while No. 53801 was one of many engines given their new BR numbers in LMS style characters during the early part of 1948. *Ivo Peters.*

Right *(Plate 452):* This detailed cab view of No. 53809 shows another ex-SDJR 2—8—0 to be given its new BR number in LMS characters during 1948. Note also the '7F', faintly discernible on the upper cabside panel. *Ivo Peters.*

1966 is a fair testimony to their quality. The last withdrawals were in 1964 and Nos. 53808/9 are preserved, the later having achieved main line operational status since going into private preservation as LMS Nos. 13809.

The LMS always painted them black and when in the 96XX series, several (probably most) received hand-painted characters (*Plate 449*). Thereafter, normal transfer figures were used (*Plate 451*. When photographed they were never in particularly clean condition and the following positively-confirmed examples are the best which can be achieved. From this it seems likely that plain insignia with 10in figures was the most common livery form employed before the war, with red shading thereafter. It is possible that some never received red-shaded characters during this difficult time. Letter spacing seems to have been more commonly at greater than 40in centres but insufficient evidence exists on which to generalise.

Top & above *(Plates 453 & 454)*: **These two views show the earlier and later configurations of former SDJR 2—8—0 No. 53807, one of the 1925-built series of engines. The first view (top) taken at Bath on April 21 1951 shows the engine in its original large-boilered form wearing the first BR standard livery with the lion and wheel tender emblem, the second, post-rebuilding view (above), illustrates the small-boilered conversion, carrying the later BR emblem.** *Ivo Peters.*

LIVERY SAMPLES:	
CODE C13	13800-2/5/7
CODE C14	9671/80
*CODE C16	9672/3/8
CODE C21	13801-2/6

* Hand-painted characters

APPENDIX 1

CORRECTIONS AND ADDITIONS TO PREVIOUS VOLUMES

WE are again indebted to eagle-eyed and interested readers for drawing our attention to the following errors. Fortunately none are serious and most are typographical. We invite readers to continue the good work.

Volume 2

Page 22, Plate 48: For *Moorhen* read *Moor Hen*.

Page 27, Plate 60: *Prospero* was the last 'Experiment' in the LMS number series, not the last to be built.

Page 37, line 7: Opposite Code C15, No. 26730 should read 25730.

Page 53, Plate 117: LNWR number of LMS 6641 may have been 408 not 406 as stated — confirmation lacking.

Page 55, Plate 122: For 6979 read 6797.

Page 61, Plate 135: On last line of caption, former LNWR number of LMS 6970 should be 962, not 960 as stated.

Page 63, 0—4—0 Tanks: In para 1, line 2, 16 should read 17. On penultimate line, the works 0—4—0Ts were 3013-5/9.

Page 66, Para 2: On lines 3 and 4, No. 3210 should read 3310. It later became Carriage Dept. No. 5.

Page 86, Para 1: The last BR survivor (line 2) was No. 47877 (scrapped 1953) not No. 47881 as stated.

Page 86, Plate 193: LMS 7875 was ex-LNWR 1494, not as stated.

Page 88, Plate 197: No. 47884 was renumbered in 1948, not 1949.

Page 100, Plate 224: Although the number is part obscured, it is now believed this engine is No. 28450, not No. 28458 as stated. The latter was a round-top boiler engine!

Page 104, Para 1: In line 2, 1908 should read 1906.

Page 127, Plate 280: In line 2, first LMS renumbering date should be 1928 not 1927.

Page 129, Para 1: In line 2, LMS 9626 was ex-LNWR 2048, not as stated.

Page 137, Para 4: In penultimate line, No. 27253 should read No. 27523.

Page 141, Para 3: In line 2, LMS 6761 was ex-LNWR 284, not as stated.

Page 143, Plate 312: LMS 6776 was ex-Wirral No. 3, not 31.

Page 144, LMS 6850-1: This paragraph is misleading. The Wirral Railway did indeed introduce the first 4—4—4Ts in Britain (in 1896 not 1895 as inferred) but those reaching the LMS dated from 1903.

Page 148, Para 4: In line 1, 1931 should read 1930.

Page 151, Para 2: In last line, 5013 should read 50/1/3.

Page 167: The Battery locomotive worked at a *Copper* works(!) and was withdrawn in 1964, not 1963.

Page 171, Para 3: The LYR/LNWR act of amalgamation (line 5) was dated 1921 but took effect on January 1 1922.

Page 171, Para 4: It would appear that Barton Wright took charge late in 1875 (line 4).

Page 201, Plate 411: In line 4, for 11212 read 11232.

Page 205, Para 2: In line 3, LMS 11338 was ex-LYR 562.

Page 207, Para 2: *Five* examples survived to BR: 11535-7/44/6.

Page 213, last Para: In line 3, 10515 should read 12515.

Page 215, Plate 436: In last line of caption for 'renewal' read 'removal'.

Page 219, Para 5: In line 2, for 52415 read 52413.

Page 223, Plate 450: ex-LYR number may have been 656 and not as quoted — can anyone confirm?

Page 225: Fifteen lines from the bottom of the page, the five early withdrawals should read 12700/6/28/30/50.

Page 231, Para 1: In line 3, for 'withdrawn' read 'scrapped'. It was withdrawn in 1924.

Page 242, Para 1: In line 2, the 1872 date may have been 1871 for LMS 12065 — confirmation needed.

Page 245, Para 2: In line 1, for 1929-34 read 1928-36.

Page 247, Para 2: The M&CR title was incorporated in 1837 not 1840. The railway opened for business in the latter year.

Page 247, Last line: For 1924, read 1924 and 1925.

Page 258, Plate 498: The caption is misleading. No. 5 was withdrawn before the Grouping. M&CR Nos. 3 and 23 were the two similar survivors to the LMS which did not receive their new numbers.

Volume 3

Page 3, Para 5: In line 4, for 1882-91 read 1882-90.

Page 4, Caption: In line 8, for 'late' read 'early'.

Page 10, 80 class: Power Class should be 1P — see *Volume 1* page 44.

Page 33, Para 2: In line 1, for 1934 read 1928. No. 14602 was an odd early withdrawal.

Page 44, Para 3: In line 2, for 1931-4 read 1931-5.

Page 57, Para 1: No. 15174 *did* receive its BR number, in 1951 (line 4).

Page 74, Para 1: On last line, for 1916 and 1922 read 1915 and 1921.

Page 74, Plate 141: LMS 16152 may have been ex-CR 499 and not as stated. Can any reader confirm?

Page 75, Para 1: In last line, for 1961 read 1962.

Page 87, Para 1: In line 2, for 1927 read 1928.

Page 96, Plates 187/8: LMS 17632 was ex-CR 655.

Page 98, Plate 194: LMS 17554 was ex-CR 816.

Page 100, last para: Add No. 17687 in list of pre-BR withdrawals.

Page 104, Para 2: In line 3 it is probably more accurate to read 'between 1913 and 1915' and not 'in 1913 and 1914'.

Page 105, Line 3: For 1935 read 1934.

Page 108, last para: In line 3, for 1886 read 1866.

Page 111, Para 5: In line 1, David L. Smith's records suggest 1879-81 as the introduction date.

Page 114, Plate 223: Yes, we *do* know it is ex-GSWR!

Page 119, Para 1: In line 4, for 1933 read 1934.

Page 122, last lines: It would appear that No. 14239 was another example not to receive LMS number.

Page 132, Plates 259/60: We gave GSWR No. 510 for both these engines. They were in fact Nos. 510-1.

Page 133, Para 1: One of this series, LMS 14659, lasted until 1933.

Page 138, last line: Some sources give LMS 15404 as the last survivor in 1936 — confirmation would be welcomed.

Page 146, Para 2: It would appear that No. 16377 was reinstated in 1932 and finally withdrawn in 1934.
Page 147, Line 1: For 16900-28 read 16900-27.
Page 149, 141 class: No. 17022 may have been scrapped in 1924, not 1925.
Page 154, 22 class: In Para 1, line 2, for 1890 read 1892.
Page 160, Para 2: In line 5, for '/92-6/', read '/94-6/'.
Page 170, Para 2: In line 7, for 1891 read 1892 — see three lines later!

Page 172, Plate 334: LMS 14274 was ex-HR 95.
Page 173, Line 3: Nobody spotted that we had attributed the Pickersgill chimneys to McIntosh — but see Plate 336 for proof.
Page 183, last para: In line 1, for 1913/4 read 1913.
Page 187, last line: For *McKinnon* read *Mackinnon*.
Page 198: Under Drummond 0—6—0T, para 1, line 2, for 1903 read 1903/4.
Page 205: Under Cumming 4—6—0, para 1, line 1, for 'introduced' read 'ordered'.

APPENDIX 2

INDEX OF LOCOMOTIVE CLASSES (CAPITAL STOCK) COVERED IN VOLUME FOUR

Note: Except for standard 0—6—0/0—6—0T, absorbed ex-SDJR locomotives are not included in this list but are to be found in Chapter 9.

Listed in LMS number order, but note that in the ex-MR series, there were gaps in the sequence due to withdrawals between 1907 (date of number allocations) and 1923.

(Plate 455): We think it is singularly appropriate to conclude our survey of the 'Midland' contribution to the story of LMS engines with this particularly fine study of one of them at work — former 'Somerset & Dorset' 2—8—0 No. 53806, in charge of a down freight climbing towards Chilcompton, on the 7½-mile 1 in 50 (ruling gradient) climb from Radstock to Masbury Summit, on April 16 1955. No. 53806 was the last of the 1925 series to retain a large boiler; in late 1955 the locomotive went to Derby for overhaul and returned to the 'S&D' with one of the smaller boilers. This class was probably the finest goods engine the MR ever designed, yet paradoxically, it was never adopted for the parent system. Even more symbolically, this particular example was actually built during LMS days while the new company still continued to prefer building hordes of inadequate '4Fs' for its own routes. Somehow, the 'S&D' 2—8—0s seem to us to sum up all that was simultaneously best and worst about the Midland influence on LMS locomotive matters — and at that we had perhaps better leave the subject until we conclude the story in Volume 5. Ivo Peters.